THE
ACTOR'S BOOK
OF
CONTEMPORARY
STAGE
MONOLOGUES

EDITED BY

Nina Shengold

A SMITH AND KRAUS INC. BOOK

PENGUIN BOOKS

PENGUIN BOOKS

Published by the Penguin Group

Penguin Group (USA) Inc., 375 Hudson Street, New York, New York 10014, U.S.A.

Penguin Group (Canada), 90 Eglinton Avenue East, Suite 700, Toronto,

Ontario, Canada M4P 2Y3 (a division of Pearson Penguin Canada Inc.)

Penguin Books Ltd, 80 Strand, London WC2R 0RL, England

Penguin Ireland, 25 St Stephen's Green, Dublin 2, Ireland (a division of Penguin Books Ltd)

Penguin Group (Australia), 250 Camberwell Road, Camberwell,

Victoria 3124, Australia (a division of Pearson Australia Group Pty Ltd)

Penguin Books India Pvt Ltd, 11 Community Centre, Panchsheel Park, New Delhi – 110 017, India

Penguin Group (NZ), cnr Airborne and Rosedale Roads,

Albany, Auckland 1310, New Zealand (a division of Pearson New Zealand Ltd)

Penguin Books (South Africa) (Pty) Ltd, 24 Sturdee Avenue,

Rosebank, Johannesburg 2196, South Africa

Penguin Books Ltd, Registered Offices: 80 Strand, London WC2R 0RL, England

First published in Penguin Books 1987
Published simultaneously in Canada

41 42 43 44 45 46 47 48 49 50

Copyright © Smith and Kraus Inc., 1987
All rights reserved

LIBRARY OF CONGRESS CATALOGING IN PUBLICATION DATA
The Actor's book of contemporary stage monologues.
1. Monologues.   2. Acting.   I. Shengold, Nina.
PN2080.A284   1987   812'.045'08   86-30558
ISBN 0 14 00.9649 3

Printed in the United States of America
Set in Caledonia
Designed by Robert Bull

ACKNOWLEDGMENTS

Grateful thanks to David Babcock for locating literally dozens of monologues, and to the following people for giving me scripts, suggestions, and friendship along the way: Dana Alexander, Alan Amtzis, Jeff Brown, Lou and Edith Fisher, Debra Frankel, Philip Gourevitch, Laura Harrington, Richard Krawetz, Eric Lane, Jeffrey Lane, Rick Leed, Mark Mannucci, Melanie Merians, Tina Newton, Ron Nyswaner, Ph. Data, Mary Portser, James Skofield, Eleanore Speert, Stephanie Stein, David Van Biema, Shelley Wyant, and my family. Special thanks also to Smith & Kraus, Inc., book producers, for conceiving this book and helping me through all the paperwork. Finally, thanks to the playwrights for letting us borrow your words.

CONTENTS

EDITOR'S PREFACE

By a twist of alphabetical fate, the first monologue in this collection is from a play called *The Actor's Nightmare*. For most actors, finding good monologues for auditions and classwork *is* a nightmare. I hope this collection will wake you up.

All of the plays you will find here are from the last twenty-five years (in fact, some were produced for the first time this season), and most are from Off Broadway, Off-Off Broadway, or regional theatres. From better-known writers such as Tennessee Williams, Sam Shepard, and Lanford Wilson, I chose speeches from lesser-known plays—*Small Craft Warnings* instead of *A Streetcar Named Desire; Cowboy Mouth* instead of *True West; The Madness of Lady Bright* and *The Great Nebula in Orion* instead of *Talley's Folly*. Auditioning is quite hard enough without being told you're the fifth Blanche DuBois of the day.

Beyond that, I tried to find speeches that tell a clear, self-contained story and give actors something to work with. There are monologues here in a spectrum of styles on a spectrum of subjects, from suicide to the zen of tennis. There are roles for actors of different ages, races, and character types. The Monologue Reference Chart in the back of the book will help you locate appropriate material. I have also been lucky enough to speak with Swoosie Kurtz, Lanford Wilson, Christopher Durang, and Tina Howe about the process of writing and performing monologues. All have offered fascinating ideas; plus, in these conversations, readers will find helpful suggestions about performing some of the monologues in the book. Several other playwrights have kindly contributed brief thoughts on how best to perform their pieces, and I have added some of these comments to the introductions to their monologues.

Compiling this list—getting paid to read hundreds of

plays—was a dream-come-true job for me. It gave me a chance to survey and consider what playwrights are writing these days. What struck me most was the level of bleakness and fury in most of these plays. Perhaps this is partly the nature of monologues: nobody pours out his heart for five minutes onstage unless something is urgent. But what should we make of plays like *Aunt Dan and Lemon* and *The Transfiguration of Benno Blimpie*, whose heroes have locked themselves away to starve or eat to death? Or *Serenading Louie* and *Passing Game*, in which men who "have it all" murder their families? What about *Bosoms and Neglect*, where the image of hope is a blind woman finally reaching to touch her son after he leaves?

When I skim down this list, I realize this impression of darkness is not universal. There are plenty of gentler plays too; there are romances, comedies. Interestingly, there are also a number of plays (*Still Life, Soap Opera, Talking with . . . , Kennedy's Children*) which are made up completely of monologues, and whose characters never address one another. In a world which is scared of human connection, the monologue seems a uniquely appropriate form. Every one is a soul saying, "Listen to me. Pay attention. I matter."

Although this book is conceived primarily as a resource for actors, I hope it will also help introduce readers to playwrights and plays they may not have known. Pick out a monologue, yes, but then *go read the play*. There is wonderful writing here, vibrant and varied. I hope it will serve as a springboard for wonderful acting.

—NINA SHENGOLD
New York City
September 1986

A Conversation with Swoosie Kurtz

Swoosie Kurtz made her New York debut in *Tartuffe* in 1978, and has gone on to win Tony Awards for her work in *Fifth of July* and *The House of Blue Leaves*, the Drama Desk Award for *A History of the American Film*, and Obie Awards for *Uncommon Women and Others* and *The House of Blue Leaves*. Ms. Kurtz also garnered two Emmy nominations for her role on the TV series "Love, Sidney." Her films include *True Stories*, *Against All Odds*, *Wildcats*, and *The World According to Garp*. This interview took place in Kurtz's dressing room at Broadway's Plymouth Theatre, where she was playing Bananas Shaughnessy in *The House of Blue Leaves*.

How did you start acting? When did you first fall in love with it?

In high school. A wonderful drama teacher lit the fire for me. I started reading scenes in class and realized that I'd latched on to something I did well. Acting gave me an identity.

Did you know right away that this would be your life?

Yes. I knew I *wanted* it to be.

And how easy was that?

Well, as you can see it's taken me a long time! Mine was a very slow but steady route. I built all those building blocks very slowly and painstakingly, and I think it's paid off.

I'm sure it's been a while since you walked into a general audition with a prepared monologue.

A number of years, but I did it a *lot!* I did a lot of annual T.C.G. (Theatre Communications Group) auditions. They're the liaison between actors and all the directors and casting directors from regional theatres. It's a marathon, a two-day marathon, from nine in the morning till six at night. You have your appointed time and number and day, and you know those poor bastards are vegged-out from monologues by the end of the day. It's great, though, because you have an audience of all these artistic directors from all over the country.

How do you prepare for that sea of faces?

I think you need a director. A *good* director. It's very, very hard to direct yourself in a monologue. Naturally, if you're doing it for classwork, that's different, but if you're doing an audition, I think you should get, if nothing else, a friend with a very good, objective eye, who'll be honest with you and can help you pick out what's important and what's not.

Are there any auditions that really stand out in your mind as particularly great or particularly awful experiences?

Once, at a T.C.G. audition, I got offered a job—several jobs in fact—and the director of the theatre said to me, "I didn't care for your selection at all, but I could tell you can act." (Laughs) Well, let's face it, that's the point of the audition, isn't it? Of course these were general auditions, which are quite different from specific auditions. If you want a particular part, then obviously you choose pieces very carefully to make you look as much like that character as possible. Whereas, in a general audition, you want to show off your whole range of colors, your strong points, and above all, be fascinating! Don't bore them! My ultimate advice . . . be anything, but *don't* be boring! As an audience I would rather be outraged, offended, terrorized, baffled . . . *anything* but bored!

How do you deal with the people in the room when you're doing an audition monologue?

That's very tricky. I always tended to look right above their heads.

In their direction, but not making eye contact?

Right. I think it makes casting people very uncomfortable to make eye contact. Now, there are exceptions, like Ronnie's monologue in *The House of Blue Leaves*, where he says, "Go ahead—laugh. Because you know what I think of you? (Bronx cheers)." Maybe in a case like that it's a good choice to look at them and make them uncomfortable. But I think in general it's not a good idea. They're busy watching you and don't want their reactions to be judged. Some people's faces can be very blank while they're watching, and you think, "Boy, are *they* bored," but they're not at *all* bored! That's just how they are when watching something. They might be *enthralled*! Their faces might be frozen in wonder! Also, not making eye contact helps your concentration. I think it's much harder to keep your concentration in an audition than onstage, because onstage you have your borderlines. You're in costume, you have the light on you, the set has become its own kind of world. So your concentration is much more focused, I think, than in an audition room where you're under fluorescent or God knows what kinds of lights, a phone is ringing, people are coming in early and opening the door, and you are undoubtedly nervous.

Do you still get nervous?

Not very often. When you're lucky enough to work with a great director, you have been given so many things to think about that your mind is quite occupied once you get out there. If you go onstage with your first purpose firmly in mind, and you've done your work well, it will carry you through to the next purpose and the next . . .

So rather than thinking about the audience, or the audition, you think in character, "What is the first purpose I have to accomplish?"

Think in character, exactly. The character is probably not nervous, and there are many ways of channeling your nervousness into whatever the character is feeling. If you can pump that adrenaline into some other channel, it can really work for you: the idea is to make it not nervous energy, but just plain *energy*. Then you can turn it into angry energy, or shy energy or whatever passion is driving the character. This is where technique comes in.

But auditions, yeah, there are times when I still start to shake. I mistrust people who don't get nervous at all; I sense a certain arrogance there. But I do get nervous less and less.

There's a difference between nervousness and panic.

Yes, blind panic! (Laughs) Olivier once said in an interview that a lot of drama students—especially when they're just starting out—roll their heads, relax their tongues, relax their jaws, and flop over limp, thinking they're ready to go onstage. They're "relaxed." No, no, no! Don't be relaxed, be *poised*. Poised for action. Ready to strike. Not tense, but not vegged-out, either; there's an in-between point called "poised."

Let's backtrack. Before you get backstage—before you even get in the audition room—how do you work on your monologue?

First, there is no such thing as a monologue. You have to be talking to someone, even if it's only yourself. There has to be a response to what you say, voices that are challenging, questioning, resisting, agreeing. You've either shocked them, or you've stunned them, or they think you're lying. . . . That way, the monologue becomes a scene.

Imagining these responses can also be a very useful way of breaking a monologue down into smaller pieces, so that you go moment by moment and beat by beat.

Exactly! Like everything else in acting, and life, a monologue must be broken down into manageable bits and then strung together.

I like that, "and life."

And life! I believe that! You have to break everything down or you get overwhelmed. The first day of rehearsal for something, I just go, "OH MY GOD!!!" And then the director says, very calmly, "Okay, now let's start with Scene One. Well, we're not really going to start with Scene One, we're just going to start with the first *line*." You break it down, and then only later do you string it together—hopefully seamlessly, but sometimes choppiness is what's called for.

So rather than looking at a monologue as one big chunk, you're taking it sentence by sentence and thought by thought.

Exactly. There are ebbs and flows. But even when you are prepared, monologues do hang very heavy upon the heads of actors. In *Tartuffe*, I had all these lines back and forth with Victor Garber, a wonderful love scene which was not scary, because one thing led to another, cause and effect and response. . . . But then I reached a speech where I had to beg my father—in *rhyme*—for something, which I was always afraid of. I could never relax until that speech was over. I'd think, "Uh-oh, here it comes, HERE IT COMES . . . Mount Monologue! This *thing* I have to climb and conquer and get to the top of!!!" That's why breaking it down is crucial.

In The House of Blue Leaves *you have a specific kind of acting problem, a monologue that's not only a very long speech, but that is addressed directly to the audience.*

The audience plays a big part in this play. They are another character that I'm talking to. In this case, Artie has just given a speech about my going out on the roof in my nightgown. So he's exposed me to the audience in a way, and my reply is, "Can I have my song?" which I could never understand until I realized it meant, "Let me tell my side of the story." So right off that gives me my motivation: tell the story. Don't play a character, but tell the story. And decide about your *attitude* toward the story. Is it, "You're not going to believe this, but it is the greatest thing!" Or, "This is the funniest thing you've ever heard in your life!," or, "This is the scariest thing," or, "I want to show you how brave I was; tell me if you agree with me."

In other words, why do you need to tell this story, and what do you want the listener to think of you for telling it?

Right. And technique comes in here, because you don't always get the response from the audience that you want. A tiny example: when Bananas names the four people standing on the four corners of Forty-second and Broadway . . . Cardinal Spellman, Jackie Kennedy, Bob Hope, President Johnson . . . most of the time there's a laugh which in turn makes me respond—well, if I were to verbalize it, it would be, "No, really! I'm not kidding! All carrying *suitcases!*" So the line about the suitcases comes off that audience response, off their disbelief.

Now, there are nights when they don't make a sound. But I still do the beat, because I feel them *thinking* "Oh, come on!" So I respond, "No, really! Not only were they standing on the corners, *but* they were all carrying suitcases!" And that gets me into the next beat.

And here's where a good director comes in. Jerry Zaks (the director of *The House of Blue Leaves*) is a great one for saying, "Let go of the words, let go of the words, make your points." Great piece of direction.

What do you mean by "Let go of the words?"

Let go of the words. Don't emphasize each word, don't make everything equally important.

I just wanted to make sure that doesn't come across as encouragement to paraphrase.

Oh! Don't change the lines! No! Never paraphrase. Every word is carefully, carefully chosen by the playwright and must be treated as sacred. I'm a great believer in that. But let go of the words, meaning don't hang on to them. Decide what are the important things, and play the thrust of the sentence rather than the specific word.

In an article about The House of Blue Leaves *you said that the role really clicked when you figured out the posture, the arc of your back for when Bananas is being a dog. I thought that was fascinating, because it was so specific.*

That's exactly the sort of thing that happens in acting—some specific physical choice will fill you in on the rest of your character.

That's something that actors don't always use in attacking

"Mount Monologue," *as you put it, because the words are so overwhelming.*

Yes. I think a lot of young actors tend to work almost too internally, and wait for things to happen. I've always been so helped by something physical that does something to me and makes me behave in a certain way.

You've been doing The House of Blue Leaves *for about nine months now. How do you keep a monologue fresh in a long run?*

The audience does a lot of the work for me. Especially in this play, because I'm talking to them. They're constantly surprising me. The very night I think I'm really crackling, I look out and see someone's jaw dropped open and their head back in the deepest, most refreshing sleep, saving themselves up for Act Two!

And that is the difference between acting onstage and in movies.

Or even auditioning in a room full of people. At least they have the grace to stay awake!

Is there any more general advice about auditioning that you would give to actors?

Keep it simple. Pick a monologue that you know is within your grasp, given the time and circumstances allotted. Choose something you can accomplish comfortably and well.

For class, of course, you might want to do something that's challenging, maybe something you would never, ever be cast in. But not for auditions. Be practical. If you're a twenty-one-year-old girl, don't go in and do Mary Tyrone from *Long Day's Journey*. It's just not a good idea—unless you're absolutely sensational. But even so, it throws them off, because they're looking at something that doesn't come out of *you*. It doesn't match. It doesn't *fit*. Pick a monologue that fits.

How do you avoid typecasting?

I don't know how much control we as actors have over that. I certainly managed to do it in this play. But the director and producers wouldn't have trusted me in this part had I not already established myself as an actor.

I think it often happens that actors have to start closer to home, and once they've established themselves as really good actors, people will say, "You know, she could look very different, and she's good enough to become someone else." I've certainly seen you in a very wide range of roles.

Well, you see, that's the kind of acting I love, what I always strive to do, and hopefully have accomplished to a certain extent: to be almost unrecognizable from part to part. People say, and it's the highest compliment, "I saw you in *Fifth of July*, and I thought that's who you were. And tonight I saw this."

And tomorrow they go to True Stories, *and then they remember that girl on* "Love, Sidney" . . .

Exactly! It really gives me chills, it's great! That's the kind of acting I'm always in awe of, that chameleon quality. I love that.

THE

ACTOR'S BOOK

OF

CONTEMPORARY
STAGE
MONOLOGUES

The Actor's Nightmare

Christopher Durang

Premiere: Playwrights Horizons, New York City, 1981
Setting: A theatre

An accountant named George Spelvin is baffled to find himself on the stage of a theatre. The stage manager tells him that "Eddie" (Edwin Booth) has been in a car accident and George will have to go on for him. The curtain goes up on a play which is either *Private Lives*, Samuel Beckett's *Checkmate*, or *Hamlet*. George wings it as well as he can, but is lost when his co-stars exeunt.

GEORGE

Oh don't go. (*Pause; smiles uncomfortably at the audience.*) Maybe someone else will come out in a minute. (*Pause.*) Of course, sometimes people have soliloquies in Shakespeare. Let's just wait a moment more and maybe someone will come. (*The lights suddenly change to a dim blue background and one bright, white spot center stage.* GEORGE *is not standing in the spot.*) Oh dear. (*He moves somewhat awkwardly into the spot, decides to do his best to live up to the requirements of the moment.*) To be or not to be, that is the question. (*Doesn't know any more.*) Oh maid! (*No response; remembers that actors call for "line."*) Line. Line! Ohhhh. Oh, what a rogue and peasant slave am I Whether tis nobler in the mind's eye to kill oneself, or not killing oneself, to sleep a great deal. We are such stuff as dreams are made on; and our lives are rounded by a little sleep. (*The lights change. The spot goes out, and another one comes up stage right.* GEORGE *moves into it.*) Uh, thrift, thrift, Horatio. Neither a borrower nor a lender be. But to thine own self be true. There is a special providence in the fall of a sparrow. Extraordinary how potent cheap music can be. Out, out, damn spot! I come to wive it wealthily

in Padua; if wealthily, then happily in Padua. (*Sings.*) Brush up your Shakespeare; start quoting him now; Da da . . . *
(*Lights change again. That spot goes off; another one comes on, center stage, though closer to audience.* GEORGE *moves into that.*) I wonder whose yacht that is. How was China? Very large, China. How was Japan? Very small, Japan. I pledge allegiance to the flag of the United States of America and to the republic for which it stands, one nation, under God, indivisible with liberty and justice for all. Line! Line! Oh my God. (*Gets idea.*) O my God, I am heartily sorry for having offended thee, and I detest all my sins because I dread the loss of heaven and the pains of hell. But most of all because they offend thee, my God, who art all good and deserving of all my love. And I resolve to confess my sins, to do penance, and to amend my life, Amen. (*Friendly.*) That's the act of contrition that Catholic schoolchildren say in confession in order to be forgiven their sins. Catholic adults say it too, I imagine. I don't know any Catholic adults. Line! (*Explaining.*) When you call for a line, the stage manager normally gives you your next line, to refresh your memory. Line! The quality of mercy is not strained. It droppeth as the gentle rain upon the place below, when we have shuffled off this mortal coil. Alas, poor Yorick. I knew him well. Get thee to a nunnery. Line. Nunnery. As a child, I was taught by nuns, and then in high school I was taught by Benedictine priests. I really rather liked the nuns, they were sort of warm, though they were fairly crazy too. Line. I liked the priests also. The school was on the grounds of the monastery, and my junior and senior years I spent a few weekends joining in the daily routine of the monastery—prayers, then breakfast, then prayers, then lunch, then prayers, then dinner, then prayers, then sleep. I found the predictability quite attractive. And the food was good. I was going to join the monastery after high school, but they said I was too young and should

*See Note on page 355.

wait. And then I just stopped believing in all those things, so I never did join the monastery. I became an accountant. I've studied logarithms, and cosine and tangent . . . *(Irritated.)* Line! *(Apologetic.)* I'm sorry. This is supposed to be *Hamlet* or *Private Lives* or something, and I keep rattling on like a maniac. I really do apologize. I just don't recall attending a single rehearsal. I can't imagine what I was doing. And also you came expecting to see Edwin Booth and you get me. I really am very embarrassed. Sorry. *Line!* It's a far, far better thing I do than I have ever done before. It's a far, far better place I go to than I have ever been before. *(Sings the alphabet song.)* a,b,c,d,e,f,g,h,i,j,k,l,m,n,o,p,q,r,s,t . . . *(As he starts to sing, enter* ELLEN TERRY, *dragging two large garbage cans. She puts them side by side, gets in one.)* Oh, good. Are you Ophelia? Get thee to a nunnery. *(She points to the other garbage can, indicating he should get in it.)* Get in? Okay. *(He does.)* This must be one of those modern *Hamlets*. *(Lights change abruptly to "Beckett lighting.")*

Angels Fall
Lanford Wilson

Premiere: New World Festival, Miami, 1982
Setting: An adobe mission in northwestern New Mexico
There has been a nuclear accident at a uranium mine in northwestern New Mexico, and all roads are closed. Four travelers seek sanctuary in the mission run by Father Doherty and his half-Indian foster son, Don Tabaha. The stranded travelers are a burned-out professor and his young wife, a fortyish gallery owner and her "boytoy," and a twenty-one-year-old tennis pro named Salvatore "Zappy" Zappala. Zappy is an energetic, cheerful hypochondriac ("I can't hear symptoms without getting it") who sees his gift for tennis as a

"call . . . that magic that happens and you know who you
are, you know?"

ZAP

Like when I found out I was a tennis player.
   [VITA: I love you.
   ZAP: No, no joke.] I went to church and lit a candle,
man.
   [DOHERTY: You give thanks for that light.]
Really. I said my novenas, man, 'cause it had been like a—
not a miracle that anyone would know except just me—
but it had been like when those girls saw Our Lady of
Fatima up on that hill. It was really weird. I was like in
the fifth grade and I was watching these two hamburgers
on some practice court, and they took a break and one of
them hands me his racket. So I threw up a toss like I'd
seen them do and zap! Three inches over the net, two
inches inside the line. There wasn't nobody over there, but
that was an ace, man. You should have heard those guys
razz me. I mean, you know, they say, "Man, you stink."
And all those things you can't repeat in front of a priest.
They was really on my case. And I think that's the first
time anybody ever looked at me. I mean, I was skinny,
you've never seen—most of the girls in my homeroom had
about twenty pounds on me. So this guy shows me a backhand grip and he hits one to me and zap! You mother!
Backhand! Right down the line. And the thing is, that's
where I wanted it. I saw the ball come at me, and I said
I'm gonna backhand this sucker right down the line, and I
did.
   So then they took their ball back. Which I don't blame
them, 'cause no high school hotshot is gonna get off on
being showed up by this eleven-year-old creep that's built
like a parking meter, you know?
   But that was it. I hit that first ball and I said, "This is

me. This is what I do. What I do is tennis." And once you know, then there's no way out. You've been showed something. Even if it's just tennis, you can't turn around and say you wasn't showed that.

So I went to church and said a novena for those meatballs 'cause they didn't know all the butterflies that was in my stomach, that they'd been my angels. But, man, on the way home, anybody had asked me what I did, right there I'd have said, "I play tennis." Didn't know love from lob, didn't matter. That's what I am. 'Cause once you know what you are, the rest is just work.

The Art of Dining

Tina Howe

Premiere: New York Shakespeare Festival, New York City, 1979

Setting: An intimate, elegant restaurant on the New Jersey shore

Ellen and Cal have just opened a restaurant called The Golden Carousel. It's a raw, freezing day in November, and three disparate sets of guests eat their way through the comedy and drama of one evening's meal.

Elizabeth Barrow Colt is dining with David Osslow, a hearty, self-confident publisher who admires her short stories. The meal is a nightmarish ordeal for Elizabeth, who is excruciatingly shy and so nervous she drops her lipstick in her soup. She is very nearsighted and does not wear glasses. She's also terrified of food, and when David tries to convince her to taste the dinner she's ordered, she tells him this story.

(*Note:* Though the two speeches occur in different scenes, they continue the same story and can be performed together.)

—————— **1** ——————

ELIZABETH BARROW COLT

When I was young I never even saw my mother in the kitchen. The food just appeared at mealtime as if by magic, all steaming and ready to eat. Lacey would carry it in on these big white serving platters that had a rim of raised china acorns. Our plates had the same rim. Twenty-two acorns per plate, each one about the size of a lump of chewed gum. When I was very young I used to try and pry them off with my knife. . . . We ate every night at eight o'clock sharp because my parents didn't start their cocktail hour until seven, but since dinnertime was meant for exchanging news of the day, the emphasis was always on talking . . . and not on eating. My father bolted his food, and my mother played with hers: sculpting it up into hills and then mashing it back down through her fork. To make things worse, before we sat down at the table she'd always put on a fresh smear of lipstick. I still remember the shade. It was called "Fire and Ice" . . . a dark throbbing red that rubbed off on her fork in waxy clumps that stained her food pink, so that by the end of the first course she'd have rended everything into a kind of . . . rosy puree. As my father wolfed down his meat and vegetables, I'd watch my mother thread this puree through the raised acorns on her plate, fanning it out into long runny pink ribbons. . . . I could never eat a thing. . . . "WAKE UP, AMERICA!" she'd trumpet to me. "You're not being excused from this table until you clean up that plate!" So, I'd take several mouthfuls and then when no one was looking, would spit them out into my napkin. Each night I systematically transferred everything on my plate into that lifesaving napkin. . . .

—————— **2** ——————

ELIZABETH BARROW COLT
(Looks at her bass, helpless. Sighs. A silence, then very

loud and intense.) ONE AFTERNOON WHEN I CAME HOME FROM SCHOOL, MOTHER WAS IN TEARS BECAUSE LACEY HAD QUIT, WALKED OUT IN A TORRENT OF INSULTS. "NEVER AGAIN!" MOTHER SOBBED. "FROM NOW ON, I'LL DO THE COOKING MYSELF!" . . . IT WAS A BIG MISTAKE. SHE DIDN'T KNOW HOW AND SHE WAS IN THE MIDST OF MENOPAUSE. SHE KEPT BREAKING DISHES AND CUTTING HER FINGERS WITH THE CARVING KNIFE. ONE NIGHT SHE SLICED OFF THE TIP OF HER THUMB AND GROUND IT UP IN THE GARBAGE DISPOSAL! *(HANNAH GALT lurches towards the ladies' room upstairs. The lights rise a little to reveal the other diners. They're startled by ELIZABETH's sudden outburst and stare, then turn away feigning indifference, while hanging on every word.)*

Mealtime was much the same as it had always been. . . . Father still talked a blue streak, Mother still mashed her food into a pink soup . . . and I still spit everything out into my napkin. But they were paper napkins now, and since I cleared the table, there was no chance of discovery. I breathed easier. What changed then, was the violence that went into the cooking beforehand. . . . I never saw such bloodletting over meals! If she didn't knick herself while cutting the tomatoes, she'd deliberately slice a finger while waiting for the rice to boil. "Why bother cooking?" she'd cry, holding her bleeding hands under the faucet. "We'll all be dead soon enough!" . . . It was around this time that Mother was starting to get . . . suicidal. . . . *(She starts to laugh.)* Oh dear, I shouldn't laugh. . . . It was just so . . . comical! You see, Mother was very comical. She wore hats all the time, great turban-type creations piled high with artificial flowers and papier-mâché fruits. She wore them outside and she wore them in the house. She wore them when she cooked and when she ate . . . great teetering crowns that bobbed and jingled with every move . . . poor Mother . . . I don't know what it was that made her so unhappy . . . her menopause, her cocktails before dinner, some private anguish . . . but during this period, she used to threaten to kill herself. After another bloodstained dinner, she'd throw herself face down on our driveway and beg my father to put the car in reverse and drive over her. "Don't be ridiculous, dear," he'd say. But she meant it and would lie there sobbing, "PLEASE . . . DO IT!" It was a ritual we went through every night. . . .

[DAVID OSSLOW: *(Does his best to eat his dinner, stopping only when he's too shaken to swallow.)* And did she ever? . . . I mean . . . succeed?

ELIZABETH BARROW COLT: *(Sighs.)* Oh dear.

DAVID OSSLOW: She did. . . .]

ELIZABETH BARROW COLT: Poor Mother.

[DAVID OSSLOW: How . . . awful . . .

ELIZABETH BARROW COLT: *(Sighs.)*

DAVID OSSLOW: Your father finally gave in and ran over her. . . .

ELIZABETH BARROW COLT: Not that.

DAVID OSSLOW: Sleeping pills . . .

ELIZABETH BARROW COLT: If only it had been. . . .

DAVID OSSLOW: Poor thing . . .

ELIZABETH BARROW COLT: Yes . . .

DAVID OSSLOW: She shot herself? . . .

ELIZABETH BARROW COLT: Can't you guess?

DAVID OSSLOW: How could I guess . . . with someone like . . . *that?*

ELIZABETH BARROW COLT: Think! It's so in character!

DAVID OSSLOW: She slit her throat with a carving knife?

ELIZABETH BARROW COLT: *(A bit bloodthirsty.)* Better . . .

DAVID OSSLOW: *(After a pause.)* Of course . . . I know. . . .

DAVID OSSLOW: She turned on the gas. . . .

ELIZABETH BARROW COLT: She turned on the gas. . . .]

ELIZABETH BARROW COLT: She turned on the gas and opened that big mouth of an oven door and stuck her head in . . . with her hat firmly in place. . . .

[DAVID OSSLOW: Yes of course . . . the hat!]

ELIZABETH BARROW COLT: *(Starts laughing.)* It must have been quite a sight . . . Mother down on all fours, trying to fit her head in without knocking her hat off . . .

[DAVID OSSLOW: And? . . .]

ELIZABETH BARROW COLT: Oh, dear, I shouldn't laugh. . . .

[DAVID OSSLOW: No, go on. . . .]

ELIZABETH BARROW COLT: Well, after she'd been in there for ten minutes or so, getting groggier and groggier, something went wrong. The papier-mâché trinkets on her hat began to sizzle and explode like little firecrackers. Within moments the entire hat was in flames. She came to like a shot and raced to the sink. . . . her head actually . . . *cooking!* She turned on the water full blast . . . Her hat and all of her hair was consumed . . . but she survived. *(Pause.)* She joked about it afterwards . . . after the hospital stay and plastic surgery . . . about almost having barbecued herself like some amazing delicacy . . . some exotic . . . roast! "I BET I WOULD HAVE TASTED DAMNED GOOD!" she used to say, smacking her lips. *(Long Pause.)* My mother is very beautiful, you know. . . . She's so beautiful . . . people turn around.

Aunt Dan and Lemon

Wallace Shawn

Premiere: New York Shakespeare Festival, New York City, 1985

Setting: Lemon's apartment in London, and various memory locations

A young woman named Lemon invites the audience to "come inside into my little flat, and I'll tell you everything about my life." In terms of events, there is not much to tell. Lemon is sickly, virginal, and sequestered. She lives on vegetable juices and bread, and spends most of her time "just doing nothing, or staring at the wall." Yet Lemon has a rich and twisted inner life. Among other things, she admires the Nazis for their efficiency and frankness about killing. The seminal influence in Lemon's education, and the center of most of her memories, was a vibrant, iconoclastic family friend, her "Aunt" Dan.

Aunt Dan, one of the youngest Americans ever to teach at Oxford, is a quirky and passionate woman who is equally vehement about her refusal to shout at waiters and her boundless zeal for "selfless" Henry Kissinger. She used to visit the very young Lemon in bed every night and regale her with stories about her bohemian circle of friends.

One of Dan's friends was a beautiful, amoral woman named Mindy. Mindy once auctioned her body to a rich American named Jasper—10,000 pounds to take off her blouse, 50,000 for sex. Dan threw in 5 pounds "just to watch," and when Jasper fell asleep, Mindy sat on the sofa stark naked and told Dan about a man she seduced and then murdered for money.

AUNT DAN

(To LEMON.) She had to put the guy in this plastic sack, kick him down her back stairs, haul him outside, and stick him into the trunk of a car that was parked in an alley. Apparently he'd been working with the police for some time against her friend, Freddie. (A silence.) Well. My teeth were chattering as I listened to the words of this naked goddess, whose lipstick was the dreamiest, loveliest shade of rose. Then she fell silent for a long time, and we just looked at each other. And then she sort of winked at me, I think you would call it, and I wanted to touch that lipstick with my fingers, so I did. And she sort of grabbed my hand

and gave it a big kiss, and my hand was all red. And then
we just sat there for another long time. And then, to the
music of Jasper snoring on the couch, I started to kiss her
beautiful neck. I was incredibly in love. She kissed me back.
I felt as if stars were flying through my head. She was
gorgeous, perfect. We spent the rest of the night on the
couch, and then we went out and had a great breakfast,
and we spent a wonderful week together. (*Pause.*)

[LEMON (*To* AUNT DAN.): Why only a week?

AUNT DAN: Huh?

LEMON: Why only a week? (*Pause.*)

AUNT DAN: Lemon, you know, it's because . . .
(*Pause.*)]

Because love always cries out to be somehow expressed.
(*Pause.*) But the expression of love leads somehow—nowhere. (*A silence.*) You express love, and suddenly
you've . . . you've dropped off the map you were on, in a
way, and onto another one—unrelated—like a bug being
brushed from the edge of a table and falling off onto the
rug below. The beauty of a face makes you touch a hand,
and suddenly you're in a world of actions, of experiences,
unrelated to the beauty of that face, unrelated to that face
at all, unrelated to beauty. You're doing things and saying
things you never wanted to say or do. You're suddenly
spending every moment of your life in conversations, in
encounters, that have no connection with anything you ever
wanted for yourself. What you felt was love. What you felt
was that the face was beautiful. And it was not enough for
you just to feel love, just to sit in the presence of beauty
and enjoy it. Something about your feeling itself made that
impossible. And so you just didn't ask, Well, what will
happen when I touch that hand? What will happen between
that person and me? What will even happen to the thing
I'm feeling at this very moment? Instead, you just walked
right off that table, and there was that person, with all their
qualities, and there was you, with all *your* qualities, and
there you were together. And it's always, of course, ex-

tremely fascinating for as long as you can stand it, but it
has nothing to do with the love you originally felt. Every
time, in a way, you think it will have *something* to do with
the love you felt. But it never does. It never has anything
to do with love. (*Silence.*)

Baby with the Bathwater

Christopher Durang

Premiere: American Repertory Theatre, Cambridge, Mas-
sachusetts, 1983
Setting: John and Helen's home

A young couple named John and Helen have a baby. When
John calls the newborn baby "daddy's little baked potato,"
Helen chastises him: "We don't want it to have problems
in kindergarten or marriage because you called it a baked
potato. . . . Bringing up a child is a delicate thing." They
then proceed to surround the baby, whose sex they don't
know ("The doctor said we could decide later"), with sa-
distic nannies, murderous German shepherds, poisonous
toys, and a baby-sitter who reads out loud from *Mommie
Dearest*.

Eventually, they name the baby Daisy. She spends her
childhood pretending to be an inanimate object and diving
in front of buses. Helen, who alternates trying to write
her first novel with trying to kill herself, threatens to "Shake-
n-Bake" Daisy. When Daisy's "What I Did Last Summer"
essay begins, "Dark, dank rags. Wet, fetid towels. A large
German shepherd, its innards splashed across the windshield of a car," and ends, "Help, help, help. I am drowning, I am drowning, my lungs fill with the summer ocean,
but still I do not die, this awful life goes on and on, no one
can rescue me," her teacher, Miss Pringle, decides that
the girl needs help. The lunatic principal refuses: "Help

this child! She may be the next Virginia Woolf, the next Sylvia Plath. . . . Who cares if she's dead, as long as she publishes!"

Finally, at seventeen, Daisy sees a psychiatrist. A "shy, polite tentative young man," Daisy is wearing "a simple modest dress. His haircut, shoes, and socks, though, are traditionally masculine."

DAISY

When I was eleven, I came across this medical book that had pictures in it, and I realized I looked more like a boy than a girl, but my mother had always wanted a girl or a bestseller, and I didn't want to disappoint her. But then somedays, I don't know what gets into me, I would just feel like striking out at them. So I'd wait til she was having one of her crying fits, and I took the book to her—I was twelve now—and I said, "Have you ever seen this book? Are you totally insane? Why have you named me Daisy? Everyone else has always said I was a boy, what's the *matter* with you?" And she kept crying and she said something about Judith Krantz and something about being out of Shake-n-Bake chicken, and then she said, "I want to die"; and then she said, *Perhaps* you're a boy, but we don't want to jump to any hasty conclusions, so why don't we just wait, and we'd see if I menstruated or not. And I asked her what that word meant, and she slapped me and washed my mouth out with soap. Then she apologized and hugged me, and said she was a bad mother. Then she washed *her* mouth out with soap. Then she tied me to the kitchen table and turned on all the gas jets, and said it would be just a little while longer for the both of us. Then my father came home and he turned off the gas jets and untied me. Then when he asked if dinner was ready, she lay on the kitchen floor and wouldn't move, and he said, I guess not, and then he sort of crouched next to the refrigerator and tried to read a book, but I don't think he was really reading, because he never turned any of the pages. And then eventually, since nothing else seemed to be happening, I just went to bed.

Balm in Gilead

Lanford Wilson

Premiere: La Mama Experimental Theatre Club, New York City, 1965

Setting: An all-night coffee shop and street corner on upper Broadway, New York City

The coffee shop is a gathering place for "the riffraff, the bums, the petty thieves, the scum, the lost, the desperate, the dispossessed, the cool; depending on one's attitude there are a hundred names that could describe them." There are thirty-one speaking characters. Fick is a heroin addict, has been one since he was thirteen. Recently he was mugged by "four or five" guys who were looking for money or drink. He starts telling the story to Tig, a male prostitute, and keeps on repeating it long after Tig has moved on. Fick has no coat. It is cold out.

FICK

(They sit quietly, looking up out toward the street.) I mean, I was just walking down the street and they came up on me like they was important, and they start pushing me around, you know. And they pushed me into this alley, not an alley, but this hallway and back down the end of that to this dark place at the end of the hallway and they start punching at me, and I just fell into this ball on the floor so they couldn't hurt me or nothing. But if I came down there with a couple of fighters, a couple of guys, like my friends,

it wouldn't have to be you or anything, but just a couple or three guys, big guys, like walking down the street, you know. Just so they could see I got these buddies here. See I'm on *H*, I mean, I'm flying and I gotta talk man, but I'm serious now; just a few guys and they'd leave me be, maybe, because they'd think I had these buddies that looked after me, you know: cause I—you know—they kicked me up, if I wasn't on *H*, man, they'd be pains all through me— you know—walking down the street by myself—I start looking around and wondering who's out there gonna mess me up, you know. I get scared as hell, man, walking down around here, I mean, I can't protect myself or nothing, man. You know what I mean? You know what I mean? You know what I mean? You know? I mean if I had these couple— of big buddies—fighters—you—you know—if I had a cou- ple of guys—like—big guys—that—you know, there's like nothing—I could—like, if you walked around with these buddies, I mean you could do, man—you could do any- thing. . . .

Between Daylight and Boonville

Matt Williams

Premiere: Wonderhorse Theatre, New York City, 1980
Setting: A temporary trailer court in the strip mining country of southern Indiana

Three miners' wives and their kids pass the day in the makeshift "recreation area" between two of the trailers. The youngest wife, Carla, is packing to leave her husband. Lorette, an "old floozy" who chain-smokes, says, "Carla, this is the third time this month. . . . Hell, girl, you're packed more than you're unpacked." The third wife, Mar- lene, is "a large-boned woman about thirty-five years old, although she looks somewhat older. There is a tranquil quality about her, an aura of calm. . . . She is six-and-a-half to seven months pregnant." Carla looks up to Marlene as the only person she knows who seems truly happy. Marlene tells her the secret of her marriage.

_____

MARLENE

This one time, before the kids were born, Big Jim was workin' construction before goin' to work for the company. And we were rentin' a little furnished house. I worked all day gettin' the house all cleaned up. Baked cookies. Did the wash. It was one of those days. I use to do a lot more of that stuff than I do now. Anyway, I was beat. So, I sit down on the couch and propped my feet up on the coffee table and started readin' my magazines. Well, Big Jim comes home from work mad as hell at this young, cocky foreman he's workin' for. So he takes it out on me. He had stopped and had a few beers and picked up a six-pack on his way home. And he walks in and wants to know why I've got my feet propped up on the good coffee table. I told him not to worry about it. It was rented. And he said, "Don't talk back. Take your feet down off the table." I said no. And he said you better. And I said you take them down for me. And he said, "Like hell!" And he yanked that table out from under my feet, went to the front door and threw the coffee table right out into the middle of the front yard. I didn't say a word. I got up, grabbed his six-pack and walked over and threw it right out in the front yard. Big Jim didn't say nothin'. He walked over, unplugged the floor lamp and tossed it out. So I grabbed the two wedding pictures off the wall and threw them out. He threw out the chair and I threw out all the toss pillows off the couch. We just kept throwin'. Never said a word. More we threw out, the madder we got. Finally, we got to the couch and it took both of us to throw it out. By the time we emptied the living room, we were both so tired we just stood there on the front porch tryin' to catch our breath. Then we looked at one another and I laughed. And he laughed. We both started laughin', said to hell with it. Left everything in the yard and went up to bed. And that's the secret.

[CARLA. What?]

Don't ever go to bed angry.

Birdbath

Leonard Melfi

Premiere: Theatre Genesis, New York City, 1965
Setting: New York City: a midtown cafeteria, the streets outside, and Frankie's basement apartment

It's the night before Valentine's Day. Frankie Basta, an aspiring poet, is the new cashier at the midtown cafeteria where Velma Sparrow works clearing off tables. They are attracted to each other and Velma comes over to talk. "A nervous and troubled young lady who is a rapid speaker and sometimes trembles," she tells Frankie she lives in the Bronx with her domineering mother. We will later find out that she killed her mother today with a kitchen knife that she still has in her purse.

VELMA

Well, I used to be real skinny, you know what I mean? I used to be all bones, almost like one of them skeletons. But since I been workin' here for Mr. Quincy, well, I've been puttin' on some weight. (*She pauses.*) That's why, in a way, this job isn't really that bad—because of the free meal they let you have. My mother said to me, "Velma, you take advantage of that free meal. You eat as much as you can . . . when something's free you make use of

it . . . take as much as they let you have." And so, I've
been eating pretty good lately, and Mr. Quincy, he's a nice
man, he never tells me that I'm eating too much. In fact,
I think he's a real nice man, because he hired me without
my having any experience at all. This is the first time I've
ever had a job where I cleaned off the tables and everything
when the people were through eating. Boy, at first I was
real scared about this job. I didn't think I was gonna be
able to do it right . . . you know?

[FRANKIE: You're doing okay . . .]

Although, you know what? (She starts to bite her fingernails.)

[FRANKIE: What's that, Velma?]

Well, sometimes Mr. Quincy says things to me . . . or he
gives me certain kinds of looks . . . like for instance . . .
(Embarrassed) I was his . . . girlfriend, maybe. (She looks
at FRANKIE, waiting hopefully for him to agree with her.
FRANKIE gives her a slight smile of comfort, but it is not a
smile of agreement.) I told my mother about the way Mr.
Quincy is to me sometimes, and right away she wanted to
come down and meet him. She asked me how old he was
and she wanted to know how he looked, and after I told
her everything she wanted to know, she said that some
night she would get all dressed up and then come down
here and wait for me until I got off, and while she was
waiting I could introduce her to Mr. Quincy. (She walks
away and begins to wipe the same table top over again.)
You know what she said to me, my mother? She said that
it was all up in my mind that Mr. Quincy might jist
be . . . interested . . . in me. She said that it wasn't true
and that I should jist concentrate on my job and forget
about all those pipe dreams, otherwise I would be gettin'
fired. (She pauses.) Sometimes . . . sometimes it's so hard
for me to figure my mother out . . . because right afterwards she's tellin' me that maybe I shouldn't eat so much
after all because then I would be goin' from one extreme
to the other. She said when I was real skinny I couldn't

find a nice boy, and, well, if I kept on eating the way I've
been doing lately I'd get real fat, and so it would still be
the same old story for me. (*She laughs a desperate, frantic
sort of laugh.*) My mother . . . changes her mind so much
sometimes . . . that it gives me a headache.

The Blood Knot

Athol Fugard

Premiere: The Rehearsal Room, Johannesburg, South Africa,
   1961

Setting: One-room shack in the Non-white location of
   Korsten, near Port Elizabeth, South Africa

Morris and Zachariah are brothers, sons of the same Coloured mother and different fathers. Zachariah is dark-skinned,
while Morris is light-skinned enough to be able to "pass."
Years before, Morris left home and went out in the world
to pursue his education. Now he's returned to keep house
for Zachariah, preparing his foot baths and reading each
night from the Bible.

Morris is a planner. He gets through each day with the
help of an alarm clock, which he sets to go off for each
meal, activity, or bedtime. He is saving their money to buy
a small farm. Zachariah, who works as a guard, is a man of
much simpler appetites. Before Morris came back, he spent
Friday nights dancing and drinking with a neighbor named
Minnie. Now he and Morris spend every night talking: "A
whole year of spending tonights talking, talking. I'm sick
of talking. I'm sick of this room . . . I want woman." Morris
comes up with a plan to find Zach a pen-pal. They choose
Ethel Lange, from a newspaper ad ("I am eighteen years
old and well-developed. . . . My interests are nature, rock-
and-roll, swimming, and a happy future.") The two brothers
send off a letter, Ethel writes back, and everything seems

wonderful. Then Ethel sends Zach her photograph. She is white.

Monologue One: Zach has asked Morris why he came back, why he stayed. Morris replies.

Monologue Two: Ethel writes that she's coming to town on a holiday. Unaware that her pen-pal is Coloured, she wants to meet Zach. In apartheid South Africa, interracial sex is a crime, and even dreams are dangerous. Morris forces Zach to accept the bitter truth: he is black and can never have Ethel. Zach looks at his light-skinned brother and forms a deadly idea: Morris will pass as a white man and *he* can have Ethel. Zach takes their farm savings and buys Morris a gentleman's suit, complete with hat and umbrella. Morris puts on the clothes, but still doesn't look like a white man. "It's that white something inside you, that special meaning and manner of whiteness that I've got to find." In a devastating sequence, Zach goads Morris into abusing him as a white man would, calling him "Swartgat" (nigger). Late that night, Zachariah gets out of his bed and tries on the white man's suit. He imagines he is talking to his mother.

————— 1 —————

MORRIS

We are brothers, remember.

(*A few seconds pass in silence.* MORRIS *threads his needle and then starts working on a tear in* ZACHARIAH's *coat.*) That's a word, hey! Brothers! There's a broody sound for you if ever there was. I mean. . . . Take the others. Father. What is there for us in . . . Father? We never knew him. Even Mother. Maybe a sadness in that one, though, I think, at times. Like the wind. But not much else. She died and we were young. What else is there? Sister. Sissy, they say, for short. Like something snaky in the grass, hey? But we never had one, so we can't be sure. You got to use a word a long time to know its real meaning. That's the trouble with "Mother." We never said it enough.

(He tries it.) Mother. Mother! Yes. Just a touch of sadness in it, and maybe a gray dress on Sundays, and soapsuds on brown hands. That's the lot. Father, Mother, and the sisters we haven't got. The rest is just the people of the world. Strangers, and a few friends. And none of them are blood.

But brothers! Try it. Brotherhood. Brother-in-arms, each other's arms. Brotherly love. Ah, it breeds, man! It's warm and feathery, like eggs in a nest. *(Pause.)* I'll tell you a secret now, Zach. Of all the things there are in this world, I like most to hear you call me that. Zach? *(He looks at* ZACHARIAH's *bed.)* Zachie? Zachariah!

(He is asleep. MORRIS *takes the lamp, goes to the bed, and looks down at the sleeping man. He returns to the table, picks up the Bible, and after an inward struggle speaks in a solemn, "Sunday" voice.)* "And he said: What hast thou done? The voice of thy brother's blood crieth unto me!" *(*MORRIS *drops his head in an admission of guilt.)* Oh Lord! Oh Lord! So he became a hobo and wandered away, a marked man, on a long road, until a year later, in another dream, He spake again: Maybe he needs you, He said. You better go home, man! *(Pause.)* So he turned around on the road, and came back. About this time, a year ago. Could have been today. I remember turning off the road and coming this way across the veld. The sun was on my back. Yes! I left the road because it went a longer way around . . . and I was in a hurry . . . and it was autumn. I had noticed the signs on the way. Motor-cars were fewer and fast. All of them were crowded and never stopped. Their dust was yellow. Telephone poles had lost all their birds . . . and I was alone . . . and getting worried. I needed comfort. It's only a season, I said bravely. Only the beginning of the end of another year. It happens all the time! Be patient! . . . which was hard hurrying home after all those years. . . . Don't dream at night! You must get by

without the old dreams. Maybe a few new ones will come with time . . . and in time, please! . . . because I'm getting desperate, hey! . . . I remember praying.

Then I was off the road and coming here across the veld, and I thought: It looks the same. It was. Because when I reached the first *pondokkies* and the thin dogs, the wind turned and brought the stink from the lake and tears, and a clear memory of two little *outjies* in khaki *broeks*.

No one recognized me, after all those years. I must have changed. I could see they weren't sure, and wanting to say "Sir" at the end of a sentence and ask me for work and wanting to carry my bundle for a *tickey*. At first I was glad . . . but then came a certain sadness in being a stranger in my old home township. I asked the time. It's not late, they said. Not really dark, don't worry. It always gets this way when the wind blows up the factory smoke. The birds are always fooled and settle down too soon to sleep . . . they assured me.

I also asked the way. Six down, they said, pointing to the water's edge. So then there was only time left for a few short thoughts between counting the doors. Will he be home? Will I be welcome? Be remembered? Be forgiven . . . or forgotten, after all those years? Be brave, Morris! Because I had arrived at that door here about a year ago. I remember I reached it . . . and held my breath . . . and knocked . . . and waited . . . outside in the cold . . . hearing a move inside here . . . and then there was my heart as well, the smell of the water behind my back, his steps beyond the door, the slow terrible turning of the knob, the squeak of a rusty hinge, my sweat, until at last, at long last after a lonely road he stood before me . . . frowning. *(Pause.)*

You were wearing this coat. It's been a big help to me, this warm old coat . . . then . . . and in the days that followed. But specially then. It was all I saw at first! I didn't dare look up, because your eyes were there, and down below on the ground were your sad, square feet, and coming out to me, your hands . . . your empty hands. So I looked at your coat! At the buttons. At the tears, and your pockets hanging out . . . while we talked.

And that night, in the dark, when you slept, I put it on . . . because, I've got to get to know him again, I said, this brother of mine, all over again. (MORRIS *puts on* ZACHARIAH's *coat. . . . It is several sizes too large.*) It was a big help. You get right inside the man when you can wrap up in the smell of him, and imagine the sins of idle hands in empty pockets and see the sadness of snot smears on the sleeve, while having no lining and one button had a lot to say about what it's like to be him . . . when it rains . . . and cold winds. It helped a lot. It prepared me for your flesh, Zach. Because your flesh, you see, has an effect on me. The sight of it, the feel of it . . . it . . . it feels, you see. Pain, and all those dumb dreams throbbing under the raw skin, I feel, you see. . . . I saw you again after all those years . . . and it hurt.

———— 2 ————

ZACHARIAH

Ma. Ma! Mother! Hullo. How are you, old woman? What's that? You don't recognize me? Well, well, well. Take a guess. (*Shakes his head.*) No. (*Shakes his head.*) No. Try again. (*Shakes his head.*) What's the matter with you, Ma? Don't you recognize your own son? (*Shakes his head violently.*) No, no! Not him! It's me, Zach! (*Sweeps off the hat to show his face.*) *Ja.* Zach! Didn't think I could do it, did you? Well, to tell you the truth, the whole truth so help me God, I got sick of myself and made a change. Him? At home, Ma. *Ja.* A lonely boy, as you say. A sad story, as I will tell you. He went on the road, Ma, but strange to say, he came back quite white. No tan at all. I don't recognize him no more. (*He sits.*) I'll ask you again, how are you, old woman? I see some signs of wear and tear. (*Nodding his head.*) That's true . . . such sorrow . . . tomorrow. . . .

Ja . . . it's cruel . . . it's callous . . . and your feet as well?
Still a bad fit in the shoe? *Ai ai ai!* Me? *(Pause. He struggles.)*
There's something I need to know, Ma. You see, we been
talking, me and him . . . *ja*, I talk to him, he says it
helps . . . and now we got to know. Whose mother were
you really? At the bottom of your heart, where your blood
is red with pain, tell me, whom did you really love? No
evil feelings, Ma, but, I mean, a man's got to know. You
see, he's been such a burden as a brother. *(Agitation.)* Don't
be dumb! Don't cry! It was just a question! Look! I brought
you a present, old soul. *(Holds out a hand with the fingers
lightly closed.)* It's a butterfly. A real beauty butterfly. We
were travelling fast, Ma. We hit them at ninety . . . a whole
flock. But one was still alive, and made me think
of . . . Mother. . . . So I caught it, myself, for you, remembering what I caught from you. This, old Ma of mine,
is gratitude for you, and it proves it, doesn't it? Some things
are only skin-deep, because I got it, here in my hand, I
got beauty . . . too . . . haven't I?

Blue Window

Craig Lucas

Premiere: The Production Company, New York City, 1984
Setting: Five New York City apartments
Libby is giving a dinner party for a group of friends. Scene
One is a complex fabric of interwoven scenes in different
apartments, as Libby and her six guests prepare for the
party. Scene Two is the party itself, and Scene Three is its
aftermath.

Libby is an attractive but socially paralyzed woman who
is valiantly trying to conquer her fears. Hosting a party is
trauma enough, but when she pops out a front tooth cap
while trying to open a caviar jar, she is mortified. She

spends most of the party trying to hide it from her guests by mumbling or covering her mouth when she speaks, claiming her lip "itches."

The guests are a mixed lot: a lesbian couple, an arrogant composer and his "bimbotic" girlfriend, Libby's closest male friend from group therapy, and Norbert, her skydiving instructor. (Libby has not yet been able to leave the plane.) Norbert stays after the rest of the guests to help with the dishes. When he teases Libby about her tooth, suggesting she get to her dentist, Libby starts laughing hysterically, practically crying. She tells Norbert she used to be married to her dentist.

LIBBY

Big wedding. And . . . we laughed. Marty . . . We bought a big apartment on East 71st Street—much too big for just the two of us. Brand-new building, we had a terrace and windows on three sides. It was almost the penthouse. We'd been married about three months—not quite— And . . . I think I was pregnant. I was. We talked about it and I was late. Anyway, I could have been . . . And we were standing by the window. I didn't have any clothes on. I was looking out. It was late— Late afternoon. Everything was blue— as blue as it can be before it gets black.

[NORBERT: Uh-huh?]

And Marty said, Come out on the terrace. I said, I don't have any clothes on. And he brought me this little robe. And we walked out on the terrace. (BOO *puts her hand over her eyes as if she has a headache.*) We'd only lived there two months. And he kissed me and I put my head back to look up at the sky. Our reflections were in the glass. And I put my head back; we lived on the seventh floor, there was another one above us. (GRIEVER *puts his head back as if sighing.*) And we leaned—he leaned—I set my back against the rail and it . . . just . . . We were gone; we were over. I saw us leave the window. I looked—past him, my hands reached past him to try to hold something, there wasn't anything . . . just blue . . . And I didn't black out. I thought—very clearly . . . This is bad. This is real. And it's true, you see everything pass before your eyes. Everything. Slowly, like a dream, and Marty was . . . Marty was climbing up me and screaming and we turned . . . over . . . once . . . and . . . we went through an awning . . . Sloan's . . . Which saved my life . . . And I broke every bone in my face. I have a completely new face. My teeth were all shattered; these are all caps.

[ALICE (*from off*): Now I know this is here because I just saw it.

BOO: What?

ALICE: Wait.]

I was in traction for ten months. And Tom came to see me every week. Every day sometimes. Marty's family. Who sued the building. I mean, they never even attached it to the wall. It wasn't even attached. It was just a rail—a loose rail. There was another one on another floor, the same thing could have happened . . . I landed on him. I killed him. I can't—(NORBERT *moves towards her; she flinches.*) It's seven years. I'm thirty-three years old. I can't have anybody hold me. I can never be held.

Blues for Mister Charlie

James Baldwin

Premiere: Anta Theatre, New York City, 1964

Setting: Courtyard, church, and streets of a segregated Southern town

Richard Henry, a volatile, proud black musician who has been living in the North, comes back to his Southern hometown and picks a fight with a racist white shopkeeper. The shopkeeper shoots him, claiming that Richard attempted to rape his wife. His trial divides the town sharply along racial lines. The only white man who sides with the blacks is Parnell James, an outcast newspaper editor whose liberal ethics are tarnished by guilt-ridden lust for black women.

Monologue One: The black mourners are led by Richard's minister father, Meridian Henry. A man who has preached and followed the path of nonviolence all his life, Meridian doesn't know how to forgive his son's murder. He shares his anguish with Parnell.

Monologue Two: During the few days before Richard was killed, he started a fiery affair with a black activist student, Juanita. In the moments before she steps up to the witness stand, we hear Juanita's passionate thoughts about her dead lover.

1

MERIDIAN

I'm a Christian. I've been a Christian all my life, like my Mama and Daddy before me and like their Mama and Daddy before them. Of course, if you go back far enough, you get to a point *before* Christ, if you see what I mean, *B.C.*— and at that point, I've been thinking, black people weren't raised to turn the other cheek, and in the hope of heaven. No, then they didn't have to take low. Before Christ. They walked around just as good as anybody else, and when they died, they didn't go to heaven, they went to join their ancestors. My son's dead, but he's not gone to join his ancestors. He was a sinner, so he must have gone to hell— if we're going to believe what the Bible says. Is that such an improvement, such a mighty advance over B.C.? I've been thinking, I've had to think—would I have *been* such a Christian if I hadn't been born black? Maybe I *had* to become a Christian in order to have any dignity at all. Since I wasn't a man in man's eyes, then I could be a man in the eye's of God. But that didn't protect my wife. She's dead, too soon, we don't really know how. That didn't protect my son—he's dead, we know how too well. That hasn't changed this town—this town, where you couldn't find a

white Christian at high noon on Sunday! The eyes of God—
maybe those eyes are blind—I never let myself think of
that before.

———— 2 ————

JUANITA

He lay beside me on that bed like a rock. As heavy as a
rock—like he'd fallen—fallen from a high place—fallen so
far and landed so heavy, he seemed almost to be sinking
out of sight—with one knee pointing to heaven. My God.
He covered me like that. He wasn't at all like I thought he
was. He fell on—fell on me—like life and death. My God.
His chest, his belly, the rising and the falling, the moans.
How he clung, how he struggled—life and death! Life and
death! Why did it all seem to me like tears? That he came
to me, clung to me, plunged into me, sobbing, howling,
bleeding, somewhere inside his chest, his belly, and it all
came out, came pouring out, like tears! My God, the smell,
the touch, the taste, the sound, of anguish! Richard! Why
couldn't I have held you closer? Held you, held you, borne
you, given you life again? Have made you be born again!
Oh, Richard. The teeth that gleamed, oh! when you smiled,
the spit flying when you cursed, the teeth stinging when
you bit—your breath, your hands, your weight, my God,
when you moved in me! Where shall I go now, what shall
I do? Oh. Oh. Oh. Mama was frightened. Frightened because little Juanita brought her first real lover to this house.
I suppose God does for Mama what Richard did for me.
Juanita! I don't care! I don't care! Yes, I want a lover made
of flesh and blood, of flesh and blood, like me, I don't want
to be God's mother! He can *havc* His icy, snow-white heaven!
If He is somewhere around this fearful planet, if I ever see
Him. I will spit in His face! In God's face! How *dare* He
presume to judge a living soul! A living soul. Mama is afraid
I'm pregnant. Mama is afraid of so much. I'm not afraid. I
hope I'm pregnant. I *hope* I am! One more illegitimate

black baby—that's right, you jive mothers! And I am going
to raise my baby to be a man. A *man*, you dig? Oh, let me
be pregnant, let me be pregnant, don't let it all be gone!
A man. Juanita. A man. Oh, my God, there are no more.
For me. Did this happen to Mama sometime? Did she have
a man sometime who vanished like smoke? And left her to
get through this world as best she could? Is that why she
married my father? Did this happen to Mother Henry? Is
this how we all get to be mothers—so soon? of helpless
men—because all the other men perish? No. No. No. No.
What is this world like? I will end up taking care of some
man, some day. Help me do it with love. Pete. Meridian.
Parnell. We have been the mothers for them all. It must
be dreadful to be Parnell. There is no flesh he can touch.
All of it is bloody. Incest everywhere. Ha-ha! You're going
crazy, Juanita. Oh, Lord, don't let me go mad. Let me be
pregnant! Let me be pregnant!

Bosoms and Neglect

John Guare

Premiere: Goodman Theatre, Chicago, 1979
Setting: Manhattan in August

Henny is eighty-three years old and blind. Her spirit is
very strong. For two years, she has treated her ulcerated
breast cancer by covering the sores with Kotex pads and
waving a plastic statuette of St. Jude over the infected
breast. But today she has asked her forty-year-old son Scooper
to call a doctor for her. When the doctor arrives, Henny
panics and swears it's a false alarm, "Girl who cried wolf.
April fool." But first she shows Scooper her breast. The
cancer has eaten its way through the skin. She goes straight
to the hospital.

It's August. Scooper is an analytic patient whose psychoanalyst, Dr. James, has left for vacation this morning. By chance he runs into Deirdre, another of Dr. James's patients, in a bookstore. For eleven months they have shared the same waiting room without ever talking, but now, with Dr. James gone, they cling to each other for comfort, comparing neuroses. Deirdre can't cope with her Mafioso father, and Scooper is furious with Henny for hiding her illness from him for two years. Their lives are a mess. They make love, they fight, they get hysterical and stab each other with book knives. End of Act One.

Act Two takes place in the hospital where all three characters are patients. Scooper sits in a wheelchair, his stab wounds bandaged. He is visiting Henny, who's recovering from her mastectomy ("I'm a topless dancer now. Half a topless dancer.") He talks about the mess of his life, and how much he blames his mother for his helplessness. He tells her he has a recurring dream "that you picked me up and used me as a weapon against some strange man." He wants to settle accounts with his mother; he wants her to die. He offers to help her take pills and "die with some dignity." Henny agrees, and they have a tender scene. Then she hurls the pills to the floor and screams at her son. Scooper leaves with Deirdre, pushing his empty wheelchair toward Henny's bed. Unaware that her son is no longer with her, the blind woman talks to him. (*Note:* James is Scooper's real name, which his mother has never used.)

HENNY

(*Stirs.*) James? James? Is she gone? Take my hand, James. O.K. Play the Quiet Man. Hearing the name James over and over, I keep thinking of my father. He was a wonderful man. After he died, I was lost. His dying broke me in about a million pieces but after a while I pasted myself together into some kind of new teacup and toddled off to Boston for a new drink of water. I loved Boston. They laughed at my

New York accent. It made me stand out. I met a man. Don
Walker. He was Amish. I said, "You must be nuts to love
me." He said, "No, because I have all my buttons." I said,
"Which makes you ex-Amish, seeing as how you are not
allowed to have buttons." And he said, "Well, you're no
great shakes," and I said, "Either are you or you'd still be
a Shaker." Believe me, it was funny at the time. We loved
each other. I felt my father in heaven was paying attention
to me and had sent Don to me as a heavenly present. But
Don's Quaker mother who unfortunately was still on this
earth would not have her precious ex-Amish son hitched
up with a shanty Irish Catholic girl from Manhattan. Even
though we were *very* lace curtain. Maybe rayon curtain.
But not shanty. Not trash. But only a Quaker girl was good
enough for her son. He buckled under. Stopped calling
me. Neglected to keep dates. I got the message. I moved
my broken teacup of heart back to New York. Moved into
214 Riverside Drive. Met your father in the lobby. One
disappointed person? Meet another disappointed person.
Years went by. We got married. To show we could. We
stayed together. We had you. And one day I dressed you
up and got on the morning train to Boston. I waited outside
my old office on Summer Street until Don Walker came
out for lunch. I acted like I was just passing by. I wanted
it to seem like I had just bumped into him, act casual, show
him how great my life was, show off my beautiful child that
was not his. And I saw him and I loved him so much. And
after we said hellos and fancy meetings and acted surprised,
I picked you up to show him what he missed and instead
I hit him with you. Because he wasn't your father. Because
he hadn't trusted me. Because I hadn't meant enough to
him. I kept hitting him with you, pushing your face into
his, till I realized your nose was bleeding. He was so shocked.
I kept saying, "You neglected me." I kept screaming like
some shanty Irish Banshee: "I loved you." Finally he ran
off. I wiped off your face. We got back on the next train to
New York. Your father was home. He didn't ask why we

were late, what we had done. He read his paper. Had his
drinks. Slept. I put you to bed. I took off all my clothes
and stood in front of the mirror. This body was not good
enough. It couldn't get me what I wanted . . . maybe
if . . . maybe . . . I got dressed. Sat by your bed. Stared
and stared at you. This was my prayer. A better life for
you. You woke up. You looked at me. I want that for you.
I want that for you . . . *James. (She passionately reaches
her hand out to her son, trying to make that connection.
The lights hold a moment, then come down.)*

Brontosaurus

Lanford Wilson

Premiere: Circle Repertory Company, New York City, 1977
Setting: Antique shop and antique dealer's Manhattan
   apartment, both represented only by a pair of antique
   chairs

Brontosaurus is a very simple play, written to be performed
on a nearly bare stage. The antique dealer is a rich, lonely,
compulsively verbal woman of forty-five. Her young nephew
is coming to New York to attend college, and she has invited
him to share her magnificent, empty apartment. The nephew
turns out to be a blunt and taciturn theology student. They
have nothing in common, and though the dealer does nothing but complain about her charmless houseguest, she is
desperate to gain his affection. Finally, the nephew announces that he is moving out. The dealer responds with
her customary irony, making cracks about his "calling" to
the ministry. ("Imagine a bricklayer or a fireman coming
to his family, his eyes glassed-over, saying: 'Parents! I've
seen!' ") Breaking his monosyllabic custom for the first time
in the play, the nephew relates the following story, which
he compares to the Buddhist experience of Satori.

NEPHEW

(Straightforward.) I was standing at the side of the house.
I don't remember what I had been doing. I don't remember
anything before, immediately before, or immediately after.
I stood for a while and then I went inside. I was standing
at the side of the house. I had come from around behind
in the shade and was standing in the sun; not doing anything, not going anywhere, just standing at the side of the
house in the sun. And the hand of God reached out and
touched me. That doesn't mean anything. It's abstract, isn't
it? But it's the easiest way of explaining the feeling. (DEALER
sits.) I was standing there, not thinking anything that I
would remember. There was a bush on my left and the
corner of the house on my right. Instead of just stopping
for a while and then moving on, while I was stopped I
became aware that my body was changing, or something
was happening, physically happening, inside my body. As
if all my cells were changing at the same time. Some vi-
brating sensation through my body that raised me or made
me feel like I was physically growing, like a—perhaps a
chemical change was occurring. And I started to get scared,
but instead of that happening it was gradually like I wasn't
standing there anymore. For a moment it was like I had
changed into a gas. I felt I was spreading, thinning out,
being led over the world or shown the world. Thinning out
to take it all in, to absorb it. Or I was shown what I was.
I heard people speaking in languages that I understood but
had never heard before, I heard bells—no, I didn't actually
hear anything, but I seemed to *know* about bells in church
towns, in the farm country around small towns where they
make wine, in France; and people getting up where it was
just beginning to be light, to go to work; people walking
on streets, shopping, and small things growing in the wet
and shade in rain forests. I didn't see them, I wasn't shown
them, I just knew them. Because thinning out, or whatever

it was, I *became* them. An old lady who thought in a language different from the one she spoke, dying in terrible pain in the geriatric ward of a very efficient hospital; twins just being born in the Orient; a boy my age, in India, whose job was to carry the censer with incense, swinging it, in a Catholic church: I didn't know them, I *was* them. I was *they*. They were me. We were all the same stuff, the same regenerating impulse. I just thinned out to mix with it all or to realize what I was, what I had come from, and gradually came back to my own design, my own body. But, of course, I thought about it differently, because it wasn't mine. I wasn't me. I was them. I was they. Which is grammatically correct?

[DEALER: (*Pause.*) "I was they" is correct, but it sounds all wrong, doesn't it?]

I've not tried to explain the experience before, but you asked—

Calm Down Mother
Megan Terry

Premiere: Sheridan Square Playhouse, New York City, 1964
Setting: Bare stage

Calm Down Mother is a "transformation play" in which three actresses play multiple roles. A word or a physical gesture serves as the hinge for instantaneous transition from one scene to the next. In this "theatre game" style, the actors create the physical environment for each scene without props or scenery. Here, they become a mother and two daughters washing dishes at a tenement sink. They are having a fight about birth control.

SUE

See, I got enough eggs in me for thirty years, see. That's one a month for thirty years. Twelve times thirty is—360 eggs. Three hundred and sixty possibilities. Three hundred and sixty babies could be born out of my womb. So, if I don't produce each and every one of them, which is a mathematical impossibility, should I go to hell for that? So what should I do—pray and moan on beans? So what should I do, catch eggs and save them in a test tube for when after the BOMB comes? And I'm only one bearer of the eggs. You sitting on yours, you're nineteen. You got a whole year's eggs on me still. So if God sees fit to flush them down the pipe every month if they don't meet up with an electric male shock, then who the hell are these priests and all to scream about pills and controls? Tell me that! Who the hell are they? They want to save my eggs till they can get around to making them into babies, they can line up and screw the test tubes. Yeah! That's a sight. They're welcome. But they can't shoot twins into my test tubes. And you two! You sit there in the church every Sunday, kneeling and mumbling and believing all that crap that those men tell you, and they don't even know what the hell they are talking about. And I'll bet you don't know what I'm talking about. Because I'm the only one in this whole carton of eggs what's got any brains. And I'm taking my pills and I ain't kneeling on any beans or babies' brains to make up for it.

Christmas on Mars

Harry Kondoleon

Premiere: Playwrights Horizons/New York Theatre Workshop, New York City, 1983
Setting: An empty pink room in a city apartment
Bruno, an actor in cologne commercials, has picked out a dream apartment for himself and his girlfriend Audrey. He has written to Audrey's mother Ingrid to ask for her help

with finances, and to his own roommate Nissim to inform him that he's moving out. There is trouble on both fronts. Audrey hates Ingrid; Nissim loves Bruno. When both of them find out that Audrey is pregnant, they want to move in. Ingrid craves Audrey's forgiveness, and Nissim, a recently fired airline steward, believes he's entitled to Bruno's firstborn because he once saved him from a knifing.

An extravagant character who has fainting fits and smokes imaginary cigarettes, Nissim is deeply—if unrequitedly—in love with the self-absorbed Bruno. His suffering reaches religious dimensions; he buys all his shoes "a half-size too small and filled with pain. I wear them deliberately like Christ's thorn hat to remind myself of the doubleness and falsehood." He is loyal and devoted to a fault, an ardent believer in human love.

It is Christmas. Audrey is way overdue but will not give birth: "Look at me, I'm full, I'm filled now with all goodness and purity and I will not let it go." Bruno storms out of the apartment. Ingrid, who has given up hope of reconciliation with her daughter, makes plans to leave town with a man whom she met on the subway. Nissim begs her to stay, but she goes to her room to start packing. Terrified of abandonment, Nissim picks up the doll they are using for diapering practice and starts to play under the Christmas tree.

NISSIM

You've lost faith—you can't lose faith! You haven't been reading the newspapers have you? I told you not to look at them, it's the same news over and over—they try to make you think it's some other news by making it more shocking on alternate days but it's the same thing and pieced together certainly to make us lose faith! (INGRID *exits.*) *DON'T ABANDON ME! (To himself, red alarm.)* I mustn't collapse. I must think of presents and happiness. (*He picks up the practice doll.*) Oh little play-baby, do you love me?

I love you. You do, I know you do. Why don't we open some of our presents, wouldn't that be fun? It's naughty but oh let's. What would be in this pretty box, hard to tell. *(He opens it, using occasionally the forced help of the practice doll.)* A brush and comb set for you, how nice, but we'll have to put those away for a while until you're a little less bald. What could be in this big box? Let's just see. Ooo! A coat with matching little shoes. Do you like them? Let's just try them on, okay? *(He puts the red baby coat and red shoes on the practice doll.)* How dashing, how smart! You're a clever baby, ready for school already but I'll never send you to one of those public torture chambers don't worry or one of those schools named after saints that breed devils. I will teach you everything you need to know. Ask me a question. "Where do babies come from?" From God, little baby. "Who is God?" God is everything good and holy and pure and kind and healthy and growing and generous and good and good and good, that is God, little baby. "And where is he, where is God?" Why God is right above us, little baby, looking down on us. "Why then, tell me, why won't he help us, help us all, even just for a minute?" That's enough questions. We must get on our horse and ride away very fast from these questions, very fast because they will chase us, chase us through the day. *(Practice doll in one arm,* NISSIM *rides the horse toy, galloping speedily around the room.)*

Cloud Nine

Caryl Churchill

Premiere: Joint Stock Theatre Group, London, 1979
Setting: Multiple

Act One of *Cloud Nine* takes place in British colonial Africa in Victorian times. Act Two takes place in contemporary

London, but for the play's characters it is only twenty-five years later. In this highly theatrical exploration of sex roles and identity, male actors play women, women play men, white people play black people, and adults play children. Victorian repression and contemporary sexual freedom are seen as two masks for the same human needs and confusions.

Betty is Victoria and Edward's mother. In Act Two, Edward, who is gay, forms a *ménage à trois* with his sister and her lover Lin, a lesbian mother. Betty shocks both of her children by leaving her husband Clive to move into "a little flat, that will be fun." Out on her own for the first time, she blossoms: "You appreciate the weekend when you're working. . . . And the money, I feel like a child with the money. Clive always paid everything but I do understand it perfectly well." Alone on a park bench, Betty tells the audience about her newfound freedom.

BETTY

I used to think Clive was the one who like sex. But then I found I missed it. I used to touch myself when I was very little, I thought I'd invented something wonderful. I used to do it to go to sleep with or to cheer myself up, and one day it was raining and I was under the kitchen table, and my mother saw me with my hand under my dress rubbing away, and she dragged me out so quickly I hit my head and it bled and I was sick, and nothing was said, and I never did it again till this year. I thought if Clive wasn't looking at me there wasn't a person there. And one night in bed in my flat I was so frightened I started touching myself. I thought my hand might go through into space. I touched my face, it was there, my arm, my breast, and my hand sent down where I thought it shouldn't, and I thought well there is somebody there. It felt very sweet, it was a feeling from very long ago, it was very soft, just barely touching and I felt myself gathering together more and more and I felt angry with Clive and angry with my mother and I went on and on defying them, and there was this vast feeling growing in me and all round me and they couldn't stop me and no one could stop me and I was there and coming and coming. Afterwards I thought I'd betrayed Clive. My mother would kill me. But I felt triumphant because I was a separate person from them. And I cried because I didn't want to be. But I don't cry about it any more. Sometimes I do it three times in one night and it really is great fun.

Come Back to the 5 & Dime, Jimmy Dean, Jimmy Dean

Ed Graczyk

Premiere: Players Theatre of Columbus, Ohio, 1976
Setting: A five-and-dime in McCarthy, a small town in West
   Texas, on September 30, 1975, and September 30, 1955
In a small Texas town near the film set for *Giant*, the Disciples of James Dean hold their twentieth reunion. The play is interspersed with flashbacks to a meeting twenty years earlier, when *Giant* was still being filmed and all the Disciples were teenagers. One of them, Mona, was cast as an extra. Her life changed forever, in more ways than one. She became pregnant during the filming, and twenty years later she still insists that her son, Jimmy Dean, was the love-child of her idol. A high-strung, fluttery woman with psychosomatic asthma, Mona has clung to this lie for so long that she almost believes it. She also believes that her son is brain-damaged and helpless, and treats him accordingly. Both these illusions are shattered by a surprise guest at the Disciples' reunion.

Joanne is a glamorous transsexual, formerly Mona's friend

Joe. As teenagers, they worked together at the five-and-dime, until rumors of Joe's homosexuality caused their boss to fire him. It was Joe, pretending that he was James Dean to fill both their fantasies, who fathered Mona's child. Here is Mona's version of the story, unchanged over twenty years' time.

MONA

Elizabeth Taylor's head keeps gettin' in the way . . . but, I'm there, mostly behin' her left ear in that scene where she first arrives from her papa's plantation in Virginia . . . an' they have that big barbecue picnic scene. She gets real hot an' starts to faint, grabbin' onto the branch of a mesquite tree for support . . . right as the camera comes close to her at that point . . . you can see me peekin' out from behin' her left ear. *(Pause.)* I felt like such a celebrity the way they were all fussin' over me.

[JOE: Mona, you sound like you was the only one there . . . there were so many people, I could hardly even find you.

MONA (THEN): Joe, if you aren't interested in listenin' . . . you can leave.]

(She goes on building to a desperate frenzy.) That night I laid there in the back seat of the Buick and kept thinkin' about how I was chosen above all them thousands of others . . . starin' out the window at the millions of stars an' the outline of that beautiful house way off in the distance. Suddenly, one of those stars exploded, burst away from all the millions of others an' fell from the sky . . . landin' right behin' the house . . . behin' the front of Reata. I leaned over the seat to point it out to Joe, but he had tramped off somewhere, all mad 'cause he wasn't chosen, too.

[JOE. I didn't tramp off mad. I just wanted to be alone.]

I pulled my blanket aroun' my shoulders an' started to walk to where the star had fallen to earth. I walked past the front gate down the road to the house. It was so quiet and still . . . the only sound was comin' from a far away train, blowin' its whistle an' chuggin' off into the night. When I got to the front porch, this voice comin' outta nowhere says, "Isn't it a little late to be callin' on your neighbors?" It was him. I knew it. I knew it the first minute I heard his voice. Then he said, "Don't just stand there bein' unfriendly. Come on up on the porch an' sit a spell." As I moved up the stairs, I reminded him that I was the one who gave him a match that mornin' . . . an he thanked me again. We spent that whole entire night together. . . . until the sun started to peek out from over the edge of the earth, turnin' the sky into the brightest red I ever saw.

[JOE. Mona, what are you sayin'?!]

(*Sharply to* JOE.) We walked together to the gate an' he thanked me for sharin' the night with him an' then we both walked away in separate directions.

Cowboy Mouth

Sam Shepard

Premiere: Traverse Theatre, Edinburgh, Scotland, 1971
Setting: A junked-out room with a fucked-up bed
Cavale, "a chick who looks like a crow," has kidnapped Slim, "a cat who looks like a coyote," off the streets with an old .45. She wants to make him into a rock star, "a rock-n-roll Jesus with a cowboy mouth." They've been in this room for too long and they're both mean as snakes.

Slim misses his wife and kid. Cavale sings to her dead pet crow, Raymond. She dresses in raggedy black, and has named herself after the poet Nerval, who kept a pet lobster on a pink ribbon and hanged himself on Cavale's birthday. (Cavale means "escape.") She tries to tell Slim why her vision of the rock-n-roll savior is so important: "The old

God is just too far away. He don't represent our pain no more. His words don't shake through us no more. . . . People want a street angel. They want a saint but with a cowboy mouth. Somebody to get off on when they can't get off on themselves." Slim screams at her for playing with his dreams. They have a huge fight, then lie down on the bed and exchange childhood memories.

CAVALE

You're so neat. You're such a neat guy. I wish I woulda known you when I was little. Not real little. But at the age when you start finding out stuff. When I was cracking rocks apart and looking at their sparkles inside. When I first put my finger inside me and felt wonderment. I would've took you to this real neat hideout I had where I made a waterfall with tires and shit, and my own hut. We could've taken all our clothes off and I'd look at your dinger and you could show me how far you could piss. I bet you would've protected me. People were always giving me shit. Ya know what? Once I was in a play. I was real glad I was in a play 'cause I thought they were just for pretty people and I had my dumb eyepatch and those metal plate shoes to correct my duck foot. It was "The Ugly Duckling" and I really dug that 'cause of the happy ending and shit. And I got to be the ugly duckling and I had to wear some old tattered black cloth and get shit flung at me but I didn't mind 'cause at the end I'd be that pretty swan and all. But you know what they did, Slim? At the end of the play I had to kneel on the stage and cover my head with a black shawl and this real pretty blonde-haired girl dressed in a white ballet dress rose up behind me as the swan. It was really shitty, man. I never got to be the fucking swan. I paid all the dues and up rose ballerina Cathy like the North Star. And afterwards all the parents could talk about was how pretty she looked. Boy, I ran to my hideout and cried and cried. The lousy fucks. I wish you were around then. I bet you would've protected me.

Coyote Ugly

Lynn Siefert

Premiere: Steppenwolf Theatre Company, Chicago, 1985
Setting: The rural Southwest

Dowd Pewsy brings his wife Penny back home to meet the folks. His parents, Andreas and Red, are trash-culture rednecks whose lives are made up of stolen cars, shotguns, and Hide-a-Bed sex. Andreas eats Redi-Whip straight from the cannister. Her husband Red, a mechanic, can't keep his hands off of anyone's breasts. But the real shock for Penny is twelve-year-old Scarlet, a feral little nutcase who spends her time setting traps for stray bobcats and casting spells with fire and bleached bones. She is wildly jealous of Penny, and drags her out onto the desert, tied up as a captive. The good-natured Penny, a schoolteacher from Philadelphia, thinks this is a game. Scarlet ties her up, hexes her silent, and leaves her to burn in the sun. She rushes back home to go fishing with Dowd. During the following scene, they are cleaning fish outside the house. Scarlet draws in the sand and the air with a stick.

SCARLET

I blame my whole life on that Hide-a-Bed. I was produced on it after one night of hot sex. Who knows. Ma tried to get rid of me but I was too serious about living. She took ice showers and sat out late waiting for the chill. She beat me with her fist while I was still inside her and that's why she can't lay a hand on me now. There was this creep had

pink hair and one eye name of Danny Dog used to drive
Red around before he worked for a living. This one eye of
his was glass. Just some old marble he'd stuck in. He didn't
have no brakes so he'd pick Red up by punching it from
the road, coasting to the house, sliding into a three-sixty,
swinging Red into the rear, then gunning it fast back to the
road. One day he gunned it so hard his marble eye popped
out and he drove up onto the porch. Ma come running out
screaming and hollering all pooched out with me inside
her. HEY YOU WHAT ARE YOU UP TO YOU GO ON
HOME NOW, Ma said. Danny Dog pointed to the eye in
the palm of his hand. Ma give the pickup a shove. Danny
Dog beat it to the road without a look back. Right then.
When she was least expecting me, I popped out like Danny
Dog's eyeball. Ma fell down kicking and cussing with me
still hooked up to her. I hated her already so I bit her. I
bit her and I bit her. She started running. She ran dragging
me behind her all the way to Phoenix. You want to know
what happened to my neck? She ran and I flew out behind.
She felt like nothing by then but she was driven driven
driven. She ran up the front steps of a man's house. Man's
name was Keeper. Sign on the porch said SCISSORS
SHARPENED. Ma rang the bell. I bit her feet. She pulled
on the front door. She pulled so hard the whole house came
off in her hand. That's all I remember.

Crimes of the Heart

Beth Henley

Premiere: Actors Theatre of Louisville, 1979
Setting: The Magrath sisters' kitchen in Hazlehurst,
   Mississippi
Babe Botrelle is the youngest of three Southern sisters. She
has just shot her husband, Zackery, a wealthy state senator,

in the liver. Her motive? "I just didn't like his stinking looks!" The whole town of Hazelhurst is buzzing with the gossip. Babe's oldest sister, Lenny, a stay-at-home spinster, has telegrammed the middle sister, Meg, a sexy failed singer who now lives in Hollywood. Meg comes back home, Babe gets out on bail, and the sisters share their bizarre and hilarious troubles.

It's Lenny's thirtieth birthday, and she has just learned that the horse she's had since she was ten was killed by a lightning bolt. Meg has a job paying cold-storage bills for a dog-food company, and recently cried her way into the L.A. County Hospital psychiatric ward. As for the moon-struck, saxophone-playing Babe, she was so unfulfilled by her marriage that she had an affair with a fifteen-year-old black boy named Willie Jay, after adopting his stray dog named Dog). Here Babe tells her two sisters how this led to shooting her husband.

BABE

All right, then. Let's see . . . Willie Jay was over. And it was after we'd—

[MEG: Yeah! Yeah!]

BABE. And we were just standing around on the back porch playing with Dog. Well, suddenly, Zackery comes from around the side of the house. And he startled me 'cause he's supposed to be away at the office, and there he is coming from 'round the side of the house. Anyway, he says to Willie Jay, "Hey, boy, what are you doing back here?" And I said, "He's not doing anything. You just go on home, Willie Jay! You just run right on home." Well, before he can move, Zackery comes up and knocks him once right across the face and then shoves him down the porch steps, causing him to skin up his elbow real bad on that hard concrete. Then he says, "Don't you ever come around here again, or I'll have them cut out your gizzard!" Well, Willie

Jay starts crying, these tears come streaming down his face, then he gets up real quick and runs away with Dog following off after him. After that, I don't remember much too clearly; let's see . . . I went on into the living room, and I went right up to the davenport and opened the drawer where we keep the burglar gun . . . I took it out. Then I—I brought it up to my ear. That's right. I put it right inside my ear. Why, I was gonna shoot off my own head! That's what I was gonna do. Then I heard the back door slamming and suddenly, for some reason, I thought about mama . . . how she'd hung herself. And here I was about ready to shoot myself. Then I realized—that's right I realized how I didn't want to kill myself! And she—she probably didn't want to kill herself. She wanted to kill him, and I wanted to kill him, too. I wanted to kill Zackery, not myself. 'Cause I—I wanted to live! So I waited for him to come on into the living room. Then I held out the gun, and I pulled the trigger, aiming for his heart, but getting him in the stomach. *(After a pause.)* It's funny that I really did that.

Curse of the Starving Class

Sam Shepard

Premiere: New York Shakespeare Festival, New York City, 1978
Setting: Farmhouse kitchen in California

Weston and Ella are the parents of Wesley and Emma. The family is on the rocks, emotionally and financially. When the play begins, Wesley is picking up the debris of the front door his father broke down last night. Ella comes in and starts fixing him breakfast.

Monologue One: Wesley talks to himself as he throws pieces of door in a wheelbarrow.

Monologue Two: Emma has her first period. When she

finds out that her mother has cooked the chicken she saved for a 4-H Club demonstration, and her brother has pissed on her "How to Cut a Chicken" charts, she decides to run away from home on horseback. Wesley finds out that his mother has sold their house without telling her husband. Ella leaves with her lawyer friend Taylor, and Weston comes home, staggering drunk, with a bag full of artichokes. He's sold the house too, to the man whose bar he drinks in. Both buyers make trouble. Emma gets on her horse and rides through the bar, shooting it up. She winds up in jail.

The following morning, Weston wakes up and decides to make a fresh start. He takes two baths, makes himself breakfast, and does all the laundry, newly convinced "that a family wasn't just a social thing. It was an animal thing. It was a reason of nature that we were all together under the same roof." As he folds the clean laundry, he talks to a live, maggoty lamb that he has brought into the kitchen to keep warm.

1

WESLEY

(As he throws wood into wheelbarrow.) I was lying there on my back. I could smell the avocado blossoms. I could hear the coyotes. I could hear stock cars squealing down the street. I could feel myself in my bed in my room in this house in this town in this state in this country. I could feel this country close like it was part of my bones. I could feel the presence of all the people outside, at night, in the dark. Even sleeping people I could feel. Even all the sleeping animals. Dogs. Peacocks. Bulls. Even tractors sitting in the wetness, waiting for the sun to come up. I was looking straight up at the ceiling at all my model airplanes hanging by all their thin metal wires. Floating. Swaying very quietly like they were being blown by someone's breath. Cobwebs moving with them. Dust laying on their wings. Decals peeling off their wings. My P-39. My Messerschmitt. My Jap

Zero. I could feel myself lying far below them on my bed like I was on the ocean and overhead they were on reconnaissance. Scouting me. Floating. Taking pictures of the enemy. Me, the enemy. I could feel the space around me like a big, black world. I listened like an animal. My listening was afraid. Afraid of sound. Tense. Like any second something could invade me. Some foreigner. Something undescribable. Then I heard the Packard coming up the hill. From a mile off I could tell it was the Packard by the sound of the valves. The lifters have a sound like nothing else. Then I could picture my Dad driving it. Shifting unconsciously. Downshifting into second for the last pull up the hill. I could feel the headlights closing in. Cutting through the orchard. I could see the trees being lit one after the other by the lights, then going back to black. My heart was pounding. Just from my Dad coming back. Then I heard him pull the brake. Lights go off. Key's turned off. Then a long silence. Him just sitting in the car. Just sitting. I picture him just sitting. What's he doing? Just sitting. Waiting to get out. Why's he waiting to get out? He's plastered and can't move. He's plastered and doesn't want to move. He's going to sleep there all night. He's slept there before. He's woken up with dew on the hood before. Freezing headache. Teeth covered with peanuts. Then I hear the door of the Packard open. A pop of metal. Dogs barking down the road. Door slams. Feet. Paper bag being tucked under one arm. Paper bag covering "Tiger Rose." Feet coming. Feet walking toward the door. Feet stopping. Heart pounding. Sound of door not opening. Foot kicking door. Man's voice. Dad's voice. Dad calling Mom. No answer. Foot kicking. Foot kicking harder. Wood splitting. Man's voice. In the night. Foot kicking hard through door. One foot right through door. Bottle crashing. Glass breaking. Fist through door. Man cursing. Man going insane. Feet and hands tearing. Head smashing. Man yelling. Shoulder smashing. Whole body crashing. Woman screaming. Mom screaming. Mom screaming for police. Man throwing wood.

Man throwing up. Mom calling cops. Dad crashing away.
Back down driveway. Car door slamming. Ignition grinding. Wheels screaming. First gear grinding. Wheels
screaming off down hill. Packard disappearing. Sound disappearing. No sound. No sight. Planes still hanging. Heart
still pounding. No sound. Mom crying soft. Soft crying.
Then no sound. Then softly crying. Then moving around
through house. Then no moving. Then crying softly. Then
stopping. Then, far off the freeway could be heard.

_____ 2 _____

WESTON

(To lamb as he folds clothes.) There's worse things than
maggots ya' know. Much worse. Maggots go away if they're
properly attended to. If you got someone around who can
take the time. Who can recognize the signs. Who brings
ya' in out of the cold, wet pasture and sets ya' up in a cushy
situation like this. No lamb ever had it better. It's warm.
It's free of draft, now that I got the new door up. There's
no varmints. No coyotes. No eagles. No—*(Looks over at
lamb.)* Should I tell ya' something about eagles? This is a
true story. This is a true account. One time I was out in
the fields doing the castrating, which is a thing that has to
be done. It's not my favorite job, but it's something that
just has to be done. I'd set myself up right beside the lean-
to out there. Just a little roof-shelter thing out there with
my best knife, some boiling water, and a hot iron to cau-
terize with. It's a bloody job on all accounts. Well, I had
maybe a dozen spring ram lambs to do out there. I had 'em
all gathered up away from the ewes in much the same kinda'
set up as you got right there. Similar fence structure like
that. It was a crisp, bright type a' morning. Air was real
thin and you could see all the way out across the pasture
land. Frost was still well bit down on the stems, right close
to the ground. Maybe a couple a' crows and the ewes carrying on about their babies, and that was the only sound.

Well, I was working away out there when I feel this shadow
cross over me. I could feel it even before I saw it take shape
on the ground. Felt like the way it does when the clouds
move across the sun. Huge and black and cold like. So I
look up, half expecting a buzzard or maybe a red-tail, but
what hits me across the eyes is this giant eagle. Now I'm
a flyer and I'm used to aeronautics, but this sucker was
doin' some downright suicidal antics. Real low down like
he's coming in for a landing or something, then changing
his mind and pulling straight up again and sailing out away
from me. So I watch him going small for a while, then turn
back to my work. I do a couple more lambs maybe, and
the same thing happens. Except this time he's even lower
yet. Like I could almost feel his feathers on my back. I
could hear his sound real clear. A giant bird. His wings
made a kind of cracking noise. Then up he went again. I
watched him longer this time, trying to figure out his intentions. Then I put the whole thing together. He was after
those testes. Those fresh little remnants of manlihood. So
I decided to oblige him this time and threw a few a' them
on top a' the shed roof. Then I just went back to work again,
pretending to be preoccupied. I was waitin' for him this
time though. I was listening hard for him, knowing he'd
be coming in from behind me. I was watchin' the ground
for any sign of blackness. Nothing happened for about three
more lambs, when all of a sudden he comes. Just like a
thunder clap. Blam! He's down on that shed roof with his
talons taking half the tar paper with him, wings whippin'
the air, screaming like a bred mare then climbing straight
back up into the sky again. I had to stand up on that one.
Somethin' brought me straight up off the ground and I
started yellin' my head off. I don't know why it was comin'
outa' me but I was standing there with this icy feeling up
my backbone and just yelling my fool head off. Cheerin'
for that eagle. I'd never felt like that since the first day I
went up in a B-49. After a while I sat down again and went
on workin'. And every time I cut a lamb I'd throw those

balls up on top a' the shed roof. And every time he'd come down like the Cannonball Express on that roof. And every time I got that feeling.

Daddies

Douglas Gower

Premiere: Julian Theatre, San Francisco, 1977
Setting: A West Coast apartment at Christmas; "a wistful attempt at middle-class comfort."
Laury's live-in lover George is home by himself when Carl, her ex-husband and father of both of her kids, arrives with an armload of Christmas presents. The two "daddies" are stuck entertaining each other until Laury comes home with the children. They have nothing in common but Laury. George is "self-dramatizing, sardonic, oddly formal"—and frequently hostile to Carl, who belongs to a "crackpot" religious group called the World Family. In an effort to dispel the tension between them, the two men have bought gifts for each other. George's present to Carl is a framed photograph of the children with Santa. In the photograph, four-year-old Brian is crying. George tells the story of their four-hour ordeal at Macy's.

• • •

Douglas Gower comments: "George has been waiting all of the first act to spill his guts about his awful visit to Macy's. This monologue, then, is a deliberately told story, a bit of a stand-up routine. Unfortunately, the more he tells of it, the more he relives it with the gnawing realization that he has undergone this perverse holiday experience all for the benefit of his chief rival, Carl. Thus, this is a funny story that backfires on the storyteller, making it even funnier for the audience, and hopefully also disturbing.

"The trick for the actor playing George is to accomplish three things: to focus the monologue on *Carl* and his reactions, or imagined ones; to try to tell the story to *entertain* Carl, as if it were merely a funny tale with a fabulous punch line; but to know the real events of that awful day at Macy's so completely, and be so painfully sensitized to them, that the details of the story helplessly sweep him (as George) into a state of outrage as he nears the end."

GEORGE

(*Taking the photo.*) Poor old abused Saint Nick. When we were finally ushered into his workshop, and I saw him there, collapsed on his throne, his eyes glazed over from the heat of ten thousand panting children—I wanted to weep for him. The kids had really worked him over. They'd stuck him with their saddle shoes, ground his saintly old crotch with their bony knees, and all the while chattering away madly about what the reindeer eat and how Betsy Wetsy really wetsies. (*Beat.*) Well, there we were. I pushed Kris and Brian up toward . . . what was left. And I must say Santa did try to prop himself up, he did try to mutter Merry Christmas and a few miserable ho-ho-ho's—but it was too late, he was already on the verge. I swear Carl, his face was redder than his Santa suit. He was going to have a coronary right in front of us. And the kids? A lark! They were climbing over each other to get a better look. (*Beat.*) But Kris and Brian! They had been warned, they were on their best behavior. They sat politely waiting for Santa to say something. But Carl . . . he spoke not a word . . . just sat there, wheezing a little. Oh, and his eyes moved, they'd flick back and forth like they were trapped and looking for a way out. Finally, just to get the ball rolling, Kris asked Santa: How come he gets in our house when we don't even have a chimney? A simple, childlike question, one he'd been asked a thousand times. But Santa just gazed out blankly, he didn't have the *least* notion what the hell she was talking about! Brian had to cover for him. "Santa squeezes in through the rad-i-a-tor." Well, hey, that was cute, a four-year-old child, Carl! I began to think everything might go smoothly after all. We'd made it to Santa's lap, we had our candy canes and stockings, now just *get that picture* and we'd be *home-free. (He looks around and finds a child's hand puppet.)* Carl. The photographer had this hand puppet—little pink bunny rabbit—to catch the kids' attention. "Hi'ya ever'body! Smile at Whiskers! Have we been a good widdle boy and girl *all year long?" (Significantly.) That* was the mistake. For Brian that was the Big Question: All Christmas cheer hinged on his answer. And I guess it was just too much for him—you can see, poor little guy cracked under the pressure. And just at that moment, just as Brian wound up to yowl, the shutter had to snap! A great shot of Brian's quivering tonsils! But I was determined, Carl. I wanted a nice photo—for *you*, Carl. I had gone through all that misery for *you*, and I wasn't leaving without something better. So I asked this elf if we couldn't take another shot, he could see the situation I was in. But he gets bitchy. "One to a customer!" he says. Well, I *told* him I wasn't going to wait four more hours for one lousy picture. I *demanded* they take it *then!* I refused to budge! (GEORGE *pauses mid-tirade, hunching his back, sensing a presence behind him.)* And that's when I heard it . . . this low growling behind me . . . like something ready to attack . . . an angry animal . . . and I turned around . . . and there was Santa . . . growling at me. *(Coming to life.)* He was on his *feet*, Carl! His big bulk shaking all over! His face purple with heat or rage or I don't know what! Sweat dropping from his wig, sweat pouring around his nose and drenching his white beard! And, man, Santa was *big!* And *red! Redder* than the avenging angels! And angrier—*furious*—because he had finally had it—*snapped!* And he came right for me—*he grabbed me*—and I couldn't get away—*by the arm*—Got me cornered like that in front of them all! Screaming at me, twisting me, screaming at me over and over I'll never forget—What the *fuck* do you *want* man what the *fuck* do you *want* man *what the fuck do you want!* (GEORGE *breaks loose from his imaginary attacker and reels back.*) Santa Claus asking *me* what I wanted?! He was supposed to ask the *kids!* But I told him anyway! You know what I want! *I want Christmas to be the fuck over! That's what I want!* (GEORGE *stands there seething.* CARL *watches him with utter fascination. Then* GEORGE's *rage snaps into numbness. He stares into space.*) That's . . . what . . . I want.

The Dance and the Railroad

David Henry Hwang

Premiere: New Federal Theatre, New York City, 1981
Setting: A mountaintop near the Transcontinental Railroad, 1867

It is 1867 and the Transcontinental Railroad is inching across the Sierra Nevadas. A group of Chinese laborers stage a strike to protest the long hours and low pay of their back-breaking job. One of the men, Lone, studied for eight years with the Peking Opera before his family shipped him off to work on "Gold Mountain"—the American Railroad. A haughty and disciplined man, Lone has worked on the rail-road for two years without making friends. Instead, he goes to a mountaintop every night to practice his stylized opera steps: "I look at the other Chinamen and think, 'They are dead. Their muscles work only because the white man forces them. I live because I can still force my muscles to work for me.' "

One night a brash younger worker named Ma steals up to the mountain to watch Lone practice. Lone calls him an "insect." His contempt grows by leaps and bounds when

Ma announces his intention to become an opera actor and play the coveted role of Gwan Gung, god of fighters and adventurers. Lone challenges Ma to become a duck. Ma thinks it's "stupid," but passes Lone's test by staying in character when Lone becomes a tiger and attacks him. Impressed with Ma's stubbornness, Lone challenges him further: "If you want to prove to me that you're dedicated, be a locust until morning." At first Ma says, "That's ridiculous. You think I'm gonna stay like this? If you do, you're crazy." Then he remembers that Gwan Gung once stayed up all night to prove his loyalty. He takes on the challenge. This is Ma's speech as a locust, alone on the mountain at night.

MA

Locusts travel in huge swarms, so large that when they cross the sky, they block out the sun, like a storm. Second Uncle—back home—when he was a young man, his whole crop got wiped out by locusts one year. In the famine that followed, Second Uncle lost his eldest son and his second wife—the one he married for love. Even to this day, we look around before saying the word "locust," to make sure Second Uncle is out of hearing range. About eight years ago, my brother and I discovered Second Uncle's cave in back of the stream near our house. We saw him come out of it one day around noon. Later, just before the sun went down, we sneaked in. We only looked once. Inside, there must have been hundreds—maybe five hundred or more—grasshoppers in huge bamboo cages—and around them—stacks of grasshopper legs, grasshopper heads, grasshopper antennae, grasshoppers with one leg, still trying to hop but toppling like trees coughing, grasshoppers wrapped around sharp branches rolling from side to side, grasshopper legs cut off grasshopper bodies, then tied around grasshoppers and tightened till grasshoppers died. Every conceivable kind of grasshopper in every conceivable stage of life and death, subject to every conceivable grasshopper torture. We ran out quickly, my brother and I—we knew an evil place by the thickness of the air. Now, I think of Second Uncle. How sad that the locusts forced him to take out his agony on innocent grasshoppers. What if Second Uncle could see me now? Would he cut off my legs? He might as well. I can barely feel them. But then again, Second Uncle never tortured actual locusts, just weak grasshoppers.

Danny and the Deep Blue Sea

John Patrick Shanley

Premiere: Actors Theatre of Louisville, 1984
Setting: The Bronx
Shanley describes this play as "an Apache Dance . . . a violent dance for two people, originated by the Parisian apaches. Parisian apaches are gangsters or ruffians."

Two bruised, lonely people meet in a bar, go home together, and try to discover love. Roberta is thirty-one, "physically depleted, with nervous bright eyes." She is haunted by the memory of sucking off her father when she was a girl: "I can't close my eyes, man. I can't close my eyes and see the things I see." Danny is twenty-nine, "dark and powerful. He finds it difficult to meet Roberta's gaze." He has just been in a fight, and both his hands are bruised. The guys Danny works with call him The Beast.

Monologue One: Danny and Roberta are in the bar. They have started to talk, but are sitting at separate tables.

Monologue Two: Roberta and Danny have just made love. They are lying on a mattress on the floor of Roberta's small room. It is just before dawn. A distant boat horn sounds several times.

——————— 1 ———————

DANNY

I think I killed a guy last night.

[ROBERTA: How?]

I beat him up.

[ROBERTA: Well, that's not killing a guy.

DANNY: I don't know.

ROBERTA: What happened?]

I was at this party. A guy named Skull. Everybody was getting fucked up. Somebody said there was some guys outside. I went out. There were these two guys from another neighborhood out there. I asked 'em what they were doing there. They knew somebody. One of 'em was a big guy. Real drunk. He said they wanted to go, but something about twenty dollars. I told him to give me the twenty dollars, but he didn't have it. I started hitting him. But when I hit him, it never seemed to be hard, you know? I hit him a lot in the chest and face but it didn't seem to do nothing. I had him over a car hood. His friend wanted to take him away. I said okay. They started to go down the block. And they started to fight. So I ran after them. I hit on the little guy a minute, and then I started working on the big guy again. Everybody just watched. I hit him as hard as I could for about ten minutes. It never seemed like enough. Then I looked at his face . . . His teeth were all broken. He fell down. I stomped on his fuckin' chest and I heard something break. I grabbed him under the arms and pushed him over a little fence. Into somebody's driveway. Somebody pointed to some guy and said he had the twenty dollars. I kicked him in the nuts. He went right off the ground. Then I left.

——————— 2 ———————

ROBERTA

That's a big boat goin' down some like river to the ocean.

[DANNY: Whatever you say.]

That's what it is. There's boats right up by Westchester Square. What's that, twenty blocks? Look sometime, you'll see 'em. Not the real big ones, but big. Sea boats. I met a sailor in the bar one time. In the outfit, you know? I was all over him. But he turned out to be nothin'—a pothead. He giggled a lot. It was too bad because . . . . Well, it was too bad. When we got married, me and Billy, that was my husband, we smoked a ball of opium one night. It really knocked me out. I fell asleep like immediately. And I dreamed about the ocean. It was real blue. And there was the sun, and it was real yellow. And I was out there, right in the middle of the ocean, and I heard this noise. I turned around, and whaddaya think I saw? Just about right next to me. A whale! A whale came shootin' straight outta the water! A whale! Yeah! And he opened up his mouth and closed it while he was up there in the air. And people on the boat said, Look! The whales are jumpin'! And no shit, these whales start jumpin' outta the water all over the place. And I can see them! Through one a those round windows. Or right out in the open. Whales! Gushin' outta the water, and the water gushin' outta their heads, you know, spoutin'! And then, after a while, they all stopped jumpin'. It got quiet. Everybody went away. The water smoothed out. But I kept lookin' at the ocean. So deep and blue. And different. It was different then. 'Cause I knew it had all them whales in it.

A Day in the Death of Joe Egg

Peter Nichols

Premiere: Citizens Theatre, Glasgow, Scotland, 1967
Setting: Middle-class English living room
Bri and Sheila's twelve-year-old daughter Josephine (the "Joe Egg" of the title) is helplessly disabled. She is brain-

damaged, epileptic, and paraplegic: what her father describes as "a human parsnip." Bri is a frustrated grade-school teacher with stunted dreams of painting. Sheila has filled up her life with pets, houseplants, birds, projects, hobbies. She has recently joined an amateur theatre group.

The play starts with Bri addressing the audience as his delinquent sixth-grade class. The next scene, in his living room, starts out as conventional "fourth wall" realism, but midway through the first act, Bri starts to confide his marital problems directly to the audience. Sheila follows suit, and soon they embark on a wildly funny series of music-hall skits, imitating the various doctors and priests who have given "advice" about living with Joe. While the humor may seem savage, it has been a life raft for attention-hungry Bri. He has just left the stage, and Sheila addresses the audience.

_____

SHEILA

I join in these jokes to please him. If it helps him live with her, I can't see the harm, can you? He hasn't any faith she's ever going to improve. Where I have, you see . . . I believe, even if she *showed* improvement, Bri wouldn't notice. He's dense about faith—faith isn't believing in fairy tales, it's being in a receptive state of mind. I'm always on the look-out for some sign . . . (*Looks off again to wings to make sure* BRI's *not coming.*) One day when she was—what?—about a twelve month old, I suppose, she was lying on the floor kicking her legs about and I was doing the flat. I'd made a little tower of four colored bricks—plastic bricks—on a rug near her head. I got on with my dusting and when I looked again I saw she'd knocked it down. I put the four bricks up again and this time watched her. First her eyes, usually moving in all directions, must have glanced in passing at this bright tower. Then the arm that side began to show real signs of intention . . . and her fist started clenching and—spreading with the effort. The other arm—held

there like that—(*Raises one bent arm to shoulder level.*)
didn't move. At all. You see the importance—she was using
for the first time one arm instead of both. She'd seen something, touched it and found that when she touched it what-
ever-it-was changed. Fell down. Now her bent arm started
twitching towards the bricks. Must have taken—I should
think—ten minutes'—strenuous labor—to reach them with
her fingers . . . then her hand jerked in a spasm and she
pulled down the tower. (*Reliving the episode, she puts her
hands over her face to regain composure.*) I can't tell you
what that was like. But you can imagine, can't you? Several
times the hand very nearly touched and got jerked away
by spasm . . . and she'd try again. That was the best of it—
she had a will, she had a mind of her own. Soon as Bri
came home, I told him. I think he said something stupid
like—you know—"That's great, put her down for piano
lessons." But when he tested her—putting piles of bricks
all along the circle of her reach—both arms—and even
sometimes out of reach so that she had to stretch to get
there—well, of course, he saw it was true. It wasn't *much*
to wait for—one arm movement completed—and even that
wasn't sure. She'd fall asleep, the firelight would distract
her, sometimes the effort would bring on a fit. But more
often than not she'd manage . . . and a vegetable couldn't
have done that. Visitors never believed it. They hadn't the
patience to watch so long. And it amazed me—I remember
being stunned—when I realized they thought I shouldn't
deceive myself. For one thing, it wasn't deception . . . and,
anyway, what else could I do? We got very absorbed in the
daily games. Found her colored balls and bells and a Kelly—
those clowns that won't lie down. Then she caught some
bug and was very sick . . . had fit after fit—the Grand Mal,
not the others—what amounted to a complete relapse. When
she was over it, we tried the bricks again, but she couldn't
even seem to see them. That was when Bri lost interest in
her. I still try, though of course I don't bother telling him.
I'll tell him when something happens. It seems to me only

common sense. If she did it once, she could again. I think while there's life there's hope, don't you? (*Looks to wings again.*) I wish he'd talk more seriously about her. I wonder if he ever imagines what she'd be like if her brain worked. *I* do. And Bri's mother always says, "Wouldn't she be lovely if she was running about?" which makes Bri hoot with laughter. But I think of it too. Perhaps it's being a woman.

The Days and Nights of Beebee Fenstermaker

William Snyder

Premiere: Sheridan Square Theatre, New York City, 1962
Setting: Beebee's apartment in a northern city; her family's home in the South

Barbara "Beebee" Fenstermaker is a bright-eyed, eager girl of multiple artistic leanings who moves to the city to write her first novel. The play takes place over a number of years, intercutting Beebee's new life in the city with scenes of her close-knit and smothering family back home.

Monologue One: Beebee has just arrived in the city and her downstairs neighbor Nettie Jo is helping her move in. Beebee tells Nettie Jo about her talents (besides writing and playing the piano, she says, "I have a knack for composin' and a flair for textile design too. And I studied tap dancin' for two years and toe for three, but they're just sidelines.") and her plans. ("Love and a career. They're the two things I want. . . . Love gives you somethin' to say and a career gives you a way to say it, so with the two of them you're never at a loss for what to do next.") Nettie Jo tells her, "You've come a long way to get it." Beebee responds.

Monologue Two: Beebee has been in the city for several years. She has given up on her novel, given up on her brief fling with painting school, given up on her needy romance with a domineering but weak man named Ed—she has just about given up, period. Her apartment is "a complete wreck. . . . She seems exhausted but also extremely tense." She talks to herself compulsively and refuses to answer her nightly phone from her mother. A young man named Bob knocks on Beebee's door. A good-looking, sweetly naive boy from Arkansas, he has come to the city that day and is trying to locate a friend who lives in Beebee's building. Beebee invites him in for a beer. She is so nervous she spills it all over his hands.

1

BEEBEE

I guess so. I had to get out, though. My family life was very complicated. It's funny. On the one hand I believe my future's as bright as a button and nothin' can stand in my way. But sometimes when I'm home, a little devil gets next to me and says, "Beebee, you fly mighty high in your mind's eye, honey. But if you ever took the trouble to look two inches past your nose you'd see your life was signed, sealed and delivered before you were born. And it's got nothin' to do with love or careers or flights of fancy." In one way or another my whole family's just waitin' it out. They talk about what they're gonna do or what they should have done but they're just sittin there waitin' for the ax to fall. And I must say, when I walk those streets in the dead of August, and the trees are dry as paper and the grass is burnt up crisp. And the sun's so hot and the air's so thick they shut out all the sounds. And I go to my grandmother's and see her movin' from room to room, doin' a little dab here and a little dab there. Waitin' for night to come so she can sit on the porch and do somethin' that's *nothin'*. I think there's no comfort on this porch. There's no life in this town. There's no hope in this world. And God has long since passed away. Fall in line, Beebee, fall in line. In a

hundred years who'll know the difference. Follow the path
of least resistance, act out your part and *die*. But I said no!
(Crosses to bureau.) I'm not gonna sit around waitin' for
what I dread most to happen to me. I'm not gonna be one
more ribbon on the maypole. *(Sets bureau.)* I'm cuttin'
loose! So last week when I got home from college—before
I could even give myself time to think—I cashed in my six
hundred dollars' worth of savin's bonds I'd received over
the years as prize money—packed up Miss Amelia Ear-
hart—*(Gets other suitcase and places it upstage of bureau.)*
and high-tailed it down to the Trailways Bus Station and
took off. So here I am, footloose and ready to tackle anything. I got money, an apartment and I'm free!

2

BEEBEE

Want me to tell your fortune? I'm very good at fortunes.
I've been known to predict the future very accurately for
some friends of mine. For myself too, as a matter of fact.
*(She studies his palm. She is sincerely moved, if not by
what she sees, then by what she imagines to be there.)* Oh,
I wish to goodness you'd look at this fortune. If this isn't a
fortune for you. Whooee, honey, this is a fortune and a
half. Here's health . . . wealth . . . happiness . . . long
life . . . love . . . and whatever else in this world could you
want! It's an A Number One fortune if I've ever seen one.
  [BOB: What about yours, Miss Beebee?
  BEEBEE: *(Finished with game. Drops his hand.)* Mine?
  I've already done mine. Many times. *(The pleasant mood
  is broken. She stands up abruptly and turns away from
  him.)*]
I think I hear footsteps outside. Maybe it's your friend.
Sounds like he or she is goin' on up. I guess you'll have to
go now, won't you?
  [BOB: No, ma'am.]
If he or she is expectin' you . . . I know I get absolutely

wild if I'm kept waitin' five minutes. Course, you were the one that's been kept waitin', I guess. Still and all . . . maybe you'd better go while the bloom is still on the rose. (*He rises immediately and starts for the door. She turns quickly.*) Wait! Honey, wait. Sit back down. Honey, please sit back down. (*He returns slowly to the armchair and sits.*) Honey, I'm gonna be frank with you. When you knocked on that door tonight, I was absolutely wild. I was so God-awful anxious for a change in the weather or a change in the sea or somethin', I was practically pullin' the nails out of the floorboards with my teeth. Then you walked in lookin' like God's gift and it really threw me for a loop. Honey, I'm gonna be frank. Here lately, I haven't had too much success in my relationships with people. What I mean is they been awful. Honey, I'm gonna be frank. Here lately, when I meet somebody that I'm really crazy about, I can't seem to hold up my end of things more than a few days at a time. I'm too nervous, I guess, to have much stayin' power. Men just get tired of me and that's the plain truth. Then they go off and leave me and I'm even wilder than before they came. You know the story in the Bible about the stones bein' turned into bread? Well, I turn bread into stones. Anything good that comes my way I turn into somethin' bad. And you're so nice and sweet-lookin', I don't want to take any chance with you. (*There is a long pause. Bob continues to sit and look at her.*) Well, what are you sittin' there starin' for? Why don't you say somethin'?

Death Comes to Us All, Mary Agnes

Christopher Durang

Premiere: Yale School of Drama, New Haven, 1975
Setting: A Victorian drawing room in East Haddam, Vermont

In this black-comic sendup of drawing-room comedies, the servants are foulmouthed, grandfather is dying, and grandma is chewing dead rats in the Tower. Vivien Jansen-Hubbell Pomme has come home to her father's deathbed. She is "forty-five, attractive, dressed expensively . . . has no feeling in her legs." She can't walk very well and is usually supported by her twenty-six-year-old sons, Tod and Tim, gay fraternal twins who "look like an ad from *Gentlemen's Quarterly*." Vivien once left her daughter in an orphanage for five years so she could go to Italy with Tod and Tim, and now she mistakes her for one of the maids. Here Vivien reunites with her husband Herbert. He kneels and caresses her, telling her fondly, "Oh, Vivien, I hate you." Vivien holds him.

VIVIEN

(*Tearing at the eyes.*) Oh, Herbert, we had good times, didn't we? Scurrying about the Continent, knowing dukes and earls. Do you remember how you met me? You were just seventeen and you went to your first brothel. I was just fourteen and it was my first brothel too. My first night. And I remember the Madame, Madame Leore, said to me, she said, "Vera"—she got my name wrong even then— "Vera, you'll turn many a trick in your day, but you'll never turn one like your first one." And so my heart was aglow and you came up to me and in your adolescent voice you said to me, "How much?" And I thought to myself that that was the most romantic thing I had ever heard. And so you and I retired to that little room with the cobwebs and the dank smell of urine and we sat on the bed. "Is this your first?" I asked, and when you said no I didn't believe you. "And is this your first?" you asked me, and when I said yes, you didn't believe me. And one of us was lying, and to this day I don't know which one it was, but I don't care because the night air was so fragrant and love was so new,

and we were so young. So very, very young. And then you
began very methodically to take off my clothes, which were
soaked in perspiration from my busy day and from so many
other bodies. And then I bit off your buttons, one by one,
and your eyes grew larger at every pop. And then I took
off your pants. I was very young, you understand, and I
had never seen a man, not even a statue of one because
they didn't have museums in those days and I wouldn't
have gone even if they had. And so then your slender form
got on top of my slender form and then—pump! Pump!
PUMP! You pumped away, and I gave in to my first experience of love—Oh! Oh! Ohhhhhhh-Ohhhhhhhh.
OHHHHHHHHHHHHHHHHHHH. Uh. Uh. And then
when it was all over, I got off of you, and I looked into your
blue eyes—your eyes were blue then—and I said in the
pale, frightened voice of a schoolgirl, "Herbert, it is you I
love." *(Pause.)* Do you remember, Herbert? Herbert?
(Kindly.) Children, I think your father's fallen asleep. *(She
lets go of* HERBERT, *and he falls to the ground.)* Oh. Has
he had a stroke? Do you think it's a stroke?

The Death of a Miner

Paula Cizmar

Premiere: Portland Stage Company, Portland, Maine/
American Place Theatre Women's Project, New York
City, 1982

Setting: A coal-mining town in Appalachia

Mary Alice Hager, a coal miner, has been killed in a mining
accident. Her husband Jack and daughter Sallie struggle to
come to terms with her death—and the law which denies
survivors' benefits to families of female workers. Interspersed with the family's present-tense dramas are flashbacks of Mary Alice, vibrantly alive. Here she tells Jack,

who has just proposed marriage, why she wants to work in the mine.

MARY ALICE

It's what I really want to do, Jack. I can't just sit and watch. All my life . . . I watched. I watched my daddy until he finally couldn't take it any more and—

[JACK: I don't know. I don't know.

MARY ALICE: Jack, wait! No, listen.]

Listen, I gotta do this. I gotta. . . . Let me tell you. You see, one day my brother and about ten of the boys from his class went out explorin' in the caverns one day, 'bout a mile from where we were livin'. Jack. Listen. They were in there a few hours—guess they wanted to go way back into the cave to see where it would take them. There was a flash thunderstorm and it started to flood. Well, they got divers down there . . . and the TV cameras came from the city . . . and it kept rainin' off and on, My mama dragged my daddy out to the cave . . . and all the rest of us. We all sat there, with the other families, sat there, lined up on the hillside, lookin' down into the flooded pit, the TV cameras takin our pictures . . . we sat there . . . watchin' . . . waitin' . . . watchin' . . . the divers tryin to work their way through the water and up into the cavern . . . watchin' . . . and everytime they came back with nothin'. . . . My mama just sat there. Sat there. And then she started . . . couldn't help herself,. I know, but she started with that look. . . . accusin' my daddy with her eyes. If we didn't have to live in this place, none of this woulda happened . . . . that's what that look said . . . . this is your fault . . . I wish it was you in that cave and not— . . . look at you . . . can't do nothin' . . . can't even get my boy outa that cave . . . . . . it was just flashin' outa her eyes. Finally, my daddy couldn't take it anymore. He ran down the hill, started rippin' his clothes off and jumped into the water before anyone could stop him. She didn't want anyone to stop him. She just watched. He tried gettin' into that cave about a dozen times . . . finally they talked him into tyin' a rope around himself and he kept tryin'. . . . .tried about an hour . . . she never changed her expression. My brother died in that cave. Took the bodies out about a week later. After the rains died down. And the water dried up. My daddy came into my room after he saw my brother at the funeral parlor. Said . . . I love you, Mary Alice. Said, I love you. You be happy. You can find it anywhere you want it. And he left. See?

'dentity Crisis
Christopher Durang

Premiere: Yale Repertory Theatre, New Haven, 1978
Setting: A living room decorated by a fairly insane person. Jane recently tried to kill herself by slashing her thighs with a razor blade. She lives with her mother, Edith Fromage, who claims she "invented cheese in France in the early part of the century," and someone named Robert who can't decide if he's her brother, her father, or her grandfather. Jane's psychologist, Mr. Summers, makes a house call. He asks Jane what led to her suicide attempt. Jane answers, "Well, a few days ago I woke up and I heard this voice saying, 'It wasn't enough.' "

JANE

When I was eight years old, someone brought me to a theatre with lots of other children. We had come to see a production of *Peter Pan*. And I remember something seemed wrong with the whole production, odd things kept happening. Like when the children would fly, the ropes would keep breaking and the actors would come thumping to the ground and they'd have to be carried off by the stage hands. There seemed to be an unlimited supply of understudies to take the children's places, and then *they'd* fall to the ground. And then the crocodile that chases Captain Hook seemed to be a real crocodile, it wasn't an actor, and at one point it fell off the stage, crushing several children in the front row.

[SUMMERS: What happened to the children?]

Several understudies came and took their places in the audience. And from scene to scene Wendy seemed to get fatter and fatter until finally by the second act she was immobile and had to be moved with a cart.

[SUMMERS: Where does the voice fit in?

JANE: The voice belonged to the actress playing Peter Pan.]

You remember how in the second act Tinkerbell drinks some poison that Peter's about to drink, in order to save him? And then Peter turns to the audience and he says that Tinkerbell's going to die because not enough people believe in fairies, but that if everybody in the audience claps real hard to show that they *do* believe in fairies, then maybe Tinkerbell won't die. And so then all the children started to clap. We clapped very hard and very long. My palms hurt and even started to bleed I clapped so hard. Then suddenly the actress playing Peter Pan turned to the audience and she said, "That wasn't enough. You didn't clap hard enough. Tinkerbell's dead." Uh . . . well, and . . . and then everyone started to cry. The actress stalked offstage and refused to continue with the play, and they finally had to bring down the curtain. No one could see anything through all the tears, and the ushers had to come help the children up the aisles and out into the street. I don't think any of us were ever the same after that experience.

The Effect of Gamma Rays on Man-in-the-Moon Marigolds

Paul Zindel

Premiere: Mercer O'Casey Theatre, New York City, 1970
Setting: A former vegetable store, converted to a home by "a widow of confusion"

Beatrice, a widow with two teenage daughters, is a woman of ferocious, if often misguided, raw energy. She is constantly cooking up scatterbrained schemes to make money. There is always a series of elderly boarders; right now, Beatrice is caring for Nanny, a deaf, near-blind woman who might be a century old.

The play's title comes from a science project which Beatrice's younger daughter, Matilda, has made for her school Science Fair. Tillie is shy and a bit otherworldly, obsessed with the atom. Her big sister Ruth is much brassier, the kind of teenager who smokes cigarettes and buys lipsticks called Devil's Kiss. She is also an epileptic. Late one night, during a violent thunderstorm, a nightmare propels Ruth into a fit. Beatrice soothes her with hot milk and stories. The storm has knocked out the electricity, and the scene is lit only by a flashlight Ruth is holding.

BEATRICE

My father made up for all the other men in this whole world, Ruth. If only you two could have met. He'd only be about seventy now, do you realize that? And I'll bet he'd still be selling vegetables around town. All that fun— and then I don't think I ever knew what really hit me.

[RUTH: Don't tell about—

BEATRICE: Don't worry about the horses.

RUTH: What hit you?]

It was just me and Papa . . . and your father hanging around. And then Papa got sick . . . and I drove with him up to the sanatorium. And then I came home and there were the horses—

[RUTH: Mother!]

And I had the horses . . . taken care of. And then Papa got terribly sick and he begged me to marry so that he'd be sure I'd be taken care of. (*She laughs.*) If he knew how I was taken care of he'd turn over in his grave.

And *nightmares!* Do you want to know the nightmare I used to have? I never had nightmares over the fights with your father, or the divorce, or his thrombosis—he deserved it—I never had nightmares over any of that.

Let me tell you about my nightmare that used to come back and back: *Well*, I'm on Papa's wagon, but it's newer and shinier, and it's being pulled by beautiful white horses, not dirty workhorses—these are like circus horses with long manes and tinsel—and the wagon is blue, shiny blue. And it's full—filled with yellow apples and grapes and green squash. You're going to laugh when you hear this. I'm wearing a lovely gown with jewels all over it, and my hair is piled up on top of my head with a long feather in it, and the bells are ringing. Huge bells swinging on a gold braid strung across the back of the wagon, and they're going DONG, DONG . . . DONG, DONG. And I'm yelling "APPLES! PEARS! CUCUM . . . BERS!"

[RUTH: That doesn't sound like a nightmare to me.]

And then I turn down our street and all the noise stops. This long street, with all the doors of the houses shut and everything crowded next to each other, and there's not a soul around. And then I start getting afraid that the vegetables are going to spoil . . . and that nobody's going to buy anything, and I feel as though I shouldn't be on the wagon, and I keep trying to call out.

But there isn't a sound. Not a single sound. Then I turn my head and look at the house across the street. I see an upstairs window, and a pair of hands pull the curtains slowly apart. I see the face of my father and my heart stands still . . .

Ruth . . . take the light out of my eyes.

F.O.B.

David Henry Hwang

Premiere: Stanford Asian American Theatre Project, Palo Alto, California, 1979

Setting: Back room of a small Chinese restaurant in Torrance, California

A preppie-dressed Chinese-American named Dale describes the contempt of the A.B.C. (American Born Chinese) for the F.O.B. (Fresh Off the Boat): "Clumsy, ugly, greasy F.O.B. Loud, stupid, four-eyed F.O.B. Big feet. Horny. Like Lenny in *Of Mice and Men* . . . High-water pants. Floods, to be exact. Someone you wouldn't want your sister to marry. If you are a sister, someone you wouldn't want to marry."

Grace is a journalism student at UCLA, an assimilated Chinese-American who works part-time in her family's Chinese restaurant. A Chinese-speaking customer enters, wishing to buy *chong you bing*. When Grace gives him the cold shoulder, he tells her that he is "Gwan Gung, god of warriors, writers, and prostitutes!" This is Steve, a UCLA friend of Grace's, fresh off the boat. They are planning to go out tonight with Dale, her cousin. When Steve picks up on Dale's prejudice, he behaves like a caricature of obsequious F.O.B.-dom.

Monologue One: Dale, who is so completely Americanized that he calls moo shu pork "those burrito things," tells Steve what he thinks of him.

Monologue Two: While Steve and Dale engage in a hot-sauce eating competition, Grace addresses the audience.

————— 1 —————

DALE

You feel like you're an American? Don't tell me. Lemme guess. Your father. (*He switches into a mock Hong Kong accent.*) Your fad-dah tink he sending you here so you get yo' M.B.A., den go back and covuh da world wit' trinkets and beads. Diversify. Franchise. Sell—ah—Hong Kong X-Ray glasses at tourist shop at Buckingham Palace. You know—ah—"See da Queen"? (*Switches back.*) He's hoping your American education's gonna create an empire of defective goods and breakable merchandise. Like those little cameras with the slides inside? I bought one at Disneyland once and it ended up having pictures of Hong Kong in it. You know how shitty it is to expect the Magic Kingdom and wind up with the skyline of Kowloon? Part of your dad's plan, I'm sure. But you're gonna double-cross him. Coming to America, you're gonna jump the boat. You're gonna decide you like us. Yeah—you're gonna like having fifteen theaters in three blocks, you're gonna like West Hollywood and Newport Beach. You're gonna decide to become an American. Yeah, don't deny it—it happens to the best of us. You can't hold out—you're no different. You won't even know it's coming before it has you. Before you're trying real hard to be just like the rest of us—go dinner, go movie, go motel, bang-bang. And when your father writes you that do-it-yourself acupuncture sales are down, you'll throw that letter in the basket and burn it in your brain. And you'll write that you're gonna live in Monterey Park a few years before going back home—and you'll get your green card—and you'll build up a nice little stockbroker's business and have a few American kids before your dad realizes what's happened and dies, his hopes reduced to a few chattering

teeth and a pack of pornographic playing cards. Yeah—
great things come to the U.S. out of Hong Kong.

——————— 2 ———————

GRACE

Yeah. It's tough trying to live in Chinatown. But it's tough
trying to live in Torrance, too. It's true. I don't like being
alone. You know, when Mom could finally bring me to the
U.S., I was already ten. But I never studied my English
very hard in Taiwan, so I got moved back to the second
grade. There were a few Chinese girls in the fourth grade,
but they were American-born, so they wouldn't even talk
to me. They'd just stay with themselves and compare how
much clothes they all had, and make fun of the way we all
talked. I figured I had a better chance of getting in with
the white kids than with them, so in junior high I started
bleaching my hair and hanging out at the beach—you know,
Chinese hair looks pretty lousy when you bleach it. After
a while, I knew what beach was gonna be good on any given
day, and I could tell who was coming just by his van. But
the American-born Chinese, it didn't matter to them. They
just giggled and went to their own dances. Until my senior
year in high school—that's how long it took for me to get
over this whole thing. One night I took Dad's car and drove
on Hollywood Boulevard, all the way from downtown to
Beverly Hills, then back on Sunset. I was looking and listening—all the time with the window down, just so I'd feel
like I was part of the city. And that Friday, it was—I guess—
I said, "I'm lonely. And I don't like it. I don't like being
alone." And that was all. As soon as I said it, I felt all of
the breeze—it was really cool on my face—and I heard all
of the radio—and the music sounded really good, you know?
So I drove home.

The Fairy Garden

Harry Kondoleon

Premiere: Double Image Theatre, New York City, 1982
Setting: A magically beautiful garden behind a large,
  expensive Tudor-style house

Three chic friends—a woman named Dagny, a man named
Roman, and Roman's male lover Mimi—languish photo-
genically in Dagny's garden. Dagny is tired of her rich
husband Boris and wants to run off with her mechanic.
When one of the men suggests facetiously that she go and
kill Boris, she does. She returns with his head in an ice
bucket full of blood. All three of them panic and start digging a grave in the garden with teaspoons. At which point
a fairy—an old-fashioned fairy in shimmering tulle and tiara—
appears in Dagny's garden singing fairy songs and granting
wishes. She suggests that Dagny should wish for Boris's
head to be reattached, extracts a few diamonds in payment,
and goes into the house to do her deed.

Meanwhile, Dagny and Mimi have decided that they are
in love. The fairy comes out of the house with the recon-
stituted Boris. She is dressed in contemporary clothes, and
Boris introduces her as Chantal, his new fiancée. They leave
together, Dagny and Mimi leave together, and the bro-
kenhearted Roman is left by himself.

The Mechanic enters. He is "what you would expect,
with young, blunt good looks." As it turns out, he's *not* a
mechanic, but The Mechanic, a male stripper who dresses
in a mechanic's uniform. He performs his routine for the
disinterested Roman.

THE MECHANIC

So you're sitting here all by yourself, aren't you feeling
down? Don't you need cheering up?

[ROMAN: Look, you're very nice and all that but I really
    don't want to see you strip.]

(*He follows his own stage directions.*) Oh come on, I'm so
good. You just sit there very still and I'll show you my
routine. I don't have my music here but you can imagine
it. Don't talk, just watch. Okay, first—you know, when the
music just starts—I jump out and circle around like I'm
looking at this really big car that needs a lot of work. You
get it? Then I take my hat off and I wipe my brow, all the
time a little bit swaying like this—subtle, you know, nothing faggy. Then I lift the imaginary hood and take out my
wrench and start tightening things, like this. By this time
it's as if I'm getting a little sweaty so I unbutton my shirt
a little bit, take my hat off again and wipe my brow, real
sexy. Then I take out my imaginary pump and start pumping up the car—this pumping really gets them in the audience—they go crazy—pumping my hips like this. Then
suddenly, instead of doing it real slow—I whip off my shirt
and throw it over my head—throwing it over my head
prevents the really horny ones in the audience from ripping
it to pieces—keeps my overhead down if I don't have to
replace my costume. Then I dance around a bit—this part
doesn't relate to the car very much but the bold ones all
start running up to stick tips in my pocket around now.
They love me—I guess they're all pent up and lonely or
something, I don't know, someone should do a study. Anyway, then, as if I'm on one of those thing-ees on wheels, I
get on the floor and act as if I'm sliding under the car to
play with the carburetor or something.

[ROMAN: The carburetor's on top, under the hood.

THE MECHANIC: What? Oh yeah, well then the muffler,
    whatever.]

I'm down there and I'm undoing my belt and yanking off
my trousers, meanwhile they're all screaming like the house
is on fire. I leap up—I'm wearing my jock strap, my undershirt and athletic socks and work boots—and I start
shadow boxing fast and then slow. Now I'm building up a

real sweat and the girls and the gays are throwing tens and twenties like nobody's business and I'm really going strong— the music's really loud here and I walk it around for a second so everyone can get a load of me. Then I turn around real sudden like I heard someone call my name and real slow peel off my undershirt which is good and wet: this I throw into the audience— *(The undershirt should be thrown on stage not into the actual audience.)* —everyone screams, glasses fall and I do some more of this sort of shadow boxing, get more bills stuffed this time into my jock, quickly tighten up the screws on the tires, take the ignition key, stick the key in, gas it, accelerate and Pow! Lights out. *(He collapses into a chair, using a linen napkin to wipe his sweat.)* Well, how did you like it?

Fences

August Wilson

Premiere: Yale Repertory Theatre, New Haven, 1985
Setting: The yard and porch of the Maxson household in Pittsburgh, 1957–1965.

Troy Maxson is fifty-three years old, a large man with thick heavy hands; it is this largeness that he strives to fill out and make an accommodation with. Together with his black-ness, his largeness informs his sensibilities and the choices he has made in his life. Troy works as a garbage collector in Pittsburgh. An ex-con with a talent for baseball, he firmly believes that he could have played in the big league if he wasn't black. Troy's younger son Cory plays high school football. He has been recruited for an athletic scholarship, but Troy will hear none of it. He refuses to believe that times might have changed for black athletes—or that his son might get something he didn't. He makes Cory quit the team for a job at the A & P. Ultimately, Troy's hardness and pride drives a permanent wedge between father and son.

Monologue One: Troy and his work buddy Bono are sharing their payday ritual of drinking and talk on the porch. They've been talking about baseball, and Troy vents his feelings of frustration and powerlessness between slugs of alcohol. His wife Rose warns him, "You gonna drink yourself to death," and Troy starts in about Death.

Monologue Two: Troy describes his sharecropper father. "Man would sit down and eat two chickens and give you the wing." Bono says he never even knew his father: "He came on through, but I ain't never knew him to see him . . . or what he had on his mind or where he went. Just moving on through." Troy responds.

Monologue Three: Troy and Rose have been married for eighteen years, and Rose is devoted to him. Not long ago, Troy started seeing an outside woman, a "Florida gal" named Alberta. He has not confided to anyone, not even Bono—though Bono has guessed it and disapproves. Now Troy tells Rose, "I'm gonna be somebody's daddy."

Monologue Four: It is now 1965. Troy has died, and Cory comes home to visit his mother—but not to go to his father's funeral. "One time in my life I've got to say no to him. . . . Papa was like a shadow that followed you everywhere." (*Note:* Raynell is Troy's illegitimate daughter.)

_____ **1** _____

TROY

You the one brought it up. Me and Bono was talking about baseball . . . you tell me I'm gonna drink myself to Death. Ain't that right, Bono? You know I don't drink this but one night out of the week. That's Friday night. I'm gonna drink just enough to where I can handle it. Then I cuts it loose. I leave it alone. So don't you worry about me drinking myself to death. 'Cause I ain't worried about Death. I done seen him. I done wrestled with him. Look here, Bono . . . I looked up one day and Death was marching straight at me.

Like Soldiers on Parade! The Army of Death marching straight at me. The middle of July, 1941. It got real cold just like to be winter. It seem like Death himself reached out and touched me on the shoulder. He touch me just like I touch you. I got cold as ice and Death standing there grinning at me.

[ROSE: Troy, why don't you hush that talk.]

I say, "What you want, Mr. Death? You be wanting me? You done brought your army to be getting me?" I looked him dead in the eye. I wasn't fearing nothing. I was ready to tangle. Just like I'm ready to tangle now. The Bible say be ever vigilant. That's why I don't get but so drunk. I got to keep watch.

[ROSE: Troy was right down there in Mercy Hospital. You remember he had pneumonia? Laying there with a fever talking plumb out of his head.]

Death, he ain't said nothing. He just stared at me. He had a thousand men to do his bidding and he wasn't going to get a thousand and one. Not then! Hell, I wasn't but thirty-seven years old. (*Pause.*)

Death standing there staring at me . . . carrying that sickle in his hand. Finally he say, "You want bound over for another year?" See, just like that . . . "You want bound over for another year?" I told him, "Bound over hell! Let's settle this now!" It seem like he kinda fell back when I said that, and all the cold went out of me. I reached out and grabbed that sickle and threw it just as far as I could throw it . . . and me and him commenced to wrestling. We wrestled for three days and three nights. I can't say where I found the strength from. Every time it seemed like he was gonna get the best of me, I'd reach way down deep inside myself and find the strength to do him one better.

[ROSE: Every time Troy tell that story he find different ways to tell it. Different things to make up about it.]

I ain't making up nothing. I'm telling you the facts of what happened. I wrestled with Death for three days and three nights and I'm standing here to tell you about it. (*Pause.*)

All right. At the end of the third night we done weakened each other to where both of us could hardly move. Death stood up, throwed on his robe . . . had him a white robe with a hood on it. He throwed on that robe and went off to look for his sickle. Say, "I'll be back." Just like that. "I'll be back." I told him, say, "You gonna have to find me!" I wasn't no fool. I wasn't going looking for him. Death ain't nothing to play with. And I know he's gonna get me. I know I got to join his army . . . his camp followers. But as long as I keep my strength and see him coming, as long as I keep up my vigilance, he's gonna have to fight to get me. I ain't going easy.

2

TROY

My daddy ain't had them walking blues what you talking about. He stayed right there with his family. But he was just as evil as he could be. My mama couldn't stand him . . . couldn't stand that evilness. She run off when I was about eight. She sneaked off one night after he had gone to sleep. Told me she was coming back for me. I ain't never seen her no more. All his women run off and left him. He wasn't good for nobody. When my turn come to head out, I was fourteen and got to sniffing around Joe Canewell's daughter. Had us an old mule we called Greyboy. My daddy sent me out to do some plowing and I tied up Greyboy and went to fooling around with Joe Canewell's daughter. We done found us a nice little spot, got real cozy with each other. She about thirteen and we done figured we was grown anyway, so we down there enjoying our-selves . . . ain't thinking about nothing. We didn't know Greyboy had got loose and wandered back to the house and my daddy was looking for me. We down there by the creek enjoying ourselves when my daddy come up on us, surprised us. He had them leather straps off the mule and commenced to whupping me like there as no tomorrow. I jumped up, mad and embarrassed. I was scared of my daddy. When he commenced to whupping on me, quite naturally I run to get out of the way. *(Pause.)*

Now I thought he was mad 'cause I ain't done my work. But I see where he was chasing me off so he could have the gal for himself. When I see what the matter of it was, I lost all fear of my daddy. Right there is where I become a man . . . at fourteen years of age. *(Pause.)*

Now it was my turn to run him off. I picked up the same reins that he had used on me. I picked up them reins and commenced to whupping on him. The gal jumped up and run off, and when my daddy turned to face me, I could see why the devil had never come to get him: 'cause he was the devil himself. I don't know what happened. When I woke up I was laying right there by the creek and Blue—this old dog we had—was licking my face. I thought I was blind. I couldn't see nothing. Both my eyes were swollen shut. I layed there and cried. I didn't know what I was gonna do. The only thing I knew was the time had come for me to leave my daddy's house. And right there the world suddenly got big. And it was a long time before I could cut it down to where I could handle it. Part of that cutting down was when I got to the place where I could feel him kicking in my blood and knew that the only thing that separated us was the matter of a few years.

3

ROSE

I been standing with you! I been right here with you, Troy. I got a life too. I gave eighteen years of my life to stand in the same spot with you. Don't you think I ever wanted other things? Don't you think I had dreams and hopes? What about my life? What about me? Don't you think it ever crossed my mind to want to know other men? That I wanted to lay up somewhere and forget about my responsibilities? That I wanted someone to make me laugh so I could feel good? You not the only one who's got wants and needs. But I held on to you, Troy. I took all my feelings, my wants and needs, my dreams, and I buried them inside you. I planted a seed and watched and prayed over it. I planted myself inside you and waited to bloom. And it didn't take me no eighteen years to find out the soil was hard and rocky and it wasn't never gonna bloom. But I held on to you, Troy. I held you tighter. You was my husband. I owed you everything I had. Every part of me I could find to give you. And upstairs in that room, with the darkness falling in on me, I gave everything I had to try and erase the doubt that you wasn't the finest man in the world. And wherever you was going I wanted to be there with you. 'Cause you was my husband, 'cause that's the only way I was gonna survive as your wife. You always talking about what you give and what you don't have to give. But you take too. You take and don't even know nobody's giving!

4

ROSE

You can't be nobody but who you are, Cory. That shadow wasn't nothing but you growing into yourself. You either got to grow into it or cut it down to fit you. But that's all you got to make life with. That's all you got to measure yourself against that world out there. Your daddy wanted you to be everything he wasn't . . . and at the same time he tried to make you into everything he was. I don't know if he was right or wrong, but I know he meant to do more good than he meant to do harm. He wasn't always right. Sometimes when he touched, he bruised. And sometimes when he took me in his arms, he cut. When I first met your daddy I thought, Here is a man I can lay down with and make a baby. That's the first thing I thought when I seen him. I was thirty years old and had done seen my share of men. But when he walked up to me and said, "I can dance a waltz that'll make you dizzy," I thought, Rose

Lee, here is a man that you can open yourself up to and
be filled to bursting. Here is a man that can fill all them
empty spaces you been tipping around the edges of. One
of them empty spaces was being somebody's mother. I
married your daddy and settled down to cooking his supper
and keeping clean sheets on the bed. When your daddy
walked through the house, he was so big he filled it up.
That was my first mistake. Not to make him leave some
room for me, for my part in the matter. But at that time I
wanted that. I wanted a house that I could sing in. And
that's what your daddy gave me. I didn't know to keep up
his strength I had to give up little pieces of mine. I did
that. I took on his life as mine and mixed up the pieces so
that you couldn't hardly tell which was which anymore. It
was my choice. It was my life and I didn't have to live it
like that. But that's what life offered me in the way of being
a woman, and I took it. I grabbed hold of it with both
hands. After a while he didn't seem so big no more. Sometimes I'd catch him just sitting and staring at his hands,
just sitting there staring like he was watching the silence
eat away at them. By the time Raynell came into the house,
me and your daddy had done lost touch with each other.
I didn't want to make my blessing off of nobody's misfor-
tune, but I took on to Raynell like she was all them babies
I had wanted and never had. Like I'd been blessed to relive
a part of my life. And if the Lord see fit to keep up my
strength, I'm gonna do her just like your daddy did
you . . . I'm gonna give her the best of what's in me.

The First Breeze of Summer

Leslie Lee

Premiere: Negro Ensemble Company, New York City, 1975
Setting: The Edwards' home in a small northeastern city.

Gremmar, a black woman in her seventies, has two teenage grandsons. Nate dropped out of high school to work for his father, but his younger brother Lou wants better for himself. His ambition is costing him a lot of self-hatred as he tries to deny his black roots.

Against this present-tense family drama, Gremmar remembers her own teenage years. In interspersed flashbacks, we meet Sam Green, the man who courted her when she was seventeen. He has just given Lucretia (young Gremmar) a pearl necklace—an unheard-of luxury for a poor, religious black girl. She's thrilled, but afraid that her parents will make her give the pearls back. Embarrassed, Sam finally admits they're imitations. Lucretia is even more delighted—now she can wear them! Then she realizes that Sam is not in his railroad uniform. He tells her, "I got the afternoon off. Yeah, I get the rest of my life off as far as those people are concerned." He tells her what happened.

An elderly black man named Pop worked with Sam as a porter at the railroad station. It turns out that Pop was a doctor. ("I see his—whatever they call the damn thing—his degree—all in Latin and junk! He carries it with him—no lie!—in his back pocket!") But Pop couldn't find any work. Sam continues the story.

SAM

He couldn't make it baby. You have to eat. What are you going to eat—promises? Damn right we get sick. But who the hell can pay for it? He couldn't make it. The man had to eat! A hell of a lot of sick people, but no cash, babe! (LUCRETIA *sits on bed as* SAM *crosses Stage Center.*) Colored people weren't ready for colored doctors, or maybe colored doctors weren't ready for colored people. I forget the way he put it, but something like that . . . He said he didn't mind helping folks, but he didn't realize how much it was necessary for him not to be hungry—to not be wor-

rying about next month all the time . . . *(Pauses.)* Wanted
it simple, he said . . . just plain simple, you know, babe . . .
Didn't want to have to think . . . or feel . . . or even care . . .
the hell with it . . . Gave it up . . . He's a porter, so help
me God, a porter, down at the station. *(Pause.)* He was . . .
you know . . . doing his job . . . He's pushing this cracker's
bags . . . Cracker's got enough bags for everybody in this
whole town piled up on top of Pop's cart. He's pushing the
damn thing, and it's heavy, but he's pushing, smiling and
whistling, happylike . . . And I don't know, for some reason one of the bags comes tumbling down and falls on the
floor. The thing is, it splits— A couple of things break. The
cracker claims they're from— I don't know whether he's
lying or not—from Paris or Europe, one of them damn
places. And all of a sudden, he's getting red in the face.
He's yelling and making a big stew, calling Doc names!
Calling him boy this and nigger that, and Pop—Pop is
just . . . just standing there—like he's supposed to take it,
smiling and apologizing. *(Pause.)* He's got his mind—Pop—
on what he is now, not what he was. He ain't no goddamn
porter, but he don't want nobody to change it. He's got it
all figured out! So that stupid, dumb, doctor-porter is taking
all the cracker's crap! Taking it, talking to himself, reciting
that stuff from his medical books! . . . Well, I couldn't take
it! So I hightail it over to where they standing, and—and
before I could catch myself, I'm telling this cracker off! I
got my hand, my fist, my nose into his, and I'm screaming
at him—yelling at him—calling him the names he's calling
Pop. And that stupid Pop—Doc—is pulling at me—yanking at me, because he knows, because he's made it all so
simple! And he's struggling with me! And I'm yelling at the
cracker: "This man's a doctor, goddammit! You oughta be
carrying his bags, you sonofabitch! Don't you talk to Dr.
Savage that way!" And Pop is crying almost, because I
promised I wouldn't say nothing to nobody! That's what's
getting him! He's begging me and half-crying for me to shut
up! And then all of a sudden, he pulls out that damn piece

of paper and tears it into shreds—just rips it up! *(Pauses.)* Well . . . to make a long story short . . . that's it. I mean, that's it . . . I wasn't worth a good minute after that . . . Right on the spot . . . on the damn spot! *(Pauses.)* I turn around . . . on my way out . . . and there's . . . *Pop* . . . doing penance for me . . . cleaning up that bastard's shit . . . smiling, apologizing . . . kissing ass! . . . If he's mad, he's mad at me and not at the cracker—for messing up his goddamn, stupid world . . . *(Laughing suddenly and sitting in chair Stage Center.)* Baby, I'm so miserable, it's funny . . . miserable . . .

Fishing

Michael Weller

Premiere: New York Shakespeare Festival, New York City, 1975

Setting: Somewhere on the coast of the Pacific Northwest, 1974

Robbie is crashing on the couch of Bill and Shelly's rented shack in the Northwest. Bill wants to buy a fishing boat. They have $21.57 in the bank, but the *I Ching* says, "After Initial Setbacks, Great Abundance." More important, Shelly has just scored a bag of peyote buttons. Mary-Ellen and Dane, who Robbie was crashing with before he crashed with Shelly and Bill, drive up for the day. They all do peyote. Mary-Ellen is worried about Robbie, who left their house without a word and who may be in love with her. He refuses to discuss it, deflecting her questions with his customary sarcasm until she says, "God, you're the loneliest person I ever met," and draws blood. Royally stoned, the whole gang decides to drive out to the ocean. It's foggy and dangerous driving, but Robbie insists on riding his motorcycle.

Act Two begins at a lighthouse lookout in pea-soup fog. Amid the fog and peyote strangeness, Robbie takes Bill aside and hands him an envelope. Inside is the $1500 he needs for the boat. Robbie is independently wealthy and tells Bill he gets "deep pleasure" from spending his father's money: "He doesn't really know how to enjoy it, and I do." But he warns Bill about going along on "a million beautiful trips" and blaming the rest of the world for his fuckups. "What happens if you realize that the fucking up is built right into you like an extra liver, and you're gonna have to take it with you wherever you go?" Then he gets onto his bike and roars into the fog. Mary-Ellen is frantic, thinking he's planning to kill himself. Later, Robbie admits that he was. He describes the ride.

ROBBIE

It felt so amazing in the fog. A hundred miles an hour. I could've had an accident before I had a chance to off myself. I was sort of scared but the scared went into just perfect peace. Perfect control. And I thought, O.K., do it. Just like that. All I need is a set of headlights. I went around this curve. Nothing. Still deserted. Then I started to feel kind of weird. Self-conscious. I mean, who was watching? Who was I doing this for? Who am I doing everything I'm doing for. I mean, are they watching? Who the fuck is this crowd that doesn't want me around? I mean this is pathetic, I'm going through this incredible performance and no one's watching. I was pissed off. And then I thought, Wait a minute, I'm talking to myself. I'm out in the fog on a motorcycle traveling one hundred miles an hour with the intention of committing suicide and I'm talking to myself. And then suddenly it all stopped; the voices, the intention, the trip, the day, everything, and I saw something amazing inside of me that was so clear you could almost touch it with your finger . . . . life: Stay alive. I wanted like crazy to stay alive. Which means that, in balance, there must be something in it. Under all that bullshit one simple thing. Keep on. Stay alive. Pardon my being sincere for a moment. But I'm really glad I saw that. *(Long pause.)*

The Foreigner

Larry Shue

Premiere: Milwaukee Repertory Theater, 1983
Setting: Betty Meeks's Fishing Lodge Resort, Tilghman County, Georgia

Two Englishmen arrive at an out-of-the-way fishing lodge in rural Georgia. One of them, Froggy LeSueur, is a regular guest here, a hearty and cheerful adventurer. His companion, Charlie, "seems quietly, somehow permanently, lost." Charlie is a proofreader for a science fiction magazine. His dying wife has begged him to leave her bedside because she finds him "shatteringly, profoundly boring." He is terrified of conversation. Froggy solves this by presenting him to Betty Meeks, the lodge's proprietress, as a foreigner who doesn't speak English. Betty, who's never left Georgia but loves all things foreign, is thrilled. Charlie is mortified to find himself embroiled in such a lie, but the thought of confessing is even worse, and he accepts his fate.

In no time at all, the "foreigner" finds himself privy to the private conversations of all the lodge's guests. ("Don't worry about Charlie . . . he doesn't speak English.") The sweet ex-debutante Catherine Simms tells her fiancé David that she's pregnant. David, a virtuous minister when he's with Catherine, becomes a conniving, mean redneck as soon as she's out of the room. He and his Klan buddy Owen are planning to buy up the lodge (with Catherine's money) and turn it into a "Christian men's hunting club." He also plays tricks on Catherine's slow brother Ellard to make him look more retarded than he is. Charlie hears all.

Betty and Ellard dote on Charlie and, freed from the burden of speaking, he starts to cut loose, making up "native customs" of his foreign country. Ellard starts teaching him English: important words like "grits" and "aigs." Then Catherine comes down and tells him her troubles.

CATHERINE

Mind if I sit down here? I am not going up to that yellow room again. Damn picture on the wall of some dogs playin' poker. (*To* CHARLIE.) Have a seat, what you lookin' at? People in your country bend in the middle? Have a seat. (*Gestures toward a chair.* CHARLIE *sits, hands in lap, regarding her.*) That's it. Oh, yeah. This is—this'd be a good place to hang meat. Don't you think? No, we're not supposed to talk to you, I know. (*Pause.*) You don't care. What do you care. (*Pause.*) You starin' at me for? Make me feel like a TV set. (*She picks up a newspaper.*) You want the picture section? No? Suit yourself. (*Finding the front page.*) Today's *Constitution*, my goodness. What do we—? Aww— looky here. Somebody's gone out and torched the Klan headquarters, can you beat that? Up in Atlanta. Yes, sir. Burned the place *down*. That's a switch. Some old boys aren't too pleased right now, you can bet on that. Watch out for them, mister, those Klan boys. They'll get you. You're not a hundred percent American white Christian, you're liable to find yourself some fine mornin' floppin' around in some Safeway dumpster, minus a few little things. (*Reading elsewhere in the paper.*) Debutante *ball!* Well— look at the little debutantes! Aren't they pretty? Comin' out. (*To the girls in the picture.*) The catch is, girls, you don't get to go back *in.* My, my. (*Absorbed, turning pages.*) What in the world am I doin' . . . ? I don't know. . . . What else we got here? We got—. (*She says nothing for a mo-*

ment. Then she puts down the paper and, embarrassed, presses the heels of her hands into her eyes.) Shoot. 'Scuse me. I don't ever do this. *(Clears her throat.)* I'm just a little bit—weary, this mornin'. *(Clears her throat again.)* I guess? There we go. *(Picks up the paper.)* Uh . . . *(The paper goes down again, and the hands back over the eyes.)* Shoot. *(A long pause.)* I just get sorta—uh—a little sick and tired of things, from time to time. Sometimes I just— I don't know. I don't know. Or what I'm sittin' here jab-berin' away at you for, either. You really, you don't un-derstand me at all, do you? That's why, I guess. Talkin' to Betty, or Ellard, you know, there's always that slim little chance you might be understood. Cain't have that. And David, of course, he's off someplace—instead of stickin' around here gettin' to know me. I just keep thinkin' if he— *(An odd laugh.)* if he knew me a little better, he wouldn't— Ohh, boy. You ever know anybody that—what's your name? Charlie? Charlie. Anybody that was just so good, that you just feel *vile*, most of the time? Yeah. And he is, he's so sweet, and he does for people, and he's so patient. And you get with him a while, you just realize you've spent your whole life bein' selfish and silly? Doin' dumb things like *(Picking up the paper.)* this, I was one of these little cutie-patooties, 'bout a year ago. Yeah. One year. Lord. Dressin' up, flouncin' around, boppin' all over in my daddy's plane, sippin' at drinks in revolvin' restaurants. Dumb, dumb stu-pid, useless, mindless bullshit. I miss it. I do. I don't think I was cut out to be a decent person. You know? Some people are just meant to be a waste of food, and I think I'm one of 'em. I'm good at it. And a year from now, what? I'm gonna be a mother? Probably own this house? Preacher's wife? I mean—whew! I mean, hold the damn *phone* a minute. What—how'd all this *happen*? I guess I just wish things didn't change quite so fast. But . . . they do. They surely do. You got some nice eyes, you know that? You're probably real nice. You're a good listener. You are. Say "Thank you." *(Pause.)* Hm? "Thank you?"

Gemini

Albert Innaurato

Premiere: Circle Repertory Company, New York City, 1977
Setting: The Geminiani/Weinberger backyard in South
  Philadelphia

Francis Geminiani, a scholarship student at Harvard, is
home for the summer in South Philadelphia. He's a definite
misfit in this working-class Italian ghetto, trying to drown
out the garbagemen's clatter by blasting recordings of *Tris-
tan und Isolde*. Francis's father, Fran, calls his son "Igor."
("He just sits around all day, no job, nothin'.") And Francis
is thrown into turmoil when two of his schoolmates turn
up for a twenty-first birthday surprise. Judith Hastings is
a gorgeous WASP princess, her kid brother Randy is equally
golden, and Francis does not know for certain which one
he's in love with. He's mortally humiliated to have them
discover his "roots": his tough-talking, lecherous father;
Fran's shriveled-up prude of a lady friend, Lucille Pompi;
their blowsy next-door neighbor, Bunny Weinberger; and
Bunny's peculiar son Herschel.

  Herschel is sixteen years old, "very heavy, asthmatic,
very bright, but eccentric. Obsessed with Public Trans-
portation." He makes his first entrance on a rusty kid's
tricycle, impersonating a subway engine. As Bunny says,
"Well, all geniuses is a little crazy. . . . He gotta IQ of 187
or 172, depending on which test you use." Here, Herschel
is talking to Judith.

___

HERSCHEL

One time I fell while I was having an asthma attack. My
mother called the ambulance. She has, like, an uncle who's
a driver. They rushed me to the hospital. Like, you know
the siren screaming? That was two years ago right before
I went to high school. It was St. Agnes Hospital over track

thirty-seven on the A, the AA, the AA 1 through 7 and the B express lines, maybe you passed it? I didn't get, like, hurt falling, you know. Still, my mother asked me what I wanted most in the whole world, you know? I told her and she let me ride the subway for twelve whole hours. Like, she rode them with me. She had to stay home from work for two days.

[JUDITH: *(Crosses to tent, and gets a bandana out of her knapsack. She sits down, and starts cleaning her knee, which she'd hurt in leaping off the fence.)* Why are you so interested in the subways?

HERSCHEL: *(Joins her on the ground.)* Oh, not just the subways.]

I love buses too, you know? And my favorites are, well, you won't laugh? The trolleys. They are very beautiful. There's a trolley graveyard about two blocks from here. I was thinking, like, maybe Randy would like to see that, you know? I could go see the engine any time. The trolley graveyard is well, like, I guess, beautiful, you know? Really. They're just there, like old creatures everyone's forgotten, some of them rusted out, and some of them on their sides, and one, the old thirty-two, is, like, standing straight up as though sayin', like, I'm going to stand here and be myself, no matter what. I talk to them. Oh, I shouldn't have said that. Don't tell my mother, please? It's, you know, like people who go to castles and look for, well, like knights in shining armor, you know? That past was beautiful and somehow, like, pure. The same is true of the trolleys. I follow the old thirty-two route all the time. It leads right to the graveyard where the thirty-two is buried, you know? It's like, well, fate. The tracks are half covered with filth and pitch, new pitch like the city pours on. It oozes in the summer and people walk on it, but you can see the tracks and you see like it's true like old things last, good things last, like, you know? The trolleys are all filthy and half covered and rusted out and laughed at and even though they're not much use to anybody and kind of ugly like, by most standards, they're like, they're well, I guess, beautiful, you know?

───────────────────────────

Getting Out

Marsha Norman

Premiere: Actors Theatre of Louisville/Theatre de Lys, New York City, 1979

Setting: A dingy apartment in Louisville; Pine Ridge State Prison in Alabama

Arlene Holsclaw has just been released from an eight-year stretch in prison. Her parole statement lists her crime as "the second-degree murder of a cab driver in conjunction with a filling station robbery involving attempted kidnapping of attendant. Crime occurred during escape from Lakewood State Prison where subject Holsclaw was serving three years for forgery and prostitution." In spite of this record, Arlene is determined to make a fresh start. But everyone in her life—her former pimp, her cab-driving mother, the prison guard who wants to bed her—continues to deal with her as a criminal. Arlene finds herself haunted by Arlie, her former self. (The two roles are played by two different actresses.)

Monologue One: This is our first introduction to Arlie. Norman notes, "She tells this story rather simply. She enjoys it, but its horror is not lost on her. She may be doing some semiabsorbing activity such as painting her toenails."

Monologue Two: Arlene's former pimp has tried to convince her to come to New York and go back into business with him. Her tough neighbor Ruby, an ex-con who cooks in a diner, tells Arlene to stay "outside" even if it means hard work and poverty, because, "When you make your two nickels, you can keep both of them." Arlene feels helpless and trapped. This is not the new life she had hoped for. Increasingly hysterical, she remembers a chaplain in prison and the circumstances of her decision to change.

——————— 1 ———————

ARLIE

So, there was this little kid, see, this creepy little fucker next door. Had glasses an' somethin' wrong with his foot. I don't know, seven, maybe. Anyhow, ever' time his daddy went fishin', he'd bring this kid back some frogs. They built this little fence around 'em in the backyard like they was pets or somethin'. An' we'd try to go over an' see 'em but he'd start screamin' to his mother to come out an' git rid of us. Real snotty like. So we got sick of him bein' such a goody-goody an' one night me an' June snuck over there an' put all his dumb ol' frogs in this sack. You never heared such a fuss. *(Makes croaking sounds.)* Slimy bastards, frogs. We was plannin' to let 'em go all over the place, but when they started jumpin' an' all, we just figured they was askin' for it. So, we taken 'em out front to the porch an' throwed 'em one atta time out into the street. *(Laughs.)* Some of 'em hit cars goin' by but most of 'em just got squashed, you know, runned over? It was great, seein' how far we could throw 'em, over back of our backs an' under our legs an' God, it was really fun watchin' 'em fly through the air then splat *(Claps hands.)* all over somebody's car window or somethin'. Then the next day, we was waitin' an' this little kid comes out in his backyard lookin' for his stupid frogs an' he don't see any an' he gets so crazy, cryin' an' everything. So me an' June goes over an' tells him we seen this big mess out in the street, an' he goes out and sees all them frogs' legs an' bodies an' shit all over everwhere, an', man, it was so funny. We 'bout killed ourselves laughin'. Then his mother come out an' she wouldn't let him go out an' pick up all the pieces, so he jus' had to stand there watchin' all the cars go by smushing his babies right into the street. I's gonna run an' git him a frog's head, but June yellin' at me, "Arlie, git over here 'fore some car slips on them frog guts an' crashes into you." *(Pause.)* I never had so much fun in one day in my whole life.

2

ARLENE

This chaplain said I had . . . said Arlie was my hateful self and she was hurtin' me and God would find some way to take her away. . . . And it was God's will so I could be the meek . . . the meek, them that's quiet and good an' git whatever they want . . . I forgit that word . . . they git the Earth.

[RUBY: Inherit.

ARLENE: Yeah.]

And that's why I done it.

[RUBY: Done what?

ARLENE: What I done.]

'Cause the chaplain he said . . . I'd sit up nights waitin' for him to come talk to me.

[RUBY: Arlene, what did you do? What are you talkin' about?]

They tol' me . . . after I's out an' it was all over . . . they said after the chaplain got transferred . . . I didn't know why he didn't come no more till after. . . . They said it was three whole nights at first, me screamin' to God to come git Arlie an' kill her. They give me this medicine an' thought I's better. . . . Then that night it happened, the officer was in the dorm doin' count . . . an' they didn't hear nuthin' but they come back out where I was an' I'm standin' there tellin' 'em to come see, real quiet I'm tellin' 'em, but there's all this blood all over my shirt an' I got this fork I'm holdin' real tight in my hand . . . *(Clenches one hand now, the other hand fumbling with the buttons as if she's going to show RUBY.)* this fork, they said Doris stole it from the kitchen an' give it to me so I'd kill myself and shut up botherin' her . . . an' there's all these holes all over me

where I been stabbin' myself an' I'm sayin' Arlie is dead
for what she done to me, Arlie is dead an' it's God's will . . . I
didn't scream it, I was jus' sayin' it over an' over . . . Arlie
is dead, Arlie is dead . . . they couldn't git that fork outta
my hand till . . . I woke up in the infirmary an' they said
I almost died. They said they's glad I didn't. (*Smiling.*)
They said did I feel better now an' they was real nice,
bringing me chocolate puddin' . . .

[RUBY: I'm sorry, Arlene. (*Reaches out for her, but
ARLENE pulls away sharply.*)]

I'd be eatin' or jus' lookin' at the ceiling an' git a tear in
my eye, but it'd jus' dry up, you know, it didn't run out
or nuthin'. An' then pretty soon, I's well, an' officers was
sayin' they's seein' such a change in me an' givin' me yarn
to knit sweaters an' how'd I like to have a new skirt to wear
an' sometimes lettin' me chew gum. They said things ain't
never been as clean as when I's doin' the housekeepin' at
the dorm. (*So proud.*) An' then I got in the honor cottage
an' nobody was foolin' with me no more or nuthin'. And I
didn't git mad like before or nuthin'. I just done my work
an' knit. . . . An' I don't think about it what happened,
'cept . . . (*Now losing control.*) People here keep callin'
me Arlie an' . . . (*Has trouble saying "Arlie."*) I didn't mean
to do it, what I done . . .

Glengarry Glen Ross

David Mamet

Premiere: Cottlesloe Theatre, London, 1983
Setting: A Chinese restaurant, a real estate office
Four ruthless real estate salesmen jockey for deals in a
business whose only rule is "Always be closing." The company they work for is running a sales contest. First prize
is a Cadillac; second is steak knives. The losers get fired.

The first act of *Glengarry Glen Ross* consists of three two-man scenes in a Chinese restaurant. In the first scene, Shelly "the Machine" Levene, a well-seasoned salesman whose record has started to slip, tries bribing his boss to get premium "leads" (names of interested customers). In the second, two salesmen named Moss and Aaronow talk about robbing their own office. In the third, Richard Roma, the office's top-of-the-board salesman, hits on a potential customer.

ROMA

. . . all train compartments smell vaguely of shit. It gets so you don't mind it. That's the worst thing that I can confess. You know how long it took me to get there? A long time. When you *die* you're going to regret the things you don't do. You think you're *queer* . . . ? I'm going to tell you something: we're *all* queer. You think that you're a *thief?* So *what?* You get befuddled by a middle-class moral-ity . . . ? Get *shut* of it. Shut it out. You cheated on your wife . . . ? You *did* it, *live* with it. *(Pause.)* You fuck little girls, so *be* it. There's an absolute morality? May *be*. And *then* what? If you *think* there is, then *be* that thing. Bad people go to hell? I don't *think* so. If you think that, act that way. A hell exists on earth? Yes. I won't live in it. That's *me*. You ever take a dump made you feel you'd just slept for twelve hours . . . ?

   [LINGK: Did I . . . ?

   ROMA: Yes.

   LINGK: I don't know.]

Or a *piss* . . . ? A great meal fades in reflection. Everything else gains. You know why? 'Cause it's only food. This shit we eat, it keeps us going. But it's only food. The great fucks that you may have had. What do you remember about them?

   [LINGK: What do I . . . ?

ROMA: Yes.
    LINCK: Mmmm . . .]
I don't know. For *me*, I'm saying, what it is, it's probably
not the orgasm. Some broads, forearms on your neck, something her *eyes* did. There was a *sound* she made . . . or,
me, lying, in the, I'll tell you: me lying in bed; the next
day she brought me café au lait. She gives me a cigarette,
my balls feel like concrete. Eh? What I'm saying, what is
our life? (*Pause.*) It's looking forward or it's looking back.
And that's our life. That's *it*. Where is the *moment*? (*Pause.*)
And what is it that we're afraid of? Loss. What else? (*Pause.*)
The *bank* closes. We get *sick*, my wife died on a plane, the
stock market collapsed . . . the house burnt down . . . what
of these happen . . . ? None of 'em. We worry anyway.
What does this mean? I'm not *secure*. How can I be secure?
(*Pause.*) Through amassing wealth beyond all measure? No.
And what's beyond all measure? That's a sickness. That's a
trap. There is no measure. Only greed. How can we act?
The right way, we would say, to deal with this: "There is
a one-in-a-million chance that so and so will happen. . . .
Fuck it, it won't happen to *me*. . . ." No. We know that's
not the right way I think. (*Pause.*) We say the *correct* way
to deal with this is "There is a one-in-so-and-so chance this
will happen . . . God *protect* me. I am powerless, let it not
happen to me. . . ," But no to *that*. I say. There's something else. What is it? "If it happens, AS IT MAY for that
is not within our powers, I will *deal* with it, just as I do
today with what draws my concern today." I say *this* is how
we must act. I do those things which seem correct to me
today. I trust myself. And if security concerns me, I do
that which *today* I think will make me secure. And every
day I *do* that, when that day *arrives* that I need a reserve,
(a) odds are that I have it, and (b) the *true* reserve that I
have is the strength that I have of *acting each day* without
fear. (*Pause.*) According to the dictates of my mind. (*Pause.*)
Stocks, bonds, objects of art, real estate. Now: what are
they? (*Pause.*) An opportunity. To what? To make money?

Perhaps. To *lose* money? Perhaps. To "indulge" and to
"learn" about ourselves? Perhaps. *So fucking what?* What
isn't? They're an *opportunity.* That's all. They're an *event.*
A guy comes up to you, you make a call, you send in a
brochure, it doesn't matter, "There're these *properties* I'd
like for you to see." What does it mean? What you *want* it
to mean. *(Pause.)* Money? *(Pause.)* If that's what it signifies
to you. Security? *(Pause.)* Comfort? *(Pause.)* All it is is
THINGS THAT HAPPEN TO YOU. *(Pause.)* That's all it
is. How are they different? *(Pause.)* Some poor newly married guy gets run down by a cab. Some *busboy* wins the
lottery. *(Pause.)* All it is, it's a carnival. What's special . . . what *draws* us? *(Pause.)* We're all different. *(Pause.)*
We're not the same. *(Pause.)* We are not the same. *(Pause.)*
Hmmm. *(Pause. Sighs.)* It's been a long day. *(Pause.)* What
are you drinking?

Gloria and Esperanza

Julie Bovasso

Premiere: La Mama Experimental Theatre Club, New York
  City, 1970
Setting: Multiple
This hallucinogenic play takes place in the life and mind of
one Julius Esperanza Schnadelson, a visionary poet whose
visions are seen by the audience (though not necessarily
by the other characters, who tend to think he's crazy).
Julius's showgirl lover Gloria is stealing his "secret book"
of revelations, in cahoots with Fred the mailman. Eventually, they join forces with Gloria's tacky friend Marsha,
her gay Chinese landlord, and Herr von Schtutt of the IRS,
bastardizing the book into the Vegas-style *Revelations Revue.*
Meanwhile Julius goes to a psychiatric hospital populated

by lunatic saints, the Black Prince, and the St. Teresa All-Star Women's Basketball Team.

Monologue One: Gloria's landlord, Terry Wong Fu, wants a cut of her deal with the mailman. He asks for a third of the profits and his name as author, then leaves. Gloria panics.

Monologue Two: Julius speaks to a hospital Psychiatrist, "a young Ivy-League gentleman who speaks in a decidedly Ivy-League manner, i.e., without moving his jaws. . . . The Psychiatrist is given to a habit of suddenly flashing his teeth in a grimacing smile"; he is mad as a hatter and firmly believes that "God is my pecker." It is Julius's first session. He has just described his father, the genius pornographer Zachary Schnadel, and his own wild youth in Europe. Julius has been married four times. All four wives were named Sophie.

——— 1 ———

GLORIA

Now I'm in for it. God damned blackmailing little worm. He's got me good. I'm getting in deeper and deeper. (*The telephone rings.*) Hello? . . . Yes, this is Gloria B. Gilbert. . . . Who? Internal Revenue? . . . Oh. . . . Hello, Mr. von Schtutt. How are you? Long time no see. . . . No, I still haven't got any money. . . . No, I'm not working. . . . How am I living? I don't know, but I'm still living. . . . How much is it now, with the fines and the interest? . . . Really? that much? . . . Well, I don't know what to say, I haven't got a cent. . . . Sell what mink coat? I haven't got a mink coat. . . . Wait, wait, let me get this straight: Your spy was hiding behind a tree in front of *my* house and he saw *me* come out wearing a mink coat? . . . That's ridiculous. He was standing behind the wrong tree. . . . I know your spies are well trained, but he was still standing behind the wrong tree. There is no mink coat. . . . An affidavit? Sure, why

not? . . . When would you like me to come down? . . .
You'll come here? . . . When? . . . Today? . . . Two
hours? . . . Yeh, sure, okay. Why not. Fine. . . . I'll make
some coffee. . . . Okay. I'll see you. Good-bye. *(Rushing
behind the screen.)* Two hours! *(She returns in a moment
with a mink coat bundled in her arms. She rushes around
looking for a place to hide it.)* Where? Where am I going
to hide it! That fink, he'll find it no matter what . . . *(She
has a sudden idea, crosses to the telephone and dials.)*
Hello, Marsha? . . . Look, how would you like to wear the
mink coat for a few hours today? . . . So what if it's ninety-
eight degrees outside. How often do you get a chance to
wear a four-thousand-dollar mink? . . . Well, I remember
you said that you would like to know how it feels to wear
it one day, so . . . Today's the day! . . . I don't know where
you could go in it. Go to an air-conditioned luncheonette
and have a cup of coffee. . . . Yeh, go to Goldie's. The air-
conditioning is so strong in there you need a fur coat. . . .
No, don't thank me, it's my pleasure. Can you get here in
a few minutes? . . . It has to be right now or the deal is
off. . . . I can't wait two hours. . . . So leave the rollers in
your hair. . . . Alright, good-bye. I'll see you.

2

PSYCHIATRIST

I used to know a Sophie Schnadelson. Or was it Sophie
Schnadel*man*? . . . Schnadel*son*, Schnadel*man*. . . . So-
phie Schnadelson. No, that doesn't sound right. Sophie
Schnadelman. Sophie . . . Yes, that's it. Sophie Schnadel-
man. Yes. *(Musing.)* Mm. Quite a girl. Yes. Quite a girl,
Sophie Schnadelman. To her, God was a peppermint stick.
(He laughs to himself.) Suck, suck, suck . . . Oh, well! *(He
laughs again.)* I sometimes wonder what my life would have
been like if I were Sir Isaac Newton. *(He looks at* JULIUS.*)*
I have a theory about Sir Isaac Newton. It's only a theory,

of course, but I'm convinced that he had a ding dong about so big. (*He indicates two inches with his fingers.*)

[JULIUS: How do you know that?]

I did an in-depth psychological analysis of his *Philosophiae Naturalis Principia Mathematica*. It's all there, in black and white . . . to the trained clinical eye, that is. It's quite obvious. Particularly in his Corpuscular Theory of Light. Are you familiar with it? . . . It's also known as the . . . (*He pauses in order to stress the next word.*) *Emission* theory. (*Clearing his throat.*) Well, briefly . . . Newton said that light consists of minute particles . . . *emitted* . . . from *luminous bodies* . . . and which then *travel through space*. (*He gives* JULIUS *a meaningful nod and a slow knowing wink.*)

[JULIUS: Well, what has that . . .]

What has that got to do with the size of his ding dong? I'll tell you. (*Speaking very clinically, and taking pauses before each significant point, nodding, winking, or looking assertively at* JULIUS.) It's a question of simple compensation. In the Corpuscular Theory of Light, Newton was compensating for his own sexual inadequacy. Only a man whose own . . . *emission* . . . or: *ejaculation* . . . *nich var?* . . . emission, ejaculation . . . coming from a . . . far from *luminous body* . . . yes, no? . . . and which emission and or ejaculation not having the potency to reach its mark let *alone travel through space!* could have evolved such a theory. (*He pauses.*) It's self-evident. Of course I don't mean to malign the reputation of a great scientist, but facts are facts. He was a great man, no doubt. A genius. But nonetheless, genius or no . . . his dick couldn't have been more than an inch and a half at the most. (*Pausing, reflectively again.*) Yes, I have often speculated . . . I've wondered about myself and my own genius. I'm sure that the only thing that stands between me and it is my rather formidable . . . (*He laughs.*) Ahh, well . . . ! Where were we? (*Looking through his notes.*) Four years in Europe . . . orgiastic revelers . . . flailing . . . belly of the giantess . . .

pomegranate . . . (*Looking up at* JULIUS.) and it all began
to change when you met your first wife.

━━━━━━━━━━━━━━━━━━━━━━━━━━━━━

The Great Nebula in Orion

Lanford Wilson

Premiere: Stables Theatre Club, Manchester, England, 1971
Setting: Louise's Manhattan apartment
Two women meet by chance in Bergdorf Goodman's. Louise,
a prize-winning fashion designer, is bisexual, and Carrie is
a rich, rather prim Boston housewife. Fourteen years ago
they were classmates at Bryn Mawr. Although they have
seemingly little in common, Louise invites Carrie back to
her apartment for a drink. One drink becomes several, and
soon they are sharing memories, secrets, and a profound
sense of loss.

(*Note:* Sam is Louise's rakish older brother.)

━━━━━━━━━━━━━━━━━━━━━━━━━━━━━

LOUISE

I know it must seem glamorous. I'm not very damn glamorous but everyone seems to feel I must be. There have
been some really wonderful times. There's an award. Probably you don't even know about it—it's in the trade—that
I've managed to win. Twice actually. And that was a thrill.
There's a presentation luncheon and I don't know—I
never. . . . (*Full stop, thinking.*) Well. It wasn't that I never
got along with Mom, she's very—well, I should say that
I'm quite like her. There was never any question of family
pride or any such thing—we all of us—Sam too—all of us
took each other for granted. It was a very casual sort of
family. We weren't like families. I mean I had left home
by the time I was eighteen, which isn't really terribly shock-

ing anymore, but, well, the first time she came to see me—
she didn't call or anything and I was having this torrid three-
day affair with a what-was-he-a-writer—oh, god—I mean
for the newspaper. Worse, he wrote those daily horoscope
things. Well, he was a Pisces and they're into that—and
Mom comes to the door—Pisces is in bed naked—Mom
comes to the door with a little overnight bag and a hat with
feathers or a feather, and I answer the door—I've not seen
her in a year—and she was broad-minded, you know, but
I said, "Oh, Mom, sweet, how wonderful, darling, but there
isn't a cube of ice in the house, could you run down to the
deli? It's just on the corner." And Mom said, "Oh, sure,
of course." She didn't think a thing of it. I mean we got
along. And she's a teetotaler. But really—at bottom—she
wanted me to be different from what we had been. To have
a family and not mess with a career. She didn't see much
use in it; or why I was so caught up. Well, I had two
smashing seasons in a row and was pretty much the toast
of the town that spring and I guess everyone knew I was
going to win this award. I know *I* did. But you can't really
know it until you—I mean what it's like until you do. And
all my friends were there, who have been of—well, they've
been wonderful—and I was very young; the youngest designer ever. I still was the second year I won—and—everyone *stood*. (*She is very moved.*) They were—I just didn't
expect it. I know I—I—got the award and everyone cheered
and they all stood and all I could think—stupid—all I could
think of, standing there with the award (*Crying suddenly,
covering her face.*) was: If Mother could be here, if she
could see—she could. . . . (*Out of it.*) Silly. It was the last
thing I expected to think at a time like that. I mean we
weren't even close. She didn't even like me all that much.
Well, this is silly. You're right. (*Gets up.*) It isn't a good
idea. (*Walking around.*) No, it's wonderful, it is. It's good
to see you—I need—Yes, Central Park. Fifth Avenue on
the other side. Why ever do you hate the Planetarium? I
think it's kind of lovely.

Grown Ups

Jules Feiffer

Premiere: Lyceum Theatre, New York City, 1981
Setting: Marilyn's kitchen in New Rochelle; Jake and Louise's
    apartment in New York City

Helen and Jack are doting Jewish parents. Their daughter
Marilyn is a "marvel" at hors d'oeuvres, but their son Jake
is a god. Jake writes for *The New York Times*. He is "a
master of family sleight of hand; now you see him, now you
don't. He has spent a lifetime side-stepping confrontation,
joking, kidding, getting his way through charm, distance,
outlasting or ignoring the opposition; quick on his feet."

Marilyn has prepared a big family party for Uncle Rudy's
birthday. Jake's wife Louise and their daughter Edie have
stayed home with colds. Jake and Marilyn are in Marilyn's
kitchen, taking a breather from the family circus. The two
compare notes on their parents. Marilyn feels that they
take her for granted; Jake tells her that she should stop
catering to them. He hurts his sister's feelings, and tries
to make it up to her by praising her hors d'oeuvres and
telling her a story. (*Note*: This is not necessarily tactful,
since Jake is renowned in the family for telling great stories,
and Marilyn has twice expressed her jealousy that no one
will listen to *her* stories.)

JAKE

I don't know, Marilyn. Louise! Jeez. Louise is so insanely
loyal. This is a wonderful story. I invited some *Times* colleagues over for dinner. Not such a big deal, except that
Louise hates *The New York Times* (as much as *they* think
it comes down from Mount Sinai). O.K.? Because I report
all my fights, all this interoffice crap—you know, it's no
different where you are—office politics, O.K.? But Louise
worked in an office for fifteen minutes once when she was

on vacation from Mount Holyoke, so she doesn't understand; she takes it personally. So I come home, bitch, bitch,
bitch, bitch, bitch, that's it, it's over, I go to work happy
the next morning. While Louise hates. How can they do
this to her Jake? Off with their heads! O.K.? So when I
invite my oppressors home to dinner, she goes bananas.
"How can you sit down at the same table with these pigs?
How can you eat with them?!" Right? But finally she agrees.
Grudgingly. You want to know how grudgingly? This is a
week ago Tuesday. I come home; she's got a roast chicken
in the oven, it smells marvelous. The apartment looks beautiful. I check out the dining room. There are only four
chairs. We've having eight to dinner. I say, "Louise, what
happened to the chairs?" "They are being repaired," she
says. "They broke this morning and I sent them out to be
repaired." Possibly a little hostile. O.K.? We call her brother,
Mickey. Mickey's her Mr. Fix-it. Lives three blocks away.
Comes running over with four chairs. Fine. We get through
the dinner. Louise won't talk to anybody, but no problem:
My colleagues talk too much to notice wives not talking.
Bruce Forrester is charming, Glen Applebaum is charming,
The New York Times voltage meter on charm, way up there.
Louise hates them all. "Establishment assholes," she calls
them. A ten-minute shit-fit after they leave. I'm a sell-out,
a hypocrite, she can't talk to me any more. She calls her
brother, Mickey; she wants to go over. Mickey says, "It's
midnight." "It's irrelevant," says Louise, "I'm coming over."
Mickey says, "Fine, bring the chairs." So, at 12:30, Louise
and I are struggling up West End Avenue with four chairs.
Louise is wheezing! I'm so pissed, I can't see straight. We
get up to Broadway. She goes on strike. She sits down on
a chair—(JACK *enters from garden, stands by door and
listens.* JAKE *includes him in his audience.*) What am I
supposed to do? I sit down on a chair. People start coming
out of the subway; they see us, they make cracks. It's very
strange to see two grown people sitting on chairs outside
the subway on Broadway at 12:30 in the morning. I feel

like a total ass, but Louise loves it. She cracks back at the people coming out of the subway, and soon there's a small crowd gathered around us. My wife is a hell of a better hostess on the street than at her own dinner party. Three street musicians show up—they play. Why not? There's always music on the Johnny Carson show. Here's Louise! In the end, Louise talks four guys in the crowd into carrying the chairs over to Mickey's for us.

The Homecoming

Harold Pinter

Premiere: Royal Shakespeare Company, London, 1965
Setting: An old house in North London

Max, an aging butcher, is the patriarch of a family of men. He lives in a rundown house in North London with his brother Sam and two of his three adult sons. Joey is a small-time pug boxer, and Lenny, a hoodlum and pimp. The oldest son, Teddy, is a philosophy professor who has been teaching in an American university for the past six years. Teddy brings his wife Ruth to London to meet his family. They arrive in the dead of night, when the men of the household are sleeping. Teddy goes straight to bed in his old, unchanged room, but Ruth elects for "a breath of air." When she comes back in from her walk, she meets Lenny in his pajamas, fixing a clock with a bothersome tick. They talk briefly, then Lenny asks Ruth if he can hold her hand. She asks why. He answers, "I'll tell you why," and delivers the following story.

LENNY

One night, not too long ago, one night down by the docks, I was standing alone under an arch, watching all the men jibbing the boom, out in the harbor, and playing about with the yardarm, when a certain lady came up to me and made me a certain proposal. This lady had been searching for me for days. She'd lost track of my whereabouts. However, the fact was she eventually caught up with me, and when she caught up with me she made me this certain proposal. Well, this proposal wasn't entirely out of order and normally I would have subscribed to it. I mean I would have subscribed to it in the normal course of events. The only trouble was she was falling apart with the pox. So I turned it down. Well, this lady was very insistent and started taking liberties with me down under this arch, liberties which by any criterion I couldn't be expected to tolerate, the facts being what they were, so I clumped her one. It was on my mind at the time to do away with her, you know, to kill her, and the fact is, that as killings go, it would have been a simple matter, nothing to it. Her chauffeur, who had located me for her, he'd popped round the corner to have a drink, which just left this lady and myself, you see, alone, standing underneath this arch, watching all the steamers steaming up, no one about, all quiet on the Western Front, and there she was up against this wall—well, just sliding down the wall, following the blow I'd given her. Well, to sum up, everything was in my favor, for a killing. Don't worry about the chauffeur. The chauffeur would never have spoken. He was an old friend of the family. But . . . in the end I thought . . . Aaah, why go to all the bother . . . you know, getting rid of the corpse and all that, getting yourself into a state of tension. So I just gave her another belt in the nose and a couple of turns of the boot and sort of left it at that.

The House of Blue Leaves

John Guare

Premiere: Truck & Warehouse Theatre, New York City, 1971

Setting: An apartment in Sunnyside, Queens

It is October 4, 1965, the day Pope Paul came to New York for a Mass at Yankee Stadium. Artie Shaughnessy is a zookeeper with big dreams. Asleep, he dreams his son Ronnie is Pope. Awake, he dreams of becoming a songwriter. Artie writes such lyrics as, "Where's the devil in Evelyn?" and one of his "originals" has the same tune as "White Christmas"—but he dreams.

Artie's wife Bananas is a "sick sick sickie" who recently tried to slit her wrists with spoons. He is having an affair with his downstairs neighbor, Bunny Flingus, "a pretty, pink, electric woman in her forties," who keeps warm by stuffing the *New York Post* in her plastic booties. Bunny wants Artie to leave Bananas and take her to Hollywood, where Artie's childhood friend Billy Einhorn, the famous director, can get his songs into the movies.

Monologue One: Bananas "has lived in her nightgown for the last six months. She's in her early forties and has been crying for as long as she's had her nightgown on. She walks uncertainly, as if hidden barriers lay scattered in her path." Now she sits on the edge of the stage and tells her troubles to the audience.

Monologue Two: Ronnie Shaughnessy is "very young—looks barely seventeen—his hair is all shaved off; he is tall, skinny; he speaks with a deep, suffocated, religious fervor. His eyes bulge with a strange mixture of terrifying innocence and diabolism. You can't figure out whether he'd be a gargoyle on some Gothic cathedral or a skinny cherub on some altar." He has gone AWOL from Army basic training to come home and blow up the Pope. While he speaks, he is wiring a homemade bomb.

—————— 1 ——————

BANANAS

My troubles all began a year ago—two years ago today—
two days ago today? Today. (ARTIE *plays the "Anniversary
Waltz."*) We used to have a beautiful old green Buick. The
Green Latrine! . . . I'm not allowed to drive it anymore. . . . But when I could drive it . . . the last time I
drove it, I drove into Manhattan. (ARTIE *plays "In My
Merry Oldsmobile."*) And I drive down Broadway—to the
Crossroads of the World. (ARTIE *plays "Forty-second Street."*
BANANAS *sits on the edge of the stage and talks to the
audience.*) I see a scene that you wouldn't see in your
wildest dreams. Forty-second Street. Broadway. Four corners. Four people. One on each corner. All waving for taxis.
Cardinal Spellman. Jackie Kennedy. Bob Hope. President
Johnson. All carrying suitcases. Taxi! Taxi! I stop in the
middle of the street—the middle of Broadway and I get
out of my Green Latrine and yell, "Get in. I'm a gypsy. A
gypsy cab. Get in. I'll take you where you want to go. Don't
you all know each other? Get in! Get in!" They keep waving
for cabs. I run over to President Johnson and grab him by
the arm. "Get in!" And pull Jackie Kennedy into my car
and John-John who I didn't see starts crying and Jackie hits
me and I hit her and I grab Bob Hope and push Cardinal
Spellman into the back seat, crying and laughing, "I'll take
you where you want to. Get in! Give me your suitcases—"
and the suitcases spill open and Jackie Kennedy's wigs blow
down Forty-second Street and Cardinal Spellman hits me
and Johnson screams and I hit him. I hit them all. And
then the Green Latrine blows four flat tires and sinks and
I run to protect the car and four cabs appear and all my
friends run into four different cabs. And cars are honking
at me to move. I push the car over the bridge back to
Queens. You're asleep. I turn on Johnny Carson to get my
mind off and there's Cardinal Spellman and Bob Hope whose
nose is still bleeding and they tell the story of what hap-

pened to them and everybody laughs. Thirty million people
watch Johnny Carson and they all laugh. At me. At me.
I'm nobody. I knew all those people better than me. You.
Ronnie. I know everything about them. Why can't they
love me? And then it began to snow and I went up on the
roof. . . .

<hr>

2

RONNIE

My father tell you all about me? Pope Ronnie? Charmed
life? How great I am? That's how he is with you. You should
hear him with me, you'd sing a different tune pretty quick,
and it wouldn't be "Where Is the Devil in Evelyn?" (*He
exits into his room and comes out a moment later, carrying
a large, dusty box. He opens it. From it, he takes a bright
red altar boy cassock and surplice that fit him when he was
twelve. He speaks to us as he dresses.*) I was twelve years
old and all the newspapers had headlines on my twelfth
birthday that Billy was coming to town. And *Life* was doing
stories on him and *Look* and the newsreels because Billy
was searching America to find the Ideal American Boy to
play Huckleberry Finn. And Billy came to New York and
called my father and asked him if he could stay here—Billy
needed a hideout. In Waldorf Astorias all over the country,
chambermaids would wheel silver carts to change the sheets.
And out of the sheets would hop little boys saying, "Hello,
I'm Huckleberry Finn." All over the country, little boys
dressed in blue jeans and straw hats would be sent to him
in crates, be under the silver cover covering his dinner,
his medicine cabinet in all his hotel rooms, his suitcase—
"Hello, hello, I'm Huckleberry Finn." And he was coming
here to hide out. Here—Billy coming here—I asked the
nun in school who was Huckleberry Finn—

The nun in Queen of Martyrs knew. She told me. The
Ideal American Boy. And coming home, all the store windows reflected me and the mirror in the tailor shop said,

"Hello, Huck." The butcher shop window said, "Hello, Huck. Hello, Huckleberry Finn. All America wants to meet Billy and he'll be hiding out in your house." I came home— went in there—into my room and packed my bag. . . . I knew Billy would see me and take me back to California with him that very day. This room smelled of ammonia and air freshener and these slipcovers were new that day and my parents were filling up the icebox in their brand-new clothes, filling up the icebox with food and liquor as excited as if the Pope was coming—and nervous because they hadn't seen him in a long while—Billy. They told me my new clothes were on my bed. To go get dressed. I didn't want to tell them I'd be leaving shortly to start a new life. That I'd be flying out to California with Billy on the H.M.S. *Huckleberry*. I didn't want tears from them—only trails of envy. . . . I went to my room and packed my bag and waited.

The doorbell rang. (*Starts hitting two notes on the piano.*) If you listen close, you can still hear the echoes of those wet kisses and handshakes and tears and backs getting hit and "Hello, Billy"'s, "Hello." They talked for a long time about people from their past. And then my father called out: "Ronnie, guess who? Billy, we named him after your father. Ronnie, guess who?"

I picked up my bag and said goodbye to myself in the mirror. Came out. Billy there. Smiling.

It suddenly dawned on me. You had to do things to get parts.

I began dancing. And singing. Immediately. Things I have never done in my life—before or since. I stood on my head and skipped and whirled— (*He does a cartwheel.*) spectacular leaps in the air so I could see veins in the ceiling—ran up and down the keys of the piano and sang and began laughing and crying soft and loud to show off all my emotions. And I heard music and drums that I couldn't even keep up with. And then cut off all my emotions just like that. Instantly. And took a deep bow like the Dying

Swan I saw on Ed Sullivan. I picked up my suitcase and waited by the door.

Billy turned to my parents, whose jaws were down to about there, and Billy said, "You never told me you had a mentally retarded child. You never told me I had an idiot for a godchild," and I picked up my bag and went into my room and shut the door and never came out the whole time he was here.

My only triumph was he could never find a Huckleberry Finn. Another company made the picture a few years later, but it flopped.

My father thinks I'm nothing. Billy. My sergeant. They laugh at me. You laughing at me? I'm going to fool you all. By tonight, I'll be on headlines all over the world. Cover of *Time*. *Life*. TV specials. (*Shows a picture of himself on the wall.*) I hope they use this picture of me—I look better with hair— Go ahead—laugh. Because you know what I think of you? (*Gives us hesitant Bronx cheers.*) I'm sorry you had to hear that—pay seven or eight dollars to hear that. But I don't care. I'll show you all. I'll be too big for any of you.

The House of Ramon Iglesia

José Rivera

Premiere: Ensemble Studio Theatre, New York City, 1983
Setting: The Iglesia family home in Holbrook, Long Island. Ramon and Dolores Iglesia have raised their three boys in America, and now they are packing to move back to Puerto Rico—if they can straighten out the deed to their house. To Dolores, who's never learned English, the move back home is a dream come true. To Javier, the oldest son, it smacks of failure.

Javier finished college and has a white girlfriend named

Caroline. He has just lost his job as a shipping clerk for making a thoughtless remark, and is eager to make his way up in the world. He already considers himself outside the family, referring to it as "you guys," not "we." This attitude is a source of friction with Javier's two brothers, Julio "The Beast" and Charlie ("Carlos to you, bro"). Here, Javier and Charlie are packing up boxes. When Javier makes sarcastic jokes about Puerto Rico, Charlie tells him, "Mom thinks that . . . you really dislike our people."

• • •

José Rivera comments: "When we first confront Javier, he is spiteful and dishonest. One of the few glimpses into his deep, complex feelings is provided by this monologue. Here, we are finally allowed to glimpse some of Javier's pain. Two fine actors, Giancarlo Esposito and Nick Corri, have attacked the speech in the way I think is most correct. They played *against* the pain. They were very restrained and never gave in to self-pity. And it should be remembered that Javier loves words, loves playing with words, and has a sense of humor. The speech can be done with an almost perverse sense of 'fun'—an enjoyment of the images which have haunted Javier most of his young life."

JAVIER

Charlie, I love you guys, you know I do. It's just "our people" I don't know about. I don't even know what "our people" even *means*. Is it some mass of Latin Americans on Eighth Avenue? Is it all the Puerto Ricans hanging out on Avenue D? Christ, it's so weird! Whenever I see some poor old Puerto Rican stumbling around drunk, acting like a fool, I think of Dad. If I see a bunch of guys with their numb-chucks and radios, I think of our cousins. I mean, I know exactly how these people think, what they like and dislike, what they need . . . and something in me feels like it's got to help them . . . and I will someday . . . but for now, I just want to be as far away as possible.

[CHARLIE: That's mixed up, Javier.]

Charlie, it's just me. Too many things got in between me and them.

[CHARLIE: Like what?]

Oh Charlie, like . . . I don't know . . . all the times Dad brought a live pig home and slaughtered it in the backyard the way they used to do it in Puerto Rico. And lucky me gets to hold the bucket to catch the blood I'd eat later that night in blood sausages . . .

[CHARLIE: I love blood sausages.]

(Beat.) There was my Christmas at drunk, crazy Uncle Wilfred's who beat the living shit out of his son, cousin Javier, that day. I'll never forget Javier crying, twisting around on the floor, bleeding and vomiting all over the Christmas nativity thing, a little plastic doodad the Department of Welfare had given to them. (Beat.) Or my first sexual flight to heaven. Another cousin, I won't tell you which, Charlie, the shock would kill you. She stalked into my bed one night, I was ten, she was curious, I faked sleeping, she found her way into my pants, I was scared and quiet; she was very warm. Or my second sexual flight. Another cousin, a male, who crawled into the bathtub I was innocently bathing in—he pushed me face down into the water—I was eleven, Charlie—I almost drowned— terrified—I was ripped up the way you rip up paper—then I was blasted from here to God.

In the Boom Boom Room

David Rabe

Premiere: Vivian Beaumont Theatre, New York City, 1973
Setting: Philadelphia go-go bar; Chrissy's apartment

Chrissy has just left her job at the A & P to become a go-go dancer. A sweet-natured, inarticulate woman, she is struggling to come to terms with the brutal facts of her life: a mother who tried to abort her, a father and uncles who beat and molested her as a child, and the mixed-up or violent men in her love life. The hope in her life is the pure and genuine joy that she feels while she dances. She loves and studies dancing; she dreams about being the best. Hard as Chrissy's life has been, she is fundamentally naive, too innocent to realize that the seamy world of go-go dancing will plunge her even further into the cycle of violence and degradation that she is fighting to escape.

Monologue One: Susan is the emcee of the go-go club where Chrissy dances. She is a proud, fiercely confident woman who is putting herself through college with the money from her club work. Susan is bisexual and strongly attracted to Chrissy. She tells her this story after a conversation about men and sex.

Monologue Two: Chrissy has had a semisteady relationship with a tough club patron named Al. He has just walked out on her, for a road trip with his menacing strange buddy Ralphie. Not two minutes later, Chrissy's swishy upstairs neighbor Guy appears in her doorway "to make it all right." Chrissy just wants to be by herself, but Guy is persistent. Finally she explodes at him.

------------------- **1** -------------------

SUSAN

All through my sophomore year in high school, I was in love with a boy and we were sleeping together in the back seat of his car. He was the captain of the football team and I was only a sophomore. Sometimes when my folks weren't home, we would make it on the couch, so one time toward the end of the summer after his senior year, he came by when nobody was home. I could smell beer on him, but I couldn't not do what he wanted. He asked me to take off all my clothes and went to a kitchen cabinet and came back with the butter dish. "I'm gonna cover you with butter, Susan," he said. He moved his hands real slow and soft, butter over every part of me. Then he said, "Bye-bye," and went out the door, and I remember thinking, "What is this to do to the future Homecoming Queen?" and found out the next day how he'd had his first date with a new girl that night. My father had a gun. So I waited in a little park across the street from this boy's house, and when he came I went over and said to him, "Look what I got." "What?" he said. I waved it. "Wow," he said. "That's right," I told him. And there was this Mickey Spillane book called *Vengeance Is Mine*, I had just read, so I said, "Vengeance is mine." "I got a full scholarship for football, Susan," he said. "It's a Big Ten school." And I shot him. I didn't know you could be shot and not die, so I didn't shoot him any more. I just walked away. He lived and went on to play Big Ten football after a year delay. It's somethin', though, how once you shoot a man, they're none of them the same any more, and you know how easy, if you got a gun, they fall down. You wanna go out, get somethin' to eat? I'm gonna go over to Bookbinder's and get myself an elaborate meal.

----- 2 -----

CHRISSY

Shut up! I think I said for you to shut up! Did I not say I am not in the mood? I am not in the mood! I got stuff to do I want it to be alone I do it. I gotta be makin' some resolutions about my stupid life. I can't not bite my fingernails. I can't not do it. I can't keep 'em long and red, because I'm a person and I'm a nervous person, and I diet and diet I might as well eat a barrel a marshmallows. My voice is not sexy or appealing. I try to raise it. I try to lower it. I got a list a good things to say to a man in bed, I say stupid stuff made up outa my head. My hands are too big. My stockings bag all the time. Nothin' keeps me a man I want anyway. I mean, how'm I gonna look like that? (*Seizing a glamour magazine, she thrusts the cover, the face of a beautiful woman, at him.*) I can't do it. Not ever.

[GUY: Me neither.

CHRISSY: Oh, shut up, Guy.]

And then maybe I finally get it right and my nails are long and red, I got on a new pretty dress, and I go out—I got earrings and perfume, new shiny shoes and rings all aglittery on my fingers, and they bring me back here and strip me down and a hunk of meat is all I am. Goddamn that rotten stinking Al and let him run off the end a the earth with that weird Ralphie! (*Running across the room, she collapses onto the bed.*)

Jesse and the Bandit Queen

David Freeman

Premiere: New York Shakespeare Festival, New York City, 1975

Setting: Missouri, Kansas, and the Indian Territories, from just after the Civil War until the early 1880s.

The legendary Jesse James and Belle Starr re-enact different scenes from their lives. Belle is "an attractive woman, but a little hard. A woman who has kicked around a bit." This monologue opens the play.

BELLE

(*Turns downstage on the piano stool and talks to the audience.*) I regard myself as a woman who has seen much of life. I've learned from some of it, remained blind to much of it and I guess just watched the rest lurch past me. I've always expected the worst from people and I have rarely been disappointed. The first, and the first is always the worst, was an instructor in history at The Carthage Female Academy, board and lodging, ten dollars a month. He taught history and we made a little between lessons. Or at least it felt like making history. I was eleven. He was, I don't know, twenty, twenty-one. All he ever said was "I can't keep my hands to myself." And he couldn't. He truly, truly could not. I had a horse that I loved more than any man. A mare, a brown and white mare. I called her Venus and she was better to me than I ever was to her. I was never proud of what happened to my babies and when Pearl run off, and Little Ed come at me like that I just got on Venus and rode away. I wore my lavender dress draped in black fringe and with a plume in my hat and a riding crop at my wrist, dangling . . . there. (*Rises and pulls a gun out of her cape.*) Except for the gun I always tucked into the folds of my skirt, I was one first-class lady.

Kennedy's Children
Robert Patrick

Premiere: John Golden Theatre, New York City, 1975
Setting: A bar on the Lower East Side of New York

It's a rainy February afternoon in 1974. Five different people have come to a bar to drink by themselves. Wanda is a woman obsessed by John F. Kennedy and his assassination, Mark is a Vietnam vet with a screw loose, and Rona, a hippie peace activist. Sparger is the ultimate Off-Off-Off-Broadway actor, and Carla, a model, had dreams of becoming the next Marilyn Monroe. A little while ago, she swallowed seventy-four sleeping pills; she just came to the bar "to wash them down." The five characters speak to the audience, but never to each other. Together their histories form a collage of the sixties. (*Note*: The whole play is constructed of monologues.)

* * *

Robert Patrick comments: "Sparger, like all the characters in this play, was written out of my admiration for the people of the sixties. Sparger should be played with strength, wit, courage, and gallantry. He can take on 'butch' or 'fem' characterizations at will; he is beyond mere identity. With drunkenness his deep despair pours out of him. By the way, 'Sparger' is pronounced with a hard 'G'."

Monologues One and Two: Sparger is hustling an imaginary boy. (*Note*: These two speeches are separated by several pages, but can be performed together.)

Monologue Three: Carla has just come back from the ladies' room. The pills and wine are starting to take effect; she is unsteady and "a little vague."

——————— 1 ———————

SPARGER

(*To imaginary boy.*) My name's Sparger! What's yours? Oh, have you? Why, yes, I've done a number of things this year. Maybe you've seen my name on the wall back there, on some of those stunningly mimeographed flyers for underground theatrical events of interest to the discriminating theatregoer. Let us see—(*Looking for the various flyers on the walls.*) I started out the year playing the fixed star Regulus in an astrological Halloween pageant in an abandoned garage, and then I—what's that? Oh, I always start the year with Halloween; I'm a realist—and then I did a really well-received improvised symphony concert underwater at the YWHA, and then I had a really busy week. At eight o'clock I was the left thumb in a group sensitivity demonstration called *Hands Off* at the Merrymount Episcopal Community Center, and then at ten I played a movie

projector with a twinkle-bulb in my mouth in a drag production of *Bonnie and Clyde* at the Mass Dramatists' Experimental Tavern, and then at the stroke of midnight I
was the cathectic focus of a rather tedious telepathic theatre
event in the basement of the Yoga Institute. *(Cannot find
flyer.)* Oh, right, that one wasn't advertised. We all just
sat together and tried to draw Clive Barnes to us with the
power of prayer. I try to keep busy.

2

SPARGER

(To imaginary boy.) When this Siamese dancing thing is
over—if it doesn't make Broadway—I'm supposed to tour
fourteen widely distributed colleges with an all-male musical of *Lysistrata*—in Lebanese dialect. Unless I get cast
in the Amphetamine Theatre's new production of the Third
World War. It might be smart to get into that; I think the
Third World War is coming back. The only thing is, they
don't want us to be in anything else for the entire rehearsal
period of two years. Still, it would be something to do, and
that's the important thing. If I don't get into something
really time-consuming pretty soon, my liver is going to wind
up inflammable—like a plum pudding. Alcohol is supposed
to kill brain cells. The trouble is, it's not selective enough.
It doesn't necessarily get the right ones.

3

CARLA

(Re-entering, a little vague.) What kept me sane all this
time was something I'd do when I was alone. I'd bathe,
slowly, in bath oil—scented bath oil. Then I'd wash and
condition and dry my hair and get it all fluffy and lovely.
And I'd dust myself dry with a perfumed dusting powder.
And I'd do my nails, hand and foot, with a clear—a lovely,
subtle, clear nail polish. And then I'd dress myself, slowly,

in these things I never, ever, wore anywhere else. Underwear—no, lingerie—that was all pink and black lace—and stockings of silk—not nylon at all, but silk, dark and seamless, very expensive. And a gown that looked heavy with glitter but actually was lovely and light and clinging. And then this boa that I'd gone crazy for and worked extra shifts at the Metropole to get, a huge downy soft white number that enfolded me like a cloud. And I'd stand before the mirror and remind myself of just what it was I wanted to do: the heart as big as the known world; the moon glowing to fullness within me; my great liquid eyes like the great southwestern skies; my flesh delicious as the petals of tender little flowers; my lips dark, precious, unique, the black rose . . . People were complaining that you couldn't tell one of the girls in the movies from another one, they all looked alike. Ursula Andress warmed over. And then you started hearing talk that the studios were doing it deliberately, that after the troubles they'd had with Kim Novak and Marilyn and Elizabeth Taylor and all of them, that they didn't *want* any more movie stars, no more crazy actresses to demand huge salaries, that they didn't care which woman they used, that nobody cared, because all the audiences wanted was just one supergirl after another, that the miniskirt mattered more than the girl, that James Bond didn't care who he fucked, because they were all alike! And I guess, if they felt like that about them, then *they* all were.

The Lady and the Clarinet
Michael Cristofer

Premiere: Mark Taper Forum, Los Angeles, 1980
Setting: Luba's living room
A woman named Luba has hired a clarinetist to provide background music for a very special candlelight dinner. She

drinks wine as she prepares for her guest, all the while telling the clarinet player about the men in her past. "I've only had three men in my life. I've had *more* than three, but three, only three were—are still—do still mean anything." As the evening progresses, we meet all three: Paul, Luba's gawky first lover; Jack, a married ad executive with whom she had an affair; and George, her eventual husband. The clarinet underscores everything.

Monologue One: In this memory scene, Jack and Luba have now been involved for two years. He tells her, "I hate my whole life. . . . I have everything I ever wanted, and I hate it all." But he won't leave his wife. After he goes, Luba laces into the clarinet player. "Cut the music, will you? What are you, feeling sentimental? You were really getting into that one."

Monologue Two: Right after Luba's monologue, Jack arrives at her door with a suitcase and a mile-wide grin.

———— 1 ————

LUBA

Don't give me that crap. You're all the same. Cut from the same piece of chintz. I didn't hear from him again for seven weeks. Seven weeks. Not a phone call. Nothing. Not even a message from his constipated secretary. She was having a field day. Very polite at first. "No, I'm sorry, Mr. Evert isn't here today. Can I take a message?" Very careful. Trying to sound like she didn't know who I was. Trying to sound like she didn't know that I was the same person who called an hour ago. The same person who called three times yesterday and twice the day before and God knows how many humiliating times before that. I went down there one day. I went right to his office. Face it, I said to myself, get it over with. I went into the building, up the elevator, up to the desk. The secretary is sitting there, guarding the door. She doesn't know who I am, we've never met. She says, "Can I help you?" and I freeze. I'm afraid to talk, I'm afraid she'll recognize my voice if I open my mouth. And even if she didn't, what do I say? "Can I help you?" she says again. I don't move. Maybe I'm not here, maybe I can disappear. "Is anything wrong?" she says. And I want to say, yes, something is wrong, yes. I wouldn't be standing here with my tongue in pieces if something wasn't wrong. I stood there in front of the desk, staring at the secretary—she was getting nervous by now—I pulled myself together. Christ, old Jack is not worth losing my mind over. I leaned forward. I put both my hands down on her desk. The secretary leaned toward me. She was ready to listen. I was ready to speak. I was gaining confidence. I said to myself, you're okay now. Everything's fine. I took a deep breath and threw up all over her desk. Confident, easy, in control, lovely to look at, delightful to hold. I always wanted to be like that. I'm a jackass. I do everything ass-backwards. My mother used to say I had the touch of a blacksmith. But I felt better. After that. I felt a lot better. *(The doorbell rings.)* I really did pull myself together. I got back to work. I started seeing somebody else. A plumber. Yeah. No brains. Lots of money. No problems. No expectations. *(Two quick rings.)* I was on the road to recovery. Back on the track.

2

JACK

Thank God, hi, Jesus, I was afraid you weren't home, I've been, here let me just, I didn't have time to call, are you, let me just put this stuff, it's late, I know, but, I just grabbed whatever, how are you, Christ, what a day, can I use your john, I'm, wait don't move . . . *(He kisses her quickly.)* . . . I'll be right back. *(LUBA closes door. He exits to the bathroom. LUBA is dumbfounded. She looks at the suitcase, the clothing. Then she takes the wine and gulps down a glass of it. JACK returns.)* Well, I did it. It's done. Finished. I finished it. I did it. Jesus. I can't believe it. Can you believe it? Just now. Really. What, ten, fifteen minutes ago. Maybe twenty. Twenty-five at the outside. I'm still shaking. Look at me. God. I feel great. I feel like a new person. I've been thinking about you every day. Every word you said ringing in my ears. You were right, you know? You were right about all of it. I knew you were right. But I didn't know what to do about it. No. I knew what to do but I didn't know *how* to do it. No. I knew how. But I couldn't. At least I didn't think I could. But I could. I did. I did it. We were sitting on the sofa. The kids were asleep. We were watching the TV. And one of my commercials came on. The one with the man swimming around in the toilet, you know. And I turned to her, I turned to Marge and I said, that's me. And she said, yeah, I know, I remember when you made it. And I said, no, I don't mean the commercial, I mean, that man, that man in the toilet, that's me. She just looked at me for a minute, and then she said, yeah. I have to get out, I said. And she said, yeah, you better, before you get pissed on. And then she laughed. She laughed so hard that I started laughing, too. And then she said— she was still laughing—what are you going to do? And I said—and I was still laughing, too—I said, I think we should separate. And we kept laughing. We haven't had a good laugh for years. We were laughing so hard we were crying. And she said, yeah, maybe we better separate. Then she kissed me and we started fooling around. The way she looked, she was smiling, laughing, she was beautiful. You should have seen her. I got so turned on, I jumped on her, it was incredible, the best it's ever been. And then, after, we went upstairs, she helped me pack, I picked up the suitcase, kissed her good-bye and here I am.

Lakeboat

David Mamet

Premiere: Court Street Theatre, Milwaukee, 1980
Setting: A Chicago lakeboat

Lakeboat is a series of interlocked scenes among various
men who work on a Great Lakes freighter. Joe is an able-
bodied seaman in his forties. He is talking to Dale, an
eighteen-year-old college student who is working as night-
cook on board the boat. They are off watch, sharing a beer
on the boatdeck.

JOE

You get paid for doing a job. You trade the work for money,
am I right? Why is it any fucking less good than being a
doctor, for example? That's one thing I never wanted to
be, a doctor. I used to want to be lots of things when I was
little. You know, like a kid. I wanted to be a ballplayer like
everyone. And I wanted to be a cop, what does a kid know,
right? And can I tell you something that I wanted to be? I
know this is going to sound peculiar, but it was a pure
desire on my part. One thing I wanted to be when I was
little (I don't mean to be bragging now, or just saying it).
If you were there you would have known, it was a pure
desire on my part. I wanted to be a dancer. That's one
thing I guard. Like you might guard the first time you got
laid, or being in love with a girl. Or winning a bike at the
movies . . . well, maybe not that. More like getting married, or winning a medal in the war. I wanted to be a dancer.
Not tap, I mean a real ballet dancer. I know they're all
fags, but I didn't think about it. I didn't *not* think about it.
That is, I didn't say, "I want to be a dancer but I do *not*
want to be a fag." It just wasn't important. I saw myself
arriving at the theater late doing *Swan Lake* at the Lyric
Opera. With a coat with one of those old-time collars. (It

was winter.) And on stage with a purple shirt and white
tights catching these girls . . . beautiful light girls. Sweat-
ing. All my muscles are covered in sweat. You know? But
it's clean. And my muscles all feel tight. Every fucking
muscle in my body. Hundreds of them. Tight and working.
And I'm standing up straight on stage with this kind of
expression on my face waiting to catch this girl. I was about
fifteen. It takes a hell of a lot of work to be a dancer. But
a dancer doesn't even fucking care if he is somebody. He
is somebody so much so it's not important. You know what
I mean? Like these passengers we get. Guests of the company. Always being important. If they're so fucking important, who gives a fuck? If they're really important why
the fuck do they got to tell you about it?

Landscape of the Body

John Guare

Premiere: Academy Festival Theatre, Lake Forest, Illinois,
1977
Setting: A ferry to Nantucket; Greenwich Village

A woman named Betty Yearn sits on the deck of the Nantucket ferry, writing notes and tossing them overboard in
bottles. A man in a false nose and glasses sits across from
her. He is Captain Marvin Holahan of New York City Hom-
icide. Five months ago, Betty's teenage son Bert was found
decapitated. Holahan accused Betty of killing her son. The
play flashes back to her interrogation, and to the events
leading up to the crime. The flashbacks are narrated by
Betty's now-dead sister Rosalie.

Betty and Rosalíe lived in Bangor, Maine, until Rosalie
moved to New York in search of the high life. In this flashback, Betty and Bert have come to the city to try to tempt

Rosalie back home to Bangor. Rosalie, who is "really good-natured, has a swell voice, moves like a stripper," tries to tempt Betty to move to New York.

ROSALIE

Honeybunch, you're hearing about the world. But hearing about don't put no notches on anyone's pistol. I'm doing. Bert, would you go out onto Christopher Street to the Li-Lac Chocolate store and request about a pound of kisses? (*She gives* BERT *money.* BERT *goes.*)

[BETTY: Bert, you be careful. Is it safe out there?]

Honeybunch, I get this call last week, would I be interested appearing in a film. Sure, why not.

[BETTY: He's never been to a city before.]

I report to a motel on Forty-second Street and Eleventh Avenue. Way west. Take elevator to the sixth floor. Knock. Go in. Flood lights. A camera. Workmen setting up. The real thing! A man said, "You the girl? Get your duds off. Sink into the feathers and go to it." Holy shit, they're loading the cameras and I'm naked and nobody's really paying attention. They say, "You all set?" Sure, why not. Lights. Camera. Action. And a door I thought was a closet opens up and it's from another room and a gorilla leaps out with a slit in his suit and this enormous erection and the gorilla jumps on me. Honeybunch, there's no surprises like that in Maine. And we're going at it and I can't believe it and after about five minooties, the director yells, "Cut!" and the gorilla rolls off me, takes off his gorilla head and it's Harry Reems from *Deep Throat* and *The Devil in Miss Jones.* What an honor to meet you, sir, I said. Christ! Go back to Bangor, Maine! Honey, you should move in with me.

Later
Corinne Jacker

Premiere: Phoenix Theatre, New York City, 1978
Setting: The Dowsons' summer house on the seacoast of
Rhode Island

Ms. Jacker says, "This is a play about women and water."
Molly's husband Malachai died during the year. Her two
adult daughters, Laurie and Kate, have come to the family's
summer house for their traditional Labor Day weekend.
Laurie is married with two young sons. Her older sister
Kate has never been able to find a relationship that meas-
ured up to her image of her parents' marriage. A self-
proclaimed neurotic, she has been seeing a therapist for
years. Old patterns are broken by Malachai's absence, and
over a weekend of clam-digging, sailing, and ocean-gazing,
all three of the women take stock of their lives.

KATE

I can sail. As well as any man. Better than most. My father
taught me—tacking, charting a course, no yawing when
I'm at the rudder. Our secret language. Malachai and me
at the boat house, while Molly sipped iced tea under her
sun umbrella and Laurie's skin shriveled up in the club
pool. A boat needs attention. Scraping, sanding, painting,
varnishing. One June day when it was hotter than this, I
worked for seven hours straight on the hull, and he hugged
me and said, "No son could've done better." I knew he
meant that if a man was going to get stuck with daughters,
he might as well have one like me. And he hauled out the
thermos with rum and tea in it, and he poured me a cupful,
and he said, "Drink it down, you'll feel cold as an icicle."
Oh, I did. It turned my veins into refrigerator coils. Goose-
flesh came out on my shoulders, and down my arms, I
started to shiver until my teeth clacked together. But he
knew what to do. He rolled the sleeves of my T-shirt down

as far as they'd go, and he stuck me into the sun, rubbing
my hands together and hugging me to stop me from shaking. And then, he said, "Oh, well, you're a girl after all,
aren't you, Katey, honey." And I lay my head against his
shoulder and wished there was a way to change that. I
never felt that cold again. Not till he was dead, and we
were alone, in the viewing room, and the air-conditioning
was blowing so fiercely. We went out, Laurie and I, to get
drunk, having dumped Molly on some cousin or other, and
I ordered rum and iced tea, because I wanted to shiver, I
wanted the temperature of my blood to go down below
zero, so it would freeze and clot, and stop. But I couldn't
get away from that music. The beat kept making my heart
pump. I got drunk. My God was I drunk, and my cheeks
got red, and the blood kept right on moving. I couldn't get
cold enough. I could have taken a bath in ice cubes and I
wouldn't have gotten cold enough. . . . Well, Katey's a girl
after all.

Life and Limb

Keith Reddin

Premiere: South Coast Repertory, Costa Mesa, California,
1984

Setting: New Jersey, Korea, Hell, 1952–1956

Franklin and Effie Clagg are a working-class American couple of the 1950s. Before Franklin leaves to fight in the
Korean War, he gets Effie's name tattooed in a heart on
his right arm. The next scene takes place in an army hospital
in Seoul, Korea, where Franklin's right arm has been am-
putated. The day he is leaving for home, Franklin meets
Tod Cartmell, an energetically evil teenage profiteer who
is working as a hospital orderly. Tod enlisted at sixteen, ("I
fucking fooled everybody. . . . I'm over here to kill me

some gooks,") and runs a black market empire out of the
hospital. Here Tod tells Franklin why he knows so much.

TOD

I am not ignorant of the facts embracing the situation. I
read *Time, Life, Look, Reader's Digest, Boy's Life, True
Confessions, Field and Stream, Guns and Ammo, Harper's,
Saturday Evening Post, The New Republic, Captain Amer-
ica, Holiday, Superman, Batman, Yale Law Review, Amer-
ican Medical Journal, MuscleMan, Detective, Redbook,
Bazaar, Jizz Magazine, Photoplay, National Geographic,
Bicycle Monthly, Stars and Stripes, Ibsen Quarterly, The-
atre Arts, Screaming Eagles, Total Surgery, The Mirror,
The Sun-Times, The Washington Post, The Examiner, The
Daily Planet, Publisher's Weekly, Variety, Shoe News,
Locksmith, Douche Bag, Norwegian Fiction, Abortion Re-
view, Girdle Gazette, Stamps for Champs, Language, Juggs,
Pussy Prose, The Catholic Layman Digest, Laces and Races,
Up Bosco Boulevard, Pens, Chicago Review, American Re-
alism, Cocks and Socks, The Shadow, Junior G-Man, The
Boston Glove, Clit,* The Yellow Pages . . . *The Kenyon Re-
view, Martyr of the Month, Crossword, Stiff, Jail Bait
Quarterly, Pig Latin, Shazam, The Mirror, The Paris Her-
ald-Tribune, Inseam News, Hemorrhoid,* and *Newsweek.*
(*Pause.*) So I know whereof I speak. You want a Life Saver?
  [FRANKLIN: No thanks.
  TOD: Suit yourself.
  FRANKLIN: Thank you.]
One thing about working in the hospital, you get to read
a lot. A lot of time to read, and everybody always leaves
me their stuff. Magazines, newspapers, flowers, candy, food,
and stuff people send 'em. I got me a shoebox full of letters
and getwell cards and pictures of naked girls people leave
here. Can't take everything with them when they get shipped
home, leave it here for me. Finders keepers, I say. I got
quite a collection. Playing cards, rubbers, packs of gum,

all kinds of things. I didn't used to smoke at all, now I smoke like the devil himself, three packs a day. 'Course I sell a lot of the shit on the black market so's I make out like a bandit most of the time. Got three gook girls working for me, don't nobody the wiser, they so beautiful, and smile and pretend they speak the American pretty good, so I give them plenty of money, cause the stuff it sells fast and they do a good job and I love 'em. When they old enough, shit, I guess I send for 'em from the States, raise 'em like my own kids I love 'em so much. I don't let anybody fuck 'em, see, I ain't no pimp. This is strictly business. You want any drugs, any painkillers, something like that for the trip home?

The Lisbon Traviata

Terrence McNally

Premiere: Theatre Off Park, New York City, 1985
Setting: Two Greenwich Village apartments with plenty of records

Mendy and Steven are opera fanatics of different styles and temperaments. Mendy is "middle-aged, attractive, takes care of himself. Wears good clothes well. Intelligent. His manner can be excessive (it often is) and may take some getting used to." His apartment is a cluttered brownstone cocoon. Steven is ten years younger, guarded in manner, and state-of-the-art high-tech in his tastes. They have gotten together at Mendy's to listen to records and air their romantic frustrations.

Both men are fanatical fans of Maria Callas. When Steven mentions, in passing, a bootleg recording of "Maria's" 1958 *Traviata*, Mendy insists he must hear it this second. He calls Steven's apartment, where Steven's estranged lover Mike is preparing to leave for a movie with Paul, his new "trick." When Paul turns out to be Portuguese, Mendy interrogates him about the Lisbon *Traviata*.

_____

MENDY

You were how old then?

[(*Covers phone, to Stephen.*) Don't pick up. (*Back into phone.*)]

But you remember your grandparents taking you to an opera? No, the one with bulls in it is *Carmen*. *Traviata*'s about a courtesan dying of consumption. A courtesan: what Stephen was before he started writing plays and an avocation to which he will soon be returning if he doesn't write another one. No, horses and camels are *Aida*. I wish you could remember the singers as well as you do the animals. It begins at a party. Everyone is drinking champagne and being very gay. I'll ignore that. And then the tenor's father, the baritone, comes in and ruins everything, as fathers will. And then there's a gambling scene and in the last act she reads a letter, "*Teneste la promessa*," and dies. You remember that much? Then you definitely remember *Traviata*. Now try to describe the soprano who was singing Violetta. Violetta is the heroine. You're making me feel like Milton Cross. Skip it. Just tell me about the soprano. Other than the fact that you didn't like her, what can you tell me about her? "Lousy" is a strong word, Paul. So is "stunk." I don't care about your opinion. It's her name I'm after. I think you heard Maria Callas. That's a good question. I just loved her so much. I still do. Everything about her. Anything. I take crumbs when it comes to Maria. She's given me so much; pleasure, ecstasy, a certain solace, I suppose, memories that don't stop. We'll never see her like again. How do you describe a miracle to someone who wasn't there? Do yourself a favor. Put on one of her records sometime. If what you hear doesn't get to you, really talk to you, touch you someplace here, I'm talking about the heart, move you, the truth of it, the intensity . . . well, I can't

imagine such a thing. I don't think we could be friends.
There's a reason we called her La Divina. But if you don't
even remember who sang *Traviata* that night, then there's
no point in going on with this even if you did hear Callas.
For people like you, it might as well have been Milanov.
Skip that one, too. Listen, thank you for your trouble. Enjoy
the movie. I don't care what your grandparents thought of
her either! The three of you heard the greatest singer who
ever lived and you don't even remember it. Yes, she's dead;
thanks to people like you. Murderer! I hope you hate the
movie. *(He hangs up.)* God, I loathe the Portuguese.

Little Footsteps

Ted Tally

Premiere: Playwrights Horizons, New York City, 1986
Setting: A renovated Manhattan brownstone
Ben and Joanie have been married for eight years and Joanie
is now six months pregnant. Ben, a television sports pro-
moter, "has an edgy charm and a relentless need for the
spotlight." His fears about fatherhood express themselves
in hyperventilated anxiety attacks and black-comic fantasies. (In one, he finds out that his newborn son is a bodyless
eyeball.) Right now, Ben is standing in a room which Joanie
is redecorating as a nursery. The walls are covered with
unfinished stencils and paintings of rainbows, flowers, the
Man in the Moon, etc. Ben addresses the audience.

• • •

Ted Tally comments: "I would suspect that Ben has several
different reasons for speaking this particular monologue (or,
more accurately, this one-sided dialogue). For one thing,
he wants to lead us into the literal world of his apartment.
Then, too, talking to us—goofing around—is more fun than

doing what he's supposed to be doing. This type of pro-
crastination, this refusal to accept responsibility, is quite
typical of Ben—a man who has remained so childlike himself, at least in certain ways, that he has an extremely difficult time accepting the idea of himself as a father. But
probably, his main goal here is to ingratiate himself with
the audience. If he can charm us enough with his cleverness
and humor, the reasonableness of his fears about having
children, then perhaps he can deflect our potential criticism
of him, and perhaps he can make us like him more than
we'll like his wife (whom we haven't yet met)."

BEN

My dining room, folks. *(Pause.)* At least it *used* to be my
dining room, before Joanie got her hands on it . . . *(He
moves into the room, looking around at the wall paintings.
He sets his cigarette pack down on the window sill.)* See,
the thing about my wife—the reason she's such a rare person—is that she's almost incredibly *nice.* I mean just look!
Oh, she hates it when people say that—says it makes her
sound like some kind of wimp. But no matter how much
she resents the label, she's still stuck with the quality.
Joanie is "nice" the way Mozart "wrote a few tunes"—you
know what I'm saying? Not a mean bone in her body. Not
a molecule of spite. Joanie . . . Joanie thinks that all human
disasters can be kept at bay, if only she writes enough thank-
you notes. *(He kneels by a pile of paints, throws a cleaning
rag over his shoulder. He selects a brush, then stirs an
open can of blue paint, using the stick that's sitting in the
can.)* But the thing is—even though she's such a good
person, I can't seem to resist being mean to her. And I
love her, I really do! But sometimes it's almost like I'm
compelled to be this total shit, just so I can admire how
well she copes with it. *(He rises, replacing the stick.)* What
can I tell you? I am *not* nice. *(He starts towards the ladder,
carrying his can of paint, then pauses.)* Oh, listen, by the

way. Joanie gets really pissed if she finds out I've been smoking, so don't tell her you saw me, okay? Thanks a lot. *(He crosses, sets down his paint on the ladder's shelf, dips his brush, then starts towards the wall. He hesitates again.)* Something else you should understand about all this. It's not that I don't like kids. Hey, I do! I'm walking in the park and I see some Dad scraping bubblegum off his little girl's shoe—it just tears me up inside. You know what I mean? *(Pause.)* The thing is, though—I like kids in the abstract. But when I have a kid, he won't *live* in the abstract. He'll live in my apartment. Right here. Which let's face it, is already crammed with one husband, one wife, eight years' worth of furniture, and enough electronic *tchotchkes* to start a Crazy Eddie's. So we're not just talking about the cosmic wonder of creation here. We're dealing with a Manhattan real estate problem. *(Still puffing on his cigarette, he turns back to the wall, raises his brush to finally start painting around one of the charcoal outlines. Then he pauses yet again.)* Which might be *one* reason why the very notion of—what? . . . engendering an offspring . . . has always struck me as an extremely hazy concept. Take for instance sperm. Oh sure, you *hear* a lot about them—but has anybody actually *seen* one? I mean, to me, sperm cells are like nuclear missiles. You know they *exist* . . . somewhere, lurking . . . you know they could make your life very, very unpleasant someday . . . so you just try not to think about them. And you pray to God they're never fired off with a serious intent. *(Sound of a door opening, off, and* JOANIE's *voice.)*

Little Murders

Jules Feiffer

Premiere: Broadhurst Theatre, New York City, 1967
Setting: The Newquist family apartment in a violent New York City

Patsy Newquist, the All-American Girl, is marrying Alfred Chamberlain, an "apathist" photographer who specializes in photos of shit. Tall, blond, and formidable, Patsy tells Alfred she loves him because "You're the first man I've ever gone to bed with where I didn't feel *he* was a lot more likely to get pregnant than I was." Patsy's family isn't so sure—especially when Alfred tells them he doesn't want any mention of God in the wedding service.

The ceremony is performed by Reverend Henry Dupas of the First Existential Church of Greenwich Village, "the one that has a sign in front that says, 'Christ died for our sins. Dare we make his martyrdom meaningless by not committing them?'" He is late to the ceremony because his motorcycle wouldn't start up.

DUPAS

(In a gentle, folksy manner.) You all know why we're here. There is often so much sham about this business of marriage. Everyone accepts it. Ritual. That's why I was so heartened when Alfred asked me to perform this ceremony. He has certain beliefs that I assume you all know. He is an atheist, which is perfectly all right. Really it is. I happen not to be, but inasmuch as this ceremony connotates an abandonment of ritual in the search for truth, I agreed to perform it. First, let me state frankly to you, Alfred, and to you, Patricia, that of the two hundred marriages I have performed, all but seven have failed. So the odds are not good. We don't like to admit it, especially at the wedding ceremony, but it's in the back of all our minds, isn't it? How long will it last? We all think that, don't we? We don't

like to bring it out in the open, but we all think that. Well, I say why *not* bring it out in the open? *Why* does one decide to marry? Social pressure? Boredom? Loneliness? Sexual appeasement? Um, love? I do not put any of these reasons down. Each, in its own way, is adequate. Each is all right. I married a musician last year who wanted to get married in order to stop masturbating. *(Guests stir.)* Please don't be startled. I am not putting it down. That marriage did not work. But the man tried. Now the man is separated, and still masturbating—but he is at peace with himself. He tried society's way. So you see, it was not a mistake, it turned out all right. Last month I married a novelist to a painter, with everyone at the wedding under the influence of hallucinogenic drugs. The drug quickened our mental responses but slowed our physical responses. It took two days to perform the ceremony. But never had the words so much meaning. *That* marriage should last. Still, if it does not—well, that will be all right. For, don't you see, *any* step that one takes is useful, is positive, *has* to be positive, because it is part of life. And negation of the previously taken step is positive. It too is part of life. And in this light, and *only* in this light, should marriage be regarded. As a small, single step. If it works—fine! If it fails—fine! Look elsewhere for satisfaction. Perhaps to more marriages— fine! As many as one likes—fine! To homosexuality—fine! To drug addiction—I won't put it down. Each of these is an *answer*—for *somebody*. For Alfred, today's answer is Patsy. For Patsy, today's answer is Alfred. I won't put them down for that. So what I implore you both, Alfred and Patricia, to dwell on as I ask the questions required by the State of New York in order to legally bind you—sinister phrase, that—is that not only are the *legal* questions I ask you meaningless but so, too, are those *inner* questions you ask of yourselves meaningless. Failing one's partner does *not* matter. Sexual disappointment does *not* matter. Nothing can hurt if we do not see it as harmful. Nothing can destroy if we will not see it as destructive. It is all part of

life. Part of what we are. So now, Alfred. Do you take
Patricia as your lawfully wedded wife, to love—whatever
that means—to honor—but is not dishonor, in a sense, a
form of honor?—to keep her in sickness, in health, in pros-
perity and adversity—what nonsense!— Forsaking all others—what a shocking invasion of privacy! Rephrase that to
more sensibly say: if you *choose* to have affairs you won't
feel guilty about them—as long as you both shall live—or
as long as you're not bored with each other?

Loose Ends

Michael Weller

Premiere: Arena Stage, Washington, D.C., 1979
Setting: Bali, Boston, New York, New Hampshire, 1970–
79

Paul Baumer and Susan Steen meet on a moonlit beach in
Bali in 1970. Paul has just finished a Peace Corps stint in
Africa, and Susan is bumming around with her flaky friend
Janice. It's a travelers' fling, but they meet again by coincidence a year later. The play covers nine years, during
which Paul and Susan get married, get rich, get bitter, and
split up.

In this scene it is 1978. Paul and Susan have a terrace
apartment on Central Park West, and Janice is visiting with
her new husband Phil. The men are inside (in fact, they
are preparing a surprise birthday cake for Susan), and Janice
and Susan are talking about relationships. Paul and Susan's
is rocky, about to get rockier. Janice is already making
apologies for her new husband: "Mostly he's just shy, I
guess." She smokes constantly, drinking a beer. (*Note:* Russell, who Susan has met in an earlier scene, was Janice's
boyfriend in 1974.)

JANICE

Like with Russell, well, you never met him, but believe
me . . . O.K. . . . a typical example of Russell. This time
we were in Boston, but you'd gone to New York and I
wanted to stop and see you. It was no big deal, real easy
to change the tickets, but he wouldn't do it. You know why?
Get this. I was too attached to the things of this world.
That's what he said. O.K. So one time we were back in San
Francisco and he saw this sports car and he bought it. I
couldn't believe it. He wasn't even into cars or if he was I
never knew about it. I never knew a lot of things about
him, but when I said what about the things of this world,
I mean, you can go buy a car, but I can't see a friend. You
know what he says? He can buy the car because he isn't
attached to it. He doesn't need it. Great. And the dumb
thing is, I believed him. Like completely. No, not completely. No, that's right, that's what I was starting to say.
   [(*Offers cigarette.*) Want one?
      SUSAN: No, I quit.
      JANICE: Oh, yeah? When.
      SUSAN: Six months ago.
      JANICE: Wow. But,]
You know . . . I really do believe there's this part of you
that knows better and all it takes is for one thing to happen.
Like with Russell we were meditating one day. Well, he
was. I couldn't get into it, so I was just sort of pretending.
I did that a lot. That's another thing. I used to wonder if
he knew I was pretending, 'cause if he's supposed to be so
spiritual he should be able to tell, right? But he never said
anything. Anyway, this one time I was telling you about,
I just started watching him, sort of squinting, and all of a
sudden he like started changing shape in front of me and
I could see the pores in his skin and all these little hairs
all over his body. It's like he just turned evil right in front
of me. I was even thinking later that maybe it was this

really ironic thing happening. You know. Like the first time
I finally had a mystical insight while I was meditating and
what I saw was the guy that had got me into it in the first
place, was this really evil creep. Anyway, I just got up and
walked out. He was still meditating. I never saw him again.
It's weird how these things work out. Oh, by the way, my
mother says hi.

Lunchtime

Leonard Melfi

Premiere: Chicago City Players, 1968
Setting: Bedroom of Avis's Greenwich Village duplex
A young married woman named Avis has asked Rex, a
furniture refinisher, to strip the woodwork in her bedroom.
It is clear from her nervous behavior that she would like
to seduce him. This is all in a day's work for Rex, who is
well aware of the double entendres of his bedroom-strip-
ping job. They talk for a long time about both their marriages, listening to Sinatra and sharing a scotch. Finally Rex
makes his move. Avis gets nervous and offers to fix him
some lunch.

AVIS

Would you like ham? Or ham and cheese? Or a triple-
decker with everything? On toast? Would you like a triple-
decker with everything on toast? That sounds good and
filling, doesn't it? And I could give you some freshly made
potato salad with it. I'm rather ashamed to confess that I
didn't make it myself, though. I bought it at a delicatessen.
Oh, and I could give you some pickles. I have sweet ones
and sour ones. And relish! Do you like relish? I could give
you that too. And afterwards I could give you a wonderful

piece of freshly made apple pie. I'm rather ashamed to admit that I didn't bake it, though. I got it at the bakery this morning. Delicious apple pie, with vanilla ice cream, if you like. And coffee. I'll even go down and make you a whole pot of freshly brewed hot coffee. Usually we only drink instant coffee around here. George never seems to have the time to wait for the coffee to perk. Oh, I almost forgot! Tuna fish! What about that? Would you like a tuna fish salad sandwich, maybe? A triple-decker tuna fish salad sandwich on toast with tomatoes and a little tartar sauce to go with it . . . and crispy lettuce too. Now that I could make for you myself. I'll just go downstairs and open up a can of tuna fish and I'll have the salad made in less than five minutes. Besides, I love to open up cans of tuna fish. There's something so . . . so *very real* about it . . . something so *very clean* and *natural* . . . about opening up a can of tuna fish. I suppose it's the combination of the crazy aroma that first comes from the can when you open it, and then afterward, the way in which the tuna fish looks, its color and its texture. Well, to be perfectly frank with you, it's a rather sensual experience for me . . . on the *very brink* of being sexual whenever I open up a can of tuna fish . . . *(She is near the door now.)*

Ma Rainey's Black Bottom

August Wilson

Premiere: Yale Repertory Theatre, New Haven, 1984
Setting: A recording studio in Chicago, March 1927
Legendary blues singer Ma Rainey is coming to record some blues standards for a white-owned "race" label. Her sidemen arrive at the studio first, to set up and rehearse for the session. Most of the players are men in their fifties who know the rules and play by them. (The trombone and

guitar player, Cutler, begins each take with the rhythmic chant, "One . . . Two . . . You know what to do.") But the trumpet player, a brash young jazzman named Levee, has ideas of his own.

Monologue One: Toledo, the piano player, "is the only one in the group who can read. He is self-taught but misunderstands and misapplies his knowledge, though he is quick to penetrate to the core of a situation and his insights are thought-provoking." He has just come in with a carton of sandwiches and starts to philosophize about eating and leftovers.

Monologue Two: Levee is in his young thirties, with a flamboyant style that "sneaks up on you. His temper is rakish and bright. He lacks fuel for himself and is something of a buffoon. But it is an intelligent buffoonery, clearly calculated to shift control of the situation to where he can grasp it. . . . He often gets his skill and talent confused with each other." Sturdyvant, the white producer, has just checked in with the band. The other musicians tease Levee for his "spooked up" manner with the white man: "The man come in here, call you a boy, tell you to get up off your ass and rehearse, and you ain't had nothing to say to him, except "Yessir!" Levee explodes at them.

Monologue Three: "Madame" Ma Rainery is a heavy, imperious woman who carries herself "like royalty." She arrives with a lesbian plaything named Dussie Mae and her stuttering nephew Sylvester. When her manager Irvin informs her they're going to use Levee's jazzy arrangement of one of her numbers, she runs him right over, insisting on getting her way. Here, Ma tells Cutler how she feels about her career.

_____ 1 _____

TOLEDO

No, I'm gonna show you how this goes . . . where you just a leftover from history. Everybody come from different places in Africa, right? Come from different tribes and things.

Soonawhile they began to make one big stew. You had the carrots, the peas, and potatoes and whatnot over here. And over there you had the meat, the nuts, the okra, corn . . . and then you mix it up and let it cook right through to get the flavors flowing together . . . then you got one thing. You got a stew.

Now you take and eat the stew. You take and make your history with that stew. All right. Now it's over. Your history's over and you done ate the stew. But you look around and you see some carrots over here, some potatoes over there. That stew's still there. You done made your history and it's still there. You can't eat it all. So what you got? You got some leftovers. That's what it is. You got leftovers and you can't do nothing with it. You already making you another history . . . cooking you another meal, and you don't need them leftovers no more. What to do?

See, we's the leftovers. The colored man is the leftovers. Now, what's the colored man gonna do with himself? That's what we waiting to find out. But first we gotta know we the leftovers. Now, who knows that? You find me a nigger that knows that and I'll turn any whichaway you want me to. I'll bend over for you. You ain't gonna find that. And that's what the problem is. The problem ain't with the white man. The white man knows you just a leftover. 'Cause he the one who done the eating and he know what he done ate. But we don't know that we been took and made history out of. Done went and filled the white man's belly and now he's full and tired and wants you to get out the way and let him be by himself. Now, I know what I'm talking about. And if you wanna find out, you just ask Mr. Irvin what he had for supper yesterday. And if he's an honest white man . . . which is asking a whole heap of a lot . . . he'll tell you he done ate your black ass and if you please I'm full up with you . . . so go on and get off the plate and let me eat something else.

2

LEVEE

Levee got to be Levee! And he don't need nobody messing
with him about the white man—cause you don't know nothing about me. You don't know Levee. You don't know
nothing about what kind of blood I got! What kind of heart
I got beating here! *(He pounds his chest.)*

I was eight years old when I watched a gang of white
mens come into my daddy's house and have to do with my
mama any way they wanted. *(Pauses.)*

We was living in Jefferson County, about eighty miles
outside of Natchez. My daddy's name was Mem-
phis . . . Memphis Lee Green . . . had him near fifty acres
of good farming land. I'm talking about good land! Grow
anything you want! He done gone off of shares and bought
this land from Mr. Hallie's widow woman after he done
passed on. Folks called him an uppity nigger 'cause he done
saved and borrowed to where he could buy this land and
be independent. *(Pauses.)* It was coming on planting time
and my daddy went into Natchez to get him some seed and
fertilizer. Called me, say, "Levee you the man of the house
now. Take care of your mama while I'm gone." I wasn't but
a little boy, eight years old. *(Pauses.)* My mama was frying
up some chicken when them mens come in that house.
Must have been eight or nine of them. She standing there
frying that chicken and them mens come and took hold of
her just like you take hold of a mule and make him do what
you want. *(Pauses.)* There was my mama with a gang of
white mens. She tried to fight them off, but I could see
where it wasn't gonna do her any good, I didn't know what
they were doing to her . . . but I figured whatever it was
they may as well do to me too. My daddy had a knife that
he kept around there for hunting and working and whatnot.
I knew where he kept it and I went and got it.

I'm gonna show you how spooked up I was by the white
man. I tried my damndest to cut one of them's throat! I hit

him on the shoulder with it. He reached back and grabbed hold of that knife and whacked me across the chest with it. (LEVEE *raises his shirt to show a long ugly scar.*) That's what made them stop. They was scared I was gonna bleed to death. My mama wrapped a sheet around me and carried me two miles down to the Furlow place and they drove me up to Doc Albans. He was waiting on a calf to be born, and say he ain't had time to see me. They carried me up to Miss Etta, the midwife, and she fixed me up.

My daddy came back and acted like he done accepted the facts of what happened. But he got the names of them mens from Mama. He found out who they was and then we announced we was moving out of that county. Said good-bye to everybody . . . all the neighbors. My daddy went and smiled in the face of one of them crackers who had been with my mama. Smiled in his face and sold him our land. We moved over with relations in Caldwell. He got us settled in and then he took off one day. I ain't never seen him since. He sneaked back, hiding up in the woods, laying to get them eight or nine men. (*Pauses.*) He got four of them before they got him. They tracked him down in the woods. Caught up with him and hung him and set him afire. (*Pauses.*)

My daddy wasn't spooked up by the white man. Nosir! And that taught me how to handle them. I seen my daddy go up and grin in this cracker's face . . . smile in his face and sell him his land. All the while he's planning how he's gonna get him and what he's gonna do to him. That taught me how to handle them. So you all just back up and leave Levee alone about the white man. I can smile and say yessir to whoever I please. I got time coming to me. You all just leave Levee alone about the white man.

3

MA RAINEY

I been doing this a long time. Ever since I was a little girl. I don't care what nobody else do. That's what gets me so

mad with Irvin. White folks try to be put out with you all
the time. Too cheap to buy me a Coca-Cola. I lets them
know it, though. Ma don't stand for no shit. Wanna take
my voice and trap it in them fancy boxes with all them
buttons and dials . . . and then too cheap to buy me a Coca-
Cola. And it don't cost but a nickel a bottle.
      [CUTLER: I knows what you mean about that.]
They don't care nothing about me. All they want is my
voice. Well, I done learned that, and they gonna treat me
like I want to be treated no matter how much it hurt them.
They back there now calling me all kinds of names . . . calling
me everything but a child of god. But they can't do nothing
else. They ain't got what they wanted yet. As soon as they
get my voice down on them recording machines, then it's
just like if I'd be some whore and they roll over and put
their pants on. Ain't got no use for me then. I know what
I'm talking about. You watch. Irvin right there with the
rest of them. He don't care nothing about me either. He's
been my manager for six years, always talking about sticking
together, and the only time he had me in his house was to
sing for some of his friends.
      [CUTLER: I know how they do.]
If you colored and can make them some money, then you
all right with them. Otherwise, you just a dog in the alley.

The Mad Dog Blues

Sam Shepard

Premiere: Theatre Genesis, New York City, 1971
Setting: Bare stage
Shepard describes *The Mad Dog Blues* as "a two-act ad-
venture show." Two rock-and-roll buddies, Kosmo and Yahoodi, get their music in visions. They get sick of the city
("too many tangents") and split up to collaborate by mail.

Yahoodi goes to the jungle, Kosmo goes to San Francisco. They call their visions "across a great expanse": visions of Marlene Dietrich cracking a whip, Mae West singing the blues like Janis Joplin, Paul Bunyan looking for Babe the Blue Ox, Captain Kidd. They travel; they talk. The bare stage becomes everywhere.

Somewhere on the road, between Paul Bunyan's North Woods and Loving, New Mexico, Kosmo hooks up with Waco Texas, "an old cowboy in an overcoat, boots, hat, with a beat-up guitar." Waco keeps singing Jimmie Rodgers's last song, "TB Blues." He tells Kosmo to "follow your heart. That's what a man's supposed to do. The only thing a man can do. Just follow your heart."

Meanwhile, Yahoodi has struck gold. Kosmo, Waco, and Mae West head for the jungle to find him, but he has gone off with Captain Kidd and Marlene Dietrich in search of a treasure island "near the Aleutian group." Kosmo's gang get their own boat and follow. When they reach the island, in "six or seven months as the crow flies," they swim ashore. Marlene Dietrich is fighting the Indian Ghost Girl who guards the treasure cave. Waco, who can't swim, is waterlogged. Kosmo tries giving him artificial respiration, but Mae says, "Leave him for the buzzards." They exit and Waco comes to.

WACO

(Sings.)
I been fightin' like a lion.
But I'm 'fraid I'm gonna lose.

What happened to my hat? I had me a hat. Given to me special. Can't see nothin' but ocean. Nothin' but the deep blue sea. Can't figure out this life. Here one minute, gone the next. Just a space traveler. Just a driftin' fool. Wake up in the mornin' and find yerself in the ocean. Now ain't that the damn truth. *(He notices the* GHOST GIRL *and goes to her.)* Well now, lookit that. A fair young maiden. Lookit that. Hey! This here's Waco talkin'. Listen to me. I'm so lonely and hungry for love that my stomach is stranglin' my backbone. And that's the truth. Feel like a mule driver eatin' nothin' but borax for a mile. Listen to me, honey. (*He sits down next to her and strokes her hair.*) Oh, my heart's just about ripped wide open just from the sight of somethin' like you. Yes sir. Good thing yer unconscious to this babble. You wouldn't believe the journeys I've made. You wouldn't believe. Say, if I told ya a secret you wouldn't tell nobody, would ya? It's somethin' I've been savin' up fer a long, long time. I never told it to nobody before. I'm the real Jimmie Rodgers. That's right. It's me. He lives in me, that's how I figure I'm him. Same thing as though he'd never died at all. I can feel him breathin' down deep inside me. You know how that is. A man gets into yer soul. Same as a woman or a piece a land. He's alive in me. And that's how I'm gonna put him back on the street. He died too fast. A man like that just doesn't come and go. He lives on. He lives in yer heart. He's alive right now. Can ya hear him? Listen: "I been fightin' like a lion. / But I'm 'fraid I'm gonna lose." Ya hear that? He's in there. I know it's him. It's gotta be him. It ain't me, that's for sure. It sure ain't me. (*He takes off his boots.*) My mind's as raggedy and tore up as this old pair a boots. Nothin' holdin' it together no more. Not even the desire left. Just follow her heart. That's what I say. Follow the heart. It'll lead ya right outa this world right into the next. I got no expectations. The world's a motherfucker, boy. I got nowheres to go and nothin' to see. Nowheres. And that's the truth.

The Madness of Lady Bright

Lanford Wilson

Premiere: Caffe Cino, New York City, 1964

Setting: A one-room apartment with autographed walls

Leslie Bright, a man about forty, is "a screaming preening queen, rapidly losing a long-kept 'beauty.' " On this hot summer afternoon, he is cooped up at home. Leslie tries calling various friends, but no one is home except Dial-a-Prayer. Consumed with loneliness, he talks to the mirror, the walls, and his memories.

LESLIE

You know nothing about loneliness. (*Long pause.*) I should go out. (*Seeing name on the wall.*) I should go out and look for you. . . . (*Creeping up on the name.*) Mich-ael De-lan-ey—(*Grabbing the wall.*) Gotcha! (*Turning from the wall.*) Good Lord—eight years ago—you would be how old by now? Oh well, old hustlers never die, they just start buying it back! (*Turning back to the wall.*) You were very good, I remember that. And who else? (*Going over the names.*) So-so; fair; clumsy, but cute anyway; too intelligent; Larry; good, I remember; A minus, and that's very good; undersized; very nice; *oversized*, but I'm not complaining. (*Suddenly angry.*) Samuel Fitch! (*Runs to the desk for a pencil.*) Samuel Fitch! (*Scratches the name off.*) No, I thought you were gone! You bitch! You liar! You vicious faggot! You *Queer!* You were not a man, you were some worm. (*Feeling better.*) Of course, you couldn't help it, you were *born* a worm. Once a worm always a worm, I always say. (*Looking back at the erased name.*) Oh. Poor Samuel. You really couldn't help it, could you? You were queer but you couldn't help it. Domineering mother, probably. What was it—that was sweet—you said. You said my body was smooth. (*The Mozart is back, softly but getting louder.*) Hairless, that's what you liked about it. You said I moved well, too, didn't you? Well, I *do* move well. I move *exceptionally* well. *(Sits on the side of the bed. Giselle music is added to the Mozart, and in a moment the rock-and-roll also begins.)* And I haven't a hair on my body. I'm as hairless and smooth as a newborn babe. I shave, of course, my underarms; no woman would go around with hair under her arms. It's just not done. Lately. In America anyway. *(Stretches his legs.)* And my legs—they're smooth. They are. *(Feeling the backs of his legs.)* I have—I *(Nervously.)* I have varicose veins in my legs. I can't wear hose. I have hideous, dreadful legs. I have blue, purple, *black* veins in my legs. They give me pain—they make me limp, they ache, they're ugly. They used to be beautiful and they are bony and ugly. Old veins. *(The* BOY *and* GIRL *begin to rub their legs and arms and to moan low.)* Old legs, dancing legs; *but the veins!* They get tired. And when they get *(Fast.)* old they get tired and when they get tired they get slow and when they get slow they get stiff and when they get stiff they get brittle and when they get brittle they break and the veins break and your bones snap and your skin sags. . . . The veins in my arms and legs—my veins are old and brittle and the arteries break—your temples explode your veins break like glass tubes—you can't walk you can't dance you can't speak; you stiffen with age. Age takes you over and buries you; it buries you under—under—*my veins*, my arms, my body, my heart, my old callused hands; my ugly hands; my face is collapsing. I'm losing my mind. *(The* BOY *finally screams a long, low,* "Oh." *The* GIRL *screams nervously,* "I'm going insane.")* I'm going insane. I'm going insane!

A Map of the World

David Hare

Premiere: Adelaide Festival, Australia, 1982
Setting: Bombay, India, in 1978; a film set in the present.
A Map of the World is constructed like a Chinese puzzle:
a box within a box within a box. The drama we watch turns
out to be a rehearsal for a film based on a novel written by
one of the drama's participants. What was real becomes
fiction, then film.

It is 1978. UNESCO is holding a conference on world
poverty in a hotel in Bombay. The keynote speaker is the
conservative Indian novelist Victor Mehta. One of the many
journalists in attendance is Stephen Andrews, a writer for
a leftwing English literary magazine. He and Victor argue
vehemently about politics, but their rivalry really heats up
when they discover that both have made dinner dates with
the same woman.

Peggy Whitton is a stunning American film actress who
has come to the conference during a short break in her
shooting schedule, hoping to meet some "witty and literate
people" who don't want to talk about films. She meets
Victor and Stephen.

After the first round of argument, Peggy accepts Victor's
dinner invitation and they become lovers. Stephen joins a
committee of African delegates who wish to ban Victor from
speaking unless he agrees to read a statement describing
his political novels as fiction, not "literal historical truth."
Victor refuses to comply, though whether on principal or
in opposition to Stephen is hard to say. Peggy challenges
the two men to debate with each other. The contest will
be judged by Elaine Le Fanu, an unflappable black TV
journalist. The winner wins Peggy. Here, she is talking to
Stephen.

Marco Polo Sings a Solo

John Guare

Premiere: New York Shakespeare Festival, New York City

PEGGY

You know life can really be quite easy, if you don't always let your emotions get in the way. (STEPHEN *looks at her a moment.*) When I was sixteen, I made a resolution. I had a girlfriend, we were talking in the Rockies, and the view, I can tell you, was something as we came over to Boulder, Colorado. And we had a six-pack right there on top of the mountain. And she was a good girl. I mean a really good girl. You could trust your life to her. And there that day we looked over the valley. We thought about our lives and relationships, and said, "Life can be simple, by will we can make it simple. From now on we are totally free. Let's not ever mess with the bad things at all." Now what's sad is I saw her six months ago. She's married to a lawyer in D.C. and he's never there, he's out overachieving all day, she doesn't like him when he is there, and so she's fucking around, so that one day, she told me, she got this terrible pain here. She was really desperate. Into the hospital. She told me for the first time in her life she prayed. And I said, "Really, what was your prayer, Elise?" And she said, "Oh God, let it not be cervical cancer. God, please. God, just do this for me. If it's not cancer, I swear I'll never cheat on Arnold again." And that . . . (*She laughs delightedly.*) I tell you that, when I come to write my novel about America, that will be its title: *Cheating on Arnold.* That will be its name. Because you see that is not what is going to happen to me. You understand? Because there is no need. (*She says this with the complete conviction of youth. Then smiles.*) Now the two of you, Victor, you, both slightly ridiculous, slightly contemptible, in my view, you see? Elaine will agree. That sort of behavior, men being jealous, men fighting, it's out of date. Outdated, Stephen. Unnecessary, Stephen. I mean, drop the bad behavior and you might get somewhere.

Marco Polo Sings a Solo

John Guare

Premiere: New York Shakespeare Festival, New York City, 1977

Setting: A garden in arctic Norway in 1999

Diane and Stony McBride are *the* golden couple of the 1990s, international and interplanetary jet-setters. They are living in an iceberg palace on the Norwegian island of Trollenthor, where Stony is directing an epic film about Marco Polo. The film is intended to be both a turn-of-the-millennium vision and a comeback vehicle for Stony's adoptive father, a rock, stage, and film star named Lusty McBride. His adoptive mother Debbie Lisa is also appearing in the film, when she's not too strung out on her junk habit. Her acting method includes a spontaneous, fully clothed jump into the Arctic Ocean.

Today is Diane and Stony's fifth anniversary. Diane's lover Tom Wintermouth, the man who solved the Mideast crisis by creating Saudi-Israel, arrives by helicopter. He has the cure for cancer strapped around his wrist, and he wants Diane to leave her husband and join him in the U.N. and the White House.

Diane was a brilliant piano prodigy, and Tom has bought all her recordings, including one made at age eight. Diane tells him how she felt about being a virtuoso, and why she has given it up.

DIANE

I really started cookin' when I was eight. I sat down at the piano as I had every day since I could walk, threw back the lid of the Knabe-Bechstein-Steinway and there on the keys was Mozart. I was never lonely playing the piano. Brahms was always there. Bach. Chopin. And here was Mozart. Hi, Mozart! Only this time, he had a raincoat on. A little raincoat. Now I had been told to beware of men in raincoats, but after all, it was Mozart. Mozart's no degenerate. Mozart's no creep. You can trust Mozart. The cool water of Mozart. He says, "Hello, little girl. You gonna bring me back to La Vie?" I said, "Golly, I'll try." And I began playing that Kochel listing I had been practising for a year with that magical imitative brilliance that children can have. The technical mastery and total noncomprehension that children can have. I lifted my hands, dug them into the eighty-eights and Mozart says: "Yeah. Give it to me." I looked down. Mozart. The raincoat. Opened. The keys became erect. Black. White. I became terrified. Mozart! This isn't a schoolyard. This is a hall named after Mr. Andrew Carnegie and I'm only eight years old and what the hell are you doing??? "More. More. More," says Mozart and he throws back his head. "Dig those digits into these eighty-eights. Bring me back to life. Bring me back to life." Mother??? Dad?? They're in the wings blowing kisses at me. Holding up signs. "You've never played better." Mozart moans. It's a short piece. It ends. Mozart spurts all over me. I'm wet. Mozart wet. Frightened. The audience roars. This child prodigy. Can't they see what's happened? I look down and hear a chorus of "yeahs" coming from all those little dead men in raincoats. There's a scuffle and Brahms leaps on the keys. "Me next! Me next! Bring me back to life." My fingers dig into Brahms. Well, I started to like it. Mozart lives. Brahms lives. For the next twenty years that was my life. Diane de la Nova and her circus of Music. Diane de la Nova and her Massage Parlor of Melody.

[TOM: You were brilliant.]

It's so easy to get brilliant reviews. You simply sit at the piano every day for twenty years with the moss growing up your legs, sparrows nesting in your hair, bringing dead men in raincoats back to life.

The Marriage of Bette and Boo
Christopher Durang

Premiere: New York Shakespeare Festival, New York City, 1985

Setting: Multiple

Matt Hudlocke (nicknamed "Skippy" after the title character in his mother's favorite movie) narrates this savage comedy of family life. The play's thirty-three scenes span as many years, often in nonchronological order. Bette Brennan is a talkative, ditsy, born housewife—the kind of woman who, following *Redbook*'s advice, refashions her wedding gown into a cocktail dress. Her husband, Boo Hudlocke, is hearty, ineffectual, and usually drunk. Bette wants children "by the dozen," but only Matt, her firstborn, survives an Rh blood-type incompatibility. Obsessed with babies, and Catholic, Bette ignores her doctor's advice and keeps trying. She miscarries again and again, Boo gets drunk, and the family disintegrates.

Monologue One: Late one night, after her second miscarriage, Bette calls up Bonnie Wilson, a childhood pal ("Bonnie Wilson was my best friend. . . . Mrs. Sullivan used to say, 'The two stupidest in math are Bonnie and Betsy. Bonnie, your grade is eight, and Betsy, yours is five.' ")

Monologue Two: By now, Bette has miscarried three times. She is pregnant again. Boo has broken his second sobriety pledge. Bette's priest, Father Donnally, invites the Hudlockes to a parish retreat for young married couples. Surrealistically, the rest of the "young married couples" turn out to be Bette and Boo's families, including Boo's dead father Paul (who sits covered by a sheet).

—————— 1 ——————

BETTE

(*On the telephone, late at night.*) Hello, Bonnie. This is Betsy. Betsy. (*To remind her.*) Bonnie, your grade is eight, and Betsy, your grade is five. Yes, it's me. How are you? Oh, I'm sorry, I woke you? Well, what time is it? Oh, I'm sorry, but isn't Florida in a different time zone than we are? Oh. I thought it was. Oh well.

Bonnie, are you married? How many children do you have? Two, that's nice. Are you going to have any more? Oh, I think you should. Yes, I'm married. To Boo. I wrote you. Oh, I never wrote you? How many years since we've spoken? Since we were fifteen. Well, I'm not a very good correspondent. Oh, dear, you're yawning, I guess it's too late to have called. Bonnie, do you remember the beach and little Jimmy Winkler? I used to dress him up as a lampshade, it was so cute. Oh. Well, do you remember when Miss Willis had me stand in the corner, and you stand in the wastebasket, and then your grandmother came to class that day? I thought you'd remember that. Oh, you want to go back to sleep?

Oh, I'm sorry. Bonnie, before you hang up, I've lost two babies. No, I don't mean misplaced, stupid, they died. I go through the whole nine-month period of carrying them, and then when it's over, they just take them away. I don't even see the bodies. Hello? Oh, I thought you weren't there. I'm sorry, I didn't realize it was so late. I thought Florida was Central Time or something. Yes, I got twelve in geography or something, you remember? Betsy, your grade is twelve and Bonnie, your grade is . . . what did you get in geography? Well, it's not important anyway. What? No, Boo's not home. Well, sometimes he just goes to a bar and then he doesn't come home until the bar closes, and some of them don't close at all and so he gets confused what time it is. Does your husband drink? Oh, that's good. What's his name? Scooter? Like bicycle? I like the name

Scooter. I love cute things. Do you remember Jackie Cooper in *Skippy* and his best friend Sukey? I cried and cried. Hello, are you still there? I'm sorry, I guess I better let you go back to sleep. Goodbye, Bonnie, it was good to hear your voice. (BETTE *hangs up.*)

2

FATHER DONNALLY

Young marrieds have many problems to get used to. For some of them this is the first person of the opposite sex the other has ever known. The husband may not be used to having a woman in his bathroom. The wife may not be used to a strong masculine odor in her boudoir. Or then the wife may not cook well enough. How many marriages have floundered on the rocks of ill-cooked bacon? (*Pauses.*) I used to amuse friends by imitating bacon in a saucepan. Would anyone like to see that? (FATHER DONNALLY *looks around.* JOAN, KARL *and* SOOT *raise their hands. After a moment,* EMILY, *rather confused, raises her hand also.* FATHER DONNALLY *falls to the ground and does a fairly good—or if not good, at least unabashedly peculiar—imitation of bacon, making sizzling noises and contorting his body to represent becoming crisp. Toward the end, he makes sputtering noises into the air. Then he stands up again. All present applaud with varying degrees of approval or incredulity.*) I also do coffee percolating. (*He does this.*) Pt. Pt. Ptptptptptptptptpt. Bacon's better. But things like coffee and bacon are important in a marriage, because they represent things that the wife does to make her husband happy. Or fat. (*Laughs.*) The wife cooks the bacon, and the husband brings home the bacon. This is how St. Paul saw marriage, although they probably didn't really eat pork back then, the curing process was not very well worked out in Christ's time, which is why so many of them followed the Jewish dietary laws even though they were Christians. I know I'm glad to be living now when we have cured pork and plumbing and showers rather than back when Christ lived. Many priests say they wish they had lived in Christ's time so they could have met Him; that would, of course, have been very nice, but I'm glad I live now and that I have a shower. (EMILY, *bothered by what he's just said, raises her hand.*) I'm not ready for questions yet, Emily. (EMILY *lowers her hand; he sips his wine.*) Man and wife, as St. Paul saw it. Now the woman should obey her husband, but that's not considered a very modern thought, so I don't even want to talk about it. All right, don't obey your husbands, but if chaos follows, don't blame me. The tower of Babel as an image of chaos has always fascinated me—

[(EMILY *raises her hand.*)

BETTE: Put your hand down, Emily.

(EMILY *does.*)

FATHER DONNALLY (*To* BETTE.): Thank you.]

Now I don't mean to get off the point. The point is husband and wife, man and woman, Adam and rib. I don't want to dwell on the inequality of the sexes because these vary from couple to couple—sometimes the man is stupid, sometimes the woman is stupid, sometimes both are stupid. The point is man and wife are joined in holy matrimony to complete each other, to populate the earth and to glorify God. That's what it's for. That's what life is for. If you're not a priest or a nun, you normally get married. (EMILY *raises her hand.*) Yes, I know, you're not married, Emily. Not everyone gets married. But my comments today are geared toward the *married* people here. (EMILY *lowers her hand.*) Man and wife are helpmates. She helps him, he helps her. In sickness and in health. Anna Karenina should not have left her husband, nor should she have jumped in front of a train. Marriage is not a step to be taken lightly. The Church does not recognize divorce; it does permit it, if you insist for legal purposes, but in the eyes of the Church you are still married and you can never be unmarried, and that's why you can never remarry after a divorce because that would be bigamy and that's a sin and illegal as well.

(*Breathes.*) So, for God's sake, if you're going to get married, pay attention to what you're doing, have conversations with the person, figure out if you *really* want to live with that person for years and years and years, because you can't change it. Priests have it easier. If I don't like my pastor, I can apply for a transfer. If I don't like a housekeeper, I can get her fired. (*Looks disgruntled.*) But a husband and wife are *stuck* together. So know what you're doing when you get married. I get so *sick* of these people coming to me after they're married, and they've just gotten to know one another *after* the ceremony, and they've discovered they have nothing in common and they hate one another. And they want me to come up with a solution. (*Throws up his hands.*) What can I do? There is no solution to a problem like that. I can't help them! It puts me in a terrible position. I can't say get a divorce, that's against God's law. I can't say go get some on the side, that's against God's law. I can't say just pretend you're happy and maybe after a while you won't know the difference because, though that's not against God's law, not that many people know how to do that, and if I suggested it to people, they'd write to the Bishop complaining about me and then he'd transfer me to some godforsaken place in Latin America without a shower, and all because these people don't know what they're doing when they get married. (*Shakes his head.*) So I mumble platitudes to these people who come to me with these insoluble problems, and I think to myself, "Why didn't they *think* before they got married? Why does no one ever *think*? Why did God make people stupid?" (*Pause.*) Are there any questions?

A Midnight Moon at the Greasy Spoon

Miguel Piñero

Premiere: Theater for the New City, New York City, 1981
Setting: An all-night luncheonette near Times Square, New York City

Joseph Scott is a vigorous man in his sixties, a former vaudevillian who runs a greasy spoon in Times Square because, as he puts it, "I may never play Broadway, so let me work on Broadway." Joe runs the place with another old-timer named Gerry and a Greek immigrant named Dominick. There's a stable of regular customers, including old Fred, Joe the cop, Jake the pimp, and other street characters. Today is the day after Dominick's wedding, a strictly business scam transaction to buy him American citizenship.

Monologue One: Zulma Samson, a chronically out-of-work actress, is one of the regulars. Here, she stops by on her way to a last-ditch round of auditions. By the end of the night, she will give it all up and find work at the greasy spoon.

Monologue Two: Joe tells Zulma about his own past in show business.

1

ZULMA

Hi, everybody . . . hot chocolate to go . . . extra milk . . . no sugar . . . is the phone working, Joe? My, Gerry, the years are taking their toll . . . potbelly, pretty soon. Stop drinking all that beer, right, Fred? Hey, Dominick . . . hello . . . this is X-87 . . . nothing . . . What? No . . . but I will . . . well if that's the way you feel about it then okay. I'll just get me another answering service . . . goodbye . . . Chocolate ready? I was going to get me another service anyway . . . I was . . . really . . . oh well, Joe, you know how it is in the business, sometimes you're up, sometimes you're down . . . but I guess I know what you're thinking once a person reaches a certain point in the struggle to reach some kind of notoriety and they don't get there then it's time to bid farewell to all that is a part of one's natural habit as is the habit to eat to breath to sleep. The nature of a prayer is to be heard by whoever is listening, I seem to have a bad connection to that certain ear wherever it is.

[JOE: What are you talking about?

GERRY: Dominick here just got married.

JOE THE COP: Would you mind repeating what you just said, I didn't get it all.]

What I'm talking about? I'm talking about David Merrick . . . Alex Cohen . . . Gower Champion . . . Joe Luggage and Frankie Suitcase, about all those guys who control the means and the manner of my existence on this planet, about *Show Business* and *Backstage* and *Variety* and all those casting notices that appear in the paper, about the Equity billboard, about the daydreams that rush through our heads as we climb the stairs to an audition, about the tears that flood out after being rejected once . . . twice . . . three times in one afternoon . . . and that's not counting the morning, or the telephone calls, the hundreds of pictures and résumés that hit the mailboxes . . . of course, I can't repeat what I said, I speak from the moment not from a script . . . as for you, Dominick who just got married, break a leg . . . well, time has it that I venture forth toward the unknown fate of a sacred audition . . . this hot chocolate will be cold by the time I reach my destination, but that's not the moment of truth . . . it comes later on in the day with the hot chicken soup that I heat in the naked cold of my lonely room . . . when the night finds me moaning over the uselessness of trying to survive in the path of glamour and beauty, for I have lost both of these elements during the course of the years, yet my talent has no end in sight and yet I am not judged by this but by the fullness of my breast. So long, guys, I will see all of you tomorrow if the lord is on my side . . . if not, send me no flowers . . . for I will venture to exploit all of me in that great casting office in the sky . . . bye. . . .

2

JOE

I was in the place a few years, couldn't get adopted . . . every Sunday in summer they would have an invited performer come to entertain the kids. Once these two black men came in and they were really funny, they made me forget all the heartaches that flowed inside my soul . . . I was never a cute kid, so no one would even take me home for the weekends . . . they came on stage and told some really funny stories and they did a song and dance number . . . I looked around me and saw all those smiling faces and I began to sing out loud with the two men on stage. They called me with them and I joined them in the song . . . not the dancing, though. I never seen anyone dance like those two guys did. Boy, they could really move . . . later that week they came back and visited with me. I was surprised, to say the least, when the administrator let them come in for the month they played in town and teach me their routine . . . that Fourth of July I went on stage with them and let me tell you, I was the happiest kid in the place . . . soon they left and I never saw them again . . . but I kept on practicing how to dance and tried different jokes and stories at night on the other kids. Soon, I never wanted to be anything else but an entertainer . . . but life being what it is, I found myself drifting as a short order cook . . . not that there's anything wrong with being a short order cook, especially being part owner . . . I always dreamt that I would . . . well, so many dreams . . . never growing old . . . ahead of death by two yards . . . yet . . . here I am . . . I can't even remember the routine that I used to do, I . . . I, well . . . life sometimes leaves no room for a celebration . . . your greatest moments become objects of torment . . . but I guess I should thank the Lord for each

dream, even if the dream never came true, at least I had
the opportunity to have dreams . . . you reach a certain
time in life . . . you find yourself wandering about in count-
less acres of flowers and one day it dawns on you . . . butterflies . . . thousands and thousands of butterflies . . .
butterflies . . . and no more flowers are growing.

The Mound Builders

Lanford Wilson

Premiere: Circle Repertory Company, New York City, 1975
Setting: A farmhouse near an archaeological dig in Blue
  Shoals, Illinois
Archaeologist August Howe stands in his office, trying to
organize "what is left of the wreckage of last summer's
expedition." As he searches through slides, dictating his
notes to a tape machine, the play flashes back to the previous summer.

August, his partner Dan Loggins, and several students
are excavating a Mississippian Indian mound site in southern Illinois. Their overstuffed household includes both of
their wives, August's eleven-year-old daughter, and his sister D. K. (Delia) Eriksen, a brilliant, wasted novelist who
is as famous for her drinking binges and public outbursts
as she is for her books. Jean Loggins, a smart, even-tem-
pered intern gynecologist, is three months pregnant with
her first child. Here, she is talking to Delia, who is still
couch-bound from her latest bender.

JEAN
I won the spelling bee. *The* spelling bee. When I was,
what? Twelve. National Champion.
  [DELIA: Dear God.]

No one in the neighborhood went to the dictionary, they all came to me. I was tutored by my grandmother so I was the only kid who used the old-fashioned English grammar school method of syllable spelling. Charmed the pants off them. It started out as a kind of phenomenon or trick—then when my teachers realized they had a certifiable freak on their hands, they made me study for it.

[DELIA: We're all freaks—all us bright sisters.]

It wasn't so bad until the competitions started. I mean, it wasn't like the little girl practicing her violin with her nose against the windowpane, watching all the other little girls at play. But I managed to work it into a nervous breakdown. (*Pause.*) I couldn't stop. Every word that was said to me, I spelled in my head. (*In an easy, flowing, but mechanical rhythm.*) Mary, go to bed. Mary, go to bed. Mary. M-A-R-Y. Mary. Go. G-O. Go. Mary, go. To. T-O. To. Mary, go to. Bed. B-E-D. Mary, go to bed. Mary, go to bed. M-A-R-Y-G-O-T-O-B-E-D. Mary, go to bed.

[DELIA: Mary?]

Mary Jean. (*She wanders to the door to gaze out.*) That, and I lost the meaning. Mary, go to bed was syllables, not sense. (*Beat.*) Then there were days when the world and its objects separated, disintegrated into their cellular structure, molecular—worse—into their atomic structure. And nothing held its form. The air was the same as the trees and a table was no more substantial than the lady sitting at it . . . Those were . . . not good days.

[DELIA: I don't imagine. But you got it together.

JEAN: Oh, yes. Juvenile resilience.

DELIA: And that led one directly into gynecology.]

That led one directly into an institution, and contact with some very sick kids. Some of them more physically ill than neurotic—who were not being particularly well cared for; and that led to an interest in medicine. And reading your books and others at an impressionable age led to gynecology. (*Beat.*) Also, living with my grandmother and her cronies, who were preoccupied with illness, kept it pretty much in my curiosity. They were always talking about friends with female troubles, problems with their organs. Of course, the only organ I knew was at church. I developed a theory of musical instruments as families. The cello was the mother, the bass was the father, and all the violins were the children. And the reason the big father organ at Grace Methodist Church made such a mournful sound was that female organs were always having something wrong with them.

Museum

Tina Howe

Premiere: Los Angeles Actors' Theatre, 1976
Setting: A gallery in a major American museum of modern art

It is the final day of "The Broken Silence," a group show by three contemporary artists. The artworks include four gigantic and identical white canvasses, a clothesline with five life-size figures hanging in their clothes, and "nine small, menacing constructions made of animal teeth, feathers, fur, claws, bone, shell, wings, horn, scales, sponge, and antennae" by Minnesota-born sculptress Agnes Vaag.

The play's forty-four characters are the art lovers, tour guides, photographers, students, guards, artists, and sycophants who pass through the exhibit. Tink Solheim and Kate Siv are "friends of the artist Agnes Vaag. They're dressed in exotic yet flattering clothes, and both exude a high-strung sensitivity. They've come to the show practically every day." Tink, in a reverie, picks up a sculpture (entitled *The Temptation and Corruption of William Blake*) and starts stroking her cheek with it. Kate sees her and screams, and Tink panics. As guards and viewers surround her, she cowers between the clothesline figures, clutching the sculpture and telling the following story.

Tink Solheim

Agnes Vaag invited me to spend a day with her in the country. Looking for her things; bones, wings . . . teeth . . .

[THE GUARD: *(Reaching up for the statue.)* WATCH IT!
CHLOE TRAPP: ALL OF HER MATERIALS ARE FOUND MATERIALS!

MICHAEL WALL: I've never seen anything like this. . . .

KATE SIV: She'll be here later, with Hilton.]

She finds all her objects in Connecticut state parks. *(Fitfully caressing her face with the statue.)* At least once a month she gets on a Greyhound bus carrying two blue suitcases filled with soft polyester batting for wrapping her objects in . . . and scours one of Connecticut's state parks. The last time she invited me to go with her. I said I'd bring along an extra suitcase and a picnic lunch. We met at the Port Authority Bus Terminal. It was so . . . odd. Going with Aggie to look for something. I mean, whenever you see her in her studio, her hands are always full: moulding something, gluing something. Her studio is bursting with the exotic: bird beaks, fish skeletons, turkey down, fox claws . . .

[KATE SIV: I'm Aggie's oldest friend, I've known her for years!]

So I just assumed she always *had* these things, that they were part of her, not something separate she had to seek out. So it was odd meeting her at Port Authority carrying those two blue suitcases stuffed with polyester batting.

[KATE SIV: She's invited me on her expeditions millions of times . . . of course I . . .]

I don't remember the name of the park we visited, but Aggie seemed to know her way around and before I realized it, we were walking through deep woods. Deep woods is the best place to find small animal skeletons, she told me. While I looked up at the trees and sky, she bent close to the ground, scooping her hands through the underbrush

like some human net. In the first hour she found a bat
skeleton, several raccoon skulls, a fresh rabbit carcass, patches
of fur. . . .

[KATE SIV: Aggie's only twenty-four, you know . . . and
so beautiful! . . .]

At one moment she was crouched out of view, the next she
was holding fragile white bones up to the sun exclaiming
over their perfect . . .

[KATE SIV: She has this amazing blonde hair. It's as
thick as rope and falls down her back in golden cas-
cades. . . .]

After awhile she had filled both her blue suitcases and asked
if she could borrow mine. We stopped for lunch and she
gave me a long speech about how calcium is formed in the
bones of vegetarian animals. . . .

[KATE SIV: And her eyes are this deep . . . green . . .]

It wasn't long before my suitcase was filled too and it was
starting to get dark. I suggested we walk back along a different route, but she said no, she couldn't stop yet.

[KATE SIV: MEN DIE OVER HER!]

It was then I noticed something . . . strange. Well, I didn't
notice it, I heard it because it was getting too dark to see.
As she was combing the underbrush, I heard this soft kind
of . . . licking noise . . . a slight kind of . . . slurping . . .
like eating, but not really chewing and swallowing . . . just
licking and tasting. "Is that you, Aggie?" I asked her. But
she never answered, and it was such a light muffled sound,
she could have been sucking on a mint. (Deep breath.) I
told her I really thought we should leave before it got any
darker and we got lost, and this time with real anger in her
voice, she said . . . NO! And then the nibbling, or kissing . . . or whatever it was . . . got louder. We reached a
clearing, the trees dropped away, the moon shone down
on Aggie's bent form as clear as day, and then I saw . . . she
was holding one of the little skeletons up to her mouth
and . . . was licking it, nibbling on it . . . running her tongue
over it. I screamed. She dropped the little thing and turned

white. The next thing I knew, she was hitting me with her fists, socking me hard all over my body, screaming and crying, "I hate you! I hate you! I HATE YOU!"

[KATE SIV: *(Near tears.)* I'm not listening to this.

BILL PLAID: Oh boy, oh boy, oh boy, all artists are *crazy!*

CHLOE TRAPP: Her perceptual gifts are extraordinary!

BILL PLAID: NUTS! ALL OF THEM!

KATE SIV: You made it up. You made it all up! That didn't happen! NONE OF IT . . . HAPPENED!

BILL PLAID: YOU HAVE TO BE NUTS TO MAKE THE STUFF!]

(Puts the sculpture back on its pedestal.) Agnes Vaag's breath reeks!

[THE GUARD: Thank you very much.]

Her breath is . . . foul!

[KATE SIV: You made it up! You've never been invited on one of her expeditions, and you know it. It's your jealousy, Tink . . . your relentless jealousy . . . and it's hateful . . . hateful . . . hateful . . .

(She runs from the room, sobbing.)]

(Giddy.) I always noticed a certain animal quality about her breath, a certain . . . rancidness . . . something sour. You know how certain people have breath that doesn't smell quite . . . human?

Native Speech

Eric Overmyer

Premiere: Los Angeles Actors' Theatre, 1983
Setting: Hungry Mother's underground radio station, and the devastated neighborhood which surrounds it

The Hungry Mother is a metaphysical disc jockey in a darkening world. His studio "is constructed from the detritus

of Western Civ: appliances, neon tubing, car parts. Junk."
As the play opens, the Mother is at the mike. He scat-sings
with the Civil Defense signal, and speaks in a "so-good-it-
hurts voice." (*Note:* There are many such monologues
throughout the play.)

. . .

Eric Overmyer comments: "This piece is not a glib riff. It
needs passion, conviction, and a sense of irony—all skills
American actors ought to cultivate. It is colloquial, but calls
for classical technique. All actors ought to have chops and
heart; this demands both."

———————

Hungry Mother

O, that's a hit. Hungry Mother plays the hits, only the hits.
I want some seafood, Mama. (*Beat.*) This is your Hungry
Mother here—and you know it. (*Lights.* HUNGRY MOTHER
*is a shambly, disheveled man in his late thirties. The Broad-
cast Indicator—a blue light bulb on the mike—is "on."
And so is* HUNGRY MOTHER.)

(*Cooool.*) Static. Dead air. Can't beat it. With a stick.
Audio entropy. In-creases ever-y-where. Home to roost.
Crack a six-pack of the ambient sound. (*Beat.*) You've been
groovin' and duckin' to the ever-popular sound of "Air Raid"—
by Victor Chinaman. Moan with the tone. A blast from the
past. With vocal variations by yours truly. The Hungry
Mother. (*Beat.*) Hard enough for you? (*A little more up
tempo.*) Hungry Mother here, your argot argonaut. Stick
with us. Solid gold and nothing but. Hungry Mother be
playing the hits, playing them hits, for you, jes' for
youuuu . . .

(*Full-out manic now.*) Uh-huh! Into the smokey blue!
Comin' at you! Get out de way! Hungry Mother gonna
hammer, gonna glide, gonna slide, gonna bop, gonna drop,
gonna dance dem ariel waves, till he get to you, yes, you!

Razzle you, dazzle you, blow you a-way! This one gonna hammer . . . gonna hammer you blue!

(Dryly.) Flatten you like a side of beef, sucker. *(Mellifluous.)* This is WTWI, it's 7:34, the weather is *dark,* dormant species are stirring, cold and warm bloods both, muck is up, and I'm the Hungry Mother. The weather outlook is for continued existential dread under cloudy skies with scattered low-grade distress. Look out for the Greenhouse Effect . . . We'll be back, but first—a word about succulents—*(Beat. Flicks switches. Then, subdued, reasonable.)* We're coming to you live, from our syncopated phone booth high above the floating bridge in violation of *several* natural laws, searching, strolling, and trolling, for the sweetest music this side of Heaven.

(Beat. Then.) Back at you! This is the Hungry Mother, just barely holding on, at WTWI, the cold-water station with the bird's-eye view, on this beautifully indeterminate morning, bringin' you monster after musical monster. Chuckin' 'em down the pike, humpin' 'em up and over the DMZ, in a never-ending effort to make a dent in that purple purple texture. And right now I've got what you've all been waiting for—Hungry Mother's HAMMER OF THE WEEK! And Mother's Hammer for this week, forty-seven with a silver bullet—"Fibreglass Felony Shoes"—something slick— by Hoover *and* the Navajos.

(Now modest, compassionate, friendly, slightly patronizing.) And, as always, behind every Mother's Hammer of the Week—there's a human being. And a human interest story. You're probably hip to this already, but I'm gonna lay it on you anyway. Hoover—is a full-blooded, red-blooded *Native American.* One of several in the annals of illustrated American Pop.

(Slight pause.) Hoover had a monster a few years back: "Fiberglass Rock"—just a giant on the Res. And elsewhere. That, *mais oui,* was before the tragic accident in which Hoover—ah, I don't know if this is public knowledge— but, o why not grovel in gore? *(Bopping.)* With the fallout

from his titanium monster, "Fiberglass Rock," Hoover put something down on a preowned dream, a Pontiac Super- chief, drive it *away*. A steal. A *machine*. Four on the floor and three on the tree, a herd of horses under the hood! *(Mock melodrama.)* Four flats. Cracked axle. Hoover—his heart as big and red as the great outdoors—goes down . . . with a wrench. The Superchief slips the jack— and pins Hoover by his . . . pickin' hand. *(Beat.)* WIPE OUT! *(Beat.)* Crushed dem bones to milk.

(Rising frenzy.) But now he's back. Back where he be- longs! With the aid of a prosthetic device! Back on the charts again! PIONEER OF PATHO-ROCK! *(Slight pause. Then warm, hip.)* Many happy returns of the day, Hoover, for you and yours.

(Flicks switches. Mellow.) The sun is up, *officially*, and all good things, according to the laws of thermodynamics, must come to an end. Join us—tomorrow—for something approaching solitude. WTWI now relents and gives up the ghost of its broadcasting day.

Oh Dad, Poor Dad, Mamma's Hung You in the Closet and I'm Feeling So Sad

Arthur Kopit

Premiere: Phoenix Theatre, New York City, 1962
Setting: A lavish hotel room in Havana, Cuba

The widowed Madame Rosepettle arrives in a Cuban hotel with her stuttering son Jonathan, a coffin, two Venus fly- traps, a giggling piranha, and five bellboys' worth of lug- gage. She keeps her dead husband on a hanger in the closet, and spends her evenings annoying lovers on the beach. Jonathan is "seventeen years old but dressed like a boy of ten. . . . He follows [his mother] about the room like a small helpless puppy trailing his master." He stays in the room at all times, feeding the plants and fish, arranging his collections of rare coins and stamps, and looking outside through a homemade telescope. Through the telescope, he spots a pretty baby-sitter named Rosalie. Jonathan begs his mother to let him meet her, and Rosalie comes to visit his room. Jonathan tells her how he made his telescope.

JONATHAN

Well, I made it out of lenses and tubing. The lenses I had because Ma-Ma-Mother gave me a set of lenses so I could see my stamps better. I have a fabulous collection of stamps, as well as a fantastic collection of coins and a simply un-believable collection of books. Well sir, Ma-Ma-Mother gave me these lenses so I could see my stamps better. She suspected that some were fake so she gave me the lenses so I might be . . . able to see. You see? Well sir, I happen to have nearly a billion sta-stamps. So far I've looked closely at 1,352,769. I've discovered three actual fakes! Number 1,352,767 was a fake. Number 1,352,768 was a fake, and number 1,352,769 was a fake. They were stuck together. Ma-Mother made me feed them im-mediately to her fly-traps. Well . . . *(He whispers.)* one day, when Mother wasn't looking . . . that is, when she was out, I heard an air-plane flying. An airplane . . . somewhere . . . far away. It wasn't very loud, but still I heard it. An airplane. Fly-ing . . . somewhere, far away. And I ran outside to the porch so that I might see what it looked like. The airplane. With hundreds of people inside it. Hundreds and hundreds and hundreds of people. And I thought to myself, if I could just see . . . if I could just see what they looked like, the people, sitting at their windows looking out . . . and flying. If I could see . . . *just* once . . . if I could see *just once* what they looked like . . . then I might . . . know what I— what I . . . *(Slight pause.)* So I . . . built a telescope in

case the plane ever . . . came back again. The tubing came
from an old blowgun (*He reaches behind the bureau and
produces a huge blowgun, easily a foot larger than he.*)
Mother brought back from her last hunting trip to Zanzibar.
The lenses were the lenses she had given me for my stamps.
So I built it. My telescope. A telescope so I might be able
to see. And . . . (*He walks out to the porch.*) and . . . and
I *could* see! I could! I COULD! I really could. For miles
and miles I could see. For miles and miles and *miles!* (*He
begins to lift it up to look through but stops, for some
reason, before he's brought it up to his eye.*) Only . . . (*He
hands it to* ROSALIE. *She takes it eagerly and scans the
horizon and the sky. She hands it back to him.*)

[ROSALIE (*With annoyance.*): There's nothing out there
to see.

JONATHAN (*Sadly.*): I know. That's the trouble.]
You take the time to build a telescope that can sa-see for
miles, then there's nothing out there to see. Ma-Mother
says it's a lesson in Life. [*Pause.*] But I'm not sorry I built
my telescope. And you know why? Because I saw you. Even
if I didn't see anything else, I did see you. And . . . and
I'm . . .very glad.

Old Times

Harold Pinter

Premiere: Royal Shakespeare Company, London, 1971
Setting: A converted farmhouse. Autumn. Night.
In this elliptical drama, three people talk about (and around)
a mysterious shared past. Kate and Anna were roommates
once, many years ago. Deeley knew both of them. Now
Kate and Deeley are married, and Anna is visiting. Each
of them seems to rewrite the past as he or she tells it. As
Anna says, "There are things one remembers even though

they may never have happened. There are things I remember which may never have happened but as I recall
them so they take place." Here Deeley remembers his first
encounter with Kate . . . or was it with Anna?

DEELEY

What happened to me was this. I popped into a fleapit to
see Odd Man Out. Some bloody awful summer afternoon,
walking in no direction. I remember thinking there was
something familiar about the neighborhood and suddenly
recalled that it was in this very neighborhood that my father
bought me my first tricycle, the only tricycle in fact I ever
possessed. Anyway, there was the bicycle shop and there
was this fleapit showing Odd Man Out and there were two
usherettes standing in the foyer and one of them was stroking her breasts and the other one was saying "dirty bitch"
and the one stroking her breasts was saying "Mmmnnn"
with a very sensual relish and smiling at her fellow usherette, so I marched in on this excruciatingly hot summer
afternoon in the middle of nowhere and watched Odd Man
Out and thought Robert Newton was fantastic. And I still
think he was fantastic. And I would commit murder for
him, even now. And there was only one other person in
the cinema, one other person in the whole of the whole
cinema, and there she is. And there she was, very dim,
very still, placed more or less I would say at the dead centre
of the auditorium. I was off centre and have remained so.
And I left when the film was over, noticing, even though
James Mason was dead, that the first usherette appeared
to be utterly exhausted, and I stood for a moment in the
sun, thinking I suppose about something and then this girl
came out and I think looked about her and I said wasn't
Robert Newton fantastic, and she said something or other,
Christ knows what, but looked at me, and I thought, Jesus
this is it, I've made a catch, this is a true-blue pickup, and
when we had sat down in the café with tea she looked into

her cup and then up at me and told me she thought Robert
Newton was remarkable. So it was Robert Newton who
brought us together and it is only Robert Newton who can
tear us apart.

Orphans

Lyle Kessler

Premiere: Matrix Theatre, Los Angeles, 1983
Setting: An old row house in North Philadelphia
Treat and Phillip are brothers. Treat is a chain-snatcher,
sullen and volatile. Phillip has lived so sheltered a life that
he seems almost retarded, a wild child. Convinced he's
allergic to "most everything: plants, grass, trees, pollen,"
he won't go outside. He's created a fantasy world out of
game shows, the people who walk past the window, and
Star-Kist Tuna.
    Their lives change drastically when Treat kidnaps Har-
old, a well-dressed Chicago "businessman" he has met in
a bar. Treat plans to hold Harold for ransom, but Harold
embraces the brothers as "Dead End Kids," and hires them
as underworld henchmen. Here, he has just come back
from the bar with Treat and is too drunk to walk. He crawls
to the foot of the couch and delivers this story before passing
out.

HAROLD

No corn beef and cabbage cooking where I come from
either . . . come from an orphanage, goddamn orphanage,
no Irish top-of-the-morning mother there either, just a big
son-of-a-bitching German, wore a chef's hat and a filthy
dirty apron. German slept right in the kitchen. Orphans
always hungry, orphans love to come down in the middle

of the night and raid the refrigerator. German slept there, one eye open, break your back if he caught you, break every bone in your body. Took a liking to me though, filled my plate with meat and potatoes, lucky for me, orphans always coughing up blood, orphans dropping dead all the time, terrible mortality rate at an orphanage! . . . Thank god for them big heaping plates of meat and pota- toes . . . thank god for that bloody fucking German son of a bitch. (HAROLD *is falling asleep.* TREAT *moves in to get the briefcase.* HAROLD *wakes.*) You know what orphans call out in the middle of the night, Treat?

[TREAT (*moves back*): No, what do they call out, Harold? (PHILLIP *peeks down the stairs.*)]

Motherless orphans, middle of the night Chicago, orphans on a big hill facing Lake Michigan. Wind come through there making a terrible sound, wind come through there going Hisssss! Orphans pulling their blankets up over their heads, frightened orphans crying out. You know what they were crying?

[TREAT: No.]

Mommy! Mommy! Honest to god! Motherless orphans don't know a mommy from a daddy, don't know a mommy from a fuckin' tangerine . . . poor motherless bastards, calling *Mommy . . . Mommy . . .*

Painting Churches

Tina Howe

Premiere: Second Stage, New York City, 1983
Setting: Living room of the Churches' Boston townhouse. Distinguished poet Gardner Church and his flamboyantly potty wife Fanny are moving from their Beacon Hill town- house to a small retirement cottage. As they pack their

belongings, their artist daughter Mags arrives from New York to paint their portrait.

Monologue One: Fanny has found an old pair of Gardner's galoshes in a carton of pots and pans. They trigger fond memories.

Monologue Two: Mags sets the stage for the portrait sitting, nailing a crimson tablecloth to the wall as a backdrop. In spite of her obvious talent and professional acclaim, Mags's preoccupied parents have trouble taking their daughter's work seriously. As they clown their way through various poses from famous works of art, Mags reminds them of how they behaved at her professional debut.

Monologue Three: Mags's visit home provides some harsh shocks. Gardner is sliding rapidly into senility, and Fanny is at the end of her rope. When Gardner refuses to pack up his study, Fanny grabs his books and papers and savagely dumps them all over the floor. Mags is appalled by her mother's behavior. Then Fanny reveals that her husband's great "critical study" is nothing more than a random assortment of retyped fragments. She starts flinging papers around, dive-bomber style, and the senile Gardner joins in. Mags is enraged: "You're making a mockery of him!" Fanny responds to her daughter.

———— 1 ————

FANNY

(Lovingly puts the galoshes on over her shoes and wiggles her feet.) God, these bring back memories! There were real snowstorms in the old days. Not these pathetic little two-inch droppings we have now. After a particularly heavy one, Daddy and I used to go sledding on the Common. This was way before you were born. . . . God, it was a hundred years ago! . . . Daddy would stop writing early, put on these galoshes and come looking for me, jingling the fasteners like castanets. It was a kind of mating call, almost. . . . *(She jingles them.)* The Common was always

deserted after a storm; we had the whole place to ourselves.
It was so romantic. . . . We'd haul the sled up Beacon Street,
stop under the State House, and aim it straight down
to the Park Street Church, which was much further
away in those days. . . . Then Daddy would lie down on
the sled, I'd lower myself on top of him, we'd rock back
and forth a few times to gain momentum and then
. . . WHOOOOOOOOOSSSSSSSHHHHH . . . down we'd
plunge like a pair of eagles locked in a spasm of lovemaking.
God, it was wonderful! . . . The city whizzing past us at
ninety miles an hour . . . the cold . . . the darkness . . .
Daddy's hair in my mouth . . . GAR . . . REMEMBER
HOW WE USED TO GO SLEDDING IN THE OLD
DAYS? . . . Sometimes he'd lie on top of me. That was
fun. I liked that even more.

_____ 2 _____

MAGS

Remember how you behaved at my first group show in
Soho? . . . Oh, come on, you remember. It was a real circus! Think back. . . . It was about six years ago. . . . Daddy
had just been awarded some presidential medal of achievement and you insisted he wear it around his neck on a
bright red ribbon, and you wore this . . . *huge* feathered
hat to match! I'll never forget it! It was the size of a giant
pizza with twenty-inch red turkey feathers shooting straight
up into the air. . . . Oh, come on, you remember, don't
you? . . .

   [FANNY: (*Leaping to her feet.*) HOLD EVERYTHING!
   THIS IS IT! THIS IS REALLY IT! Forgive me for in-
   terrupting, Mags darling, it'll just take a minute.
   (*She whispers excitedly to* GARDNER.)]

I had about eight portraits in the show, mostly of friends
of mine, except for this old one I'd done of Mrs. Crowninshield.

   [GARDNER: All right, all right . . . let's give it a whirl.

(A pause; then they mime Michelangelo's Pietà *with* GARDNER *lying across* FANNY's *lap as the dead Christ.)*

MAGS: *(Depressed.)* The *Pietà.* Terrific!

FANNY: *(Jabbing* GARDNER *in the ribs.)* Hey, we're getting good at this.

GARDNER: Of course it would help if we didn't have all these modern clothes on.

MAGS: AS I WAS SAYING . . .

FANNY: Sorry, Mags . . . sorry . . .

(Huffing and creaking with the physical exertion of it all, they return to their seats.)]

. . . As soon as you stepped foot in the gallery you spotted it and cried out, "MY GOD, WHAT'S MILLICENT CROWNINSHIELD DOING HERE?" Everyone looked up what with Daddy's clanking medal and your amazing hat which I was sure would take off and start flying around the room. A crowd gathered. . . . Through some utter fluke, you latched on to *the* most important critic in the city, I mean . . . Mr. Modern Art himself, and you hauled him over to the painting, trumpeting out for all to hear, "THAT'S MILLICENT CROWNINSHIELD! I GREW UP WITH HER. SHE LIVES RIGHT DOWN THE STREET FROM US IN BOSTON. BUT IT'S A VERY POOR LIKE-NESS, IF YOU ASK ME! HER NOSE ISN'T NEARLY THAT LARGE AND SHE DOESN'T HAVE SOME-THING QUEER GROWING OUT OF HER CHIN! THE CROWNINSHIELDS ARE REALLY QUITE GOOD LOOKING, STUFFY, BUT GOOD LOOKING NONE-THELESS!"

[GARDNER: *(Suddenly jumps up, ablaze.)* WAIT, WAIT . . . IF IT'S MICHELANGELO YOU WANT . . . I'm sorry, Mags . . . One more . . . just one more . . . please?

MAGS: Sure, why not? Be my guest.

GARDNER: *Fanny,* prepare youself!

(More whispering.)

FANNY: But I think *you* should be God.

GARDNER: Me? . . . Really?

FANNY: Yes, it's much more appropriate.

GARDNER: Well, if you say so . . . (FANNY *and* GARD
NER *ease down to the floor with some difficulty and lie
on their sides,* FANNY *as Adam,* GARDNER *as God, their
fingers inching closer and closer in the attitude of Michelangelo's* The Creation. *Finally they touch.*)

MAGS: (*Cheers, whistles, applauds.*) THREE CHEERS
. . . VERY GOOD . . . NICELY DONE, NICELY
DONE!

(*They hold the pose a moment more, flushed with pleasure; then rise, dust themselves off and grope back to
their chairs.*)

So, there we were. . . .

FANNY: Yes, *do* go on! . . .]

. . . huddled around Millicent Crowninshield, when you
whipped into your pocketbook and suddenly announced,
"HOLD EVERYTHING! I'VE GOT A PHOTOGRAPH
OF HER RIGHT HERE, THEN YOU CAN SEE WHAT
SHE REALLY LOOKS LIKE!" . . . You then proceeded
to crouch down to the floor and dump everything out of
your bag, and I mean . . . *everything!* . . . leaking packets
of sequins and gummed stars, sea shells, odd pieces of fur,
crochet hooks, a monarch butterfly embedded in plastic,
dental floss, antique glass buttons, small jingling bells,
lace . . . I thought I'd die! Just sink to the floor and quietly
die! . . . You couldn't find it, you see. I mean, you spent
the rest of the afternoon on your hands and knees crawling
through this ocean of junk muttering, "It's *got* to be here
somewhere; I know I had it with me!" . . . Then Daddy
pulled me into the thick of it all and said, "By the way,
have you met our daughter Mags yet? She's the one who
did all these pictures . . . paintings . . . portraits . . . whatever you call them." (*She drops to her hands and knees
and begins crawling out of the room.*) By this time, Mum
had somehow crawled out of the gallery and was lost on
another floor. She began calling for me . . . "YOO-HOO,

MAGS . . . WHERE ARE YOU? . . . OH, MAGS, DAR-
LING . . . HELLO? . . . ARE YOU THERE? . . . " *(She
reenters and faces them.)* This was at my *first* show.

_____ **3** _____

FANNY

*(Fatigue has finally overtaken her. She's calm, almost se-
rene.)* . . . and to you who see him once a year, if that . . .
What is he to *you?* . . . I mean, what do you give him from
yourself that costs you something? . . . Hmmmmmm?
. . . *(Imitating her.)* "Oh, hi Daddy, it's great to see you
again. How have you been? . . . Gee, I love your hair. It's
gotten so . . . *white!*" . . . What color do you expect it to
get when he's this age? . . . I mean, if you care so much
how he looks, why don't you come and see him once in a
while? . . . But oh, no . . . you have your paintings to do
and your shows to put on. You just come and see us when
the whim strikes. *(Imitating her.)* "Hey, you know what
would be really great? . . . To do a portrait of you! I've
always wanted to paint you, you're such great subjects!" . . . *Paint* us?! . . . What about opening your eyes
and really *seeing* us? . . . Noticing what's going on around
here for a change! It's all over for Daddy and me. This is
it! *"Finita la commedia!"* . . . All I'm trying to do is exit
with a little flourish; have some fun. . . . What's so terrible
about that? . . . It can get pretty grim around here, in case
you haven't noticed . . . Daddy, tap-tap-tapping out his
nonsense all day; me traipsing around to the thrift shops
trying to amuse myself . . . He never keeps me company
anymore; never takes me out anywhere. . . . I'd put a bullet through my head in a minute, but then who'd look after
him? . . . What do you think we're moving to the cottage
for? . . . So I can watch him like a hawk and make sure he
doesn't get lost. Do you think that's any thing to look forward to? . . . Being Daddy's nursemaid out in the middle
of nowhere? I'd much rather stay here in Boston with the

few friends I have left, but you can't always do what you want in this world! *"L'homme propose, Dieu dispose!"* . . . If you want to paint us so badly, you ought to paint us as we really are. There's your picture! . . . *(She points to* GARD NER, *who's quietly playing with a paper glider.)* Daddy spread out on the floor with all his toys and me hovering over him to make sure he doesn't hurt himself! *(She goes over to him.)* YOO-HOO . . . GAR? . . . HELLO? . . .

Passing Game

Steve Tesich

Premiere: American Place Theatre, New York City, 1977
Setting: Upstate New York

Two New York actors have rented cottages at a semi-deserted upstate resort. There has been a chain of unsolved killings in the area, and guests have been staying away in droves. There is no one around but the lecherous night watchman Andrew, who's trying to shoot his old dog; Andrew's young nephew Randy; Debbie, the hard-to-get girl he's pursuing; two actors; two wives.

The two actors have never met, but know each other's faces from the audition circuit. Henry, a black man, has only been successful in dog food commercials. Richard, who's white, has not even succeeded at that—in fact, lately he's lost out to Henry on several commercial auditions. They take out their hostility in savagely competitive one-on-one basketball. Eventually, competitiveness yields to bonding, and they share their darker secrets. Both blame their wives for pumping them full of great expectations about their careers, and both are half-hoping their wives will be "taken care of" by the mysterious killer. Henry once tried to run over his wife in a car "accident," and

Richard has come to the cottage this week with a gun. They make plans to murder each other's wives.

Richard describes his wife Julie: "When I first saw her, she seemed like some wide-eyed angel who had plopped down from heaven to this cocktail party . . . she seemed so spanking sparkling new and unsoiled." Throughout the play Julie expresses her craving for change. Early one morning in bed, she addresses her husband, whom she believes is still sleeping.

JULIE

Richard . . . are you awake? (*We see his eyes open and his hand, neither of which she can see, move as a signal that he is awake. The rest of him does not move. She waits a second for a reply.*) I think you are awake but you don't have to say anything. You can pretend you're asleep . . . You can pretend, if you want, that I am a dream you are having . . . it might be better that way because I seem to be unable to say what I want to say when you are looking at me . . . your eyes squint ever so slightly when you look at me . . . as if you were taking aim at my words . . . and all I can do is squirm under your stare and camouflage myself. It's exhausting me, Richard. There is a beautiful life dying inside both of us and it is not in my power to counteract what's happening. It takes energy to break out of this pattern and I just don't have it on my own, Richard. All I seem to want now, my one desire, is to compress all of it . . . all the meals I'll have . . . all the periods, all the lovemaking and the baths and the looks out of the window . . . just compress all of them and get them over with . . . I try. Every morning I want to start anew. I open my eyes and it feels within my power to do so . . . and then I see my slip draped over a chair . . . something sticking out of a drawer—my wristwatch is waiting for my wrist, and by the time I put it on it's too late. All these thoughts

I am told are not real. I am told there is no soul. I am told
there is no God. There are only glands secreting . . . and
even the little shred of unhappiness that I thought I could
claim as my own . . . even that . . . I am told is nothing
more than a case of glands . . . and hormones . . . secreting or undersecreting. I am more than fluids, Richard . . . more . . . I am wounded, I feel, and life is trickling
out of me and your lies . . . yes, I know about them . . . your
lies will not let the wound heal. I could be a glorious woman.
There is so much that is beautiful in me. I beg you, don't
keep killing me like this. Let me live. Richard?

Pastorale

Deborah Eisenberg

Premiere: Second Stage, New York City, 1982
Setting: A New England farmhouse

Melanie and Steve had rented a farmhouse somewhere in
New England. Rachel comes up from the city for the weekend and stays for ten months. The characters are "in their
mid-twenties. It may seem to you that they are younger,
but they are not." They work various odd jobs at pottery
shops and construction, and the biggest decisions are whether
or not to go swimming ("I don't think I can really handle
getting all undressed and then having to get dressed again.
I feel like I've done it so often recently"), and whether to
take out the cats' dead mice or just put coffee cups over
them. People drift in and out of the house without much
introduction. A guy named John is visiting. Rachel, who's
just dropped some acid, is rambling about her fear of touching strangers. John tells a story.

JOHN

(As MELANIE *pours gin in his glass, he runs his hand up her leg. They remain thus affiliated for the first part of his speech.)* I remember once I was at this concert, and there was this chick sitting in the seat next to me. And she was, like, older, but she was pretty good-looking, and she looked really, really sad. Well, I remember I had just washed my hair, which was pretty long then, and it was all sort of electric. And I realized it was sort of brushing against this woman when I'd turn around, and I wondered if it was annoying her. But then I noticed she was beginning to lean a bit towards me when I'd turn, and also I saw that she was sort of looking at my hands. I mean, I really wasn't sure, so I rolled up my sleeves, really slowly. Like this . . . And I sort of stretched my arms out on the arm rests. Well she was definitely looking at my arms. No question about it. So, I was staring at the stage like I was really absorbed in the concert, and I leaned my head just a little bit towards her. Well, first she put her arm sort of over the back of my seat, like she was just sitting there, but pretty soon her hand started, just really, really gently playing with my hair, and I pretended not to notice, but I sort of moved my head around a bit. *(He reaches out and pulls the transfixed* MELANIE *onto his lap.)* That's right, honey. Climb on aboard. So anyway, after a bit she was really getting into it, you know? And so I just, like I didn't notice what I was doing, put my hand down, right so the back of my hand was just touching her leg, and then I moved it. Just a bit, but noticeably. Well, she practically just melted over into my seat with me, and she was crying like crazy, but completely silent. Oh, God, it was so weird—her tears were sort of pouring around my neck, and she was unbuttoning my shirt, and running her hand, like inside the top of my jeans, just sobbing away, but completely quiet. Christ, was that freaky.

A Prayer for My Daughter

Thomas Babe

Premiere: New York Shakespeare Festival, New York City, 1978

Setting: The dilapidated squad room of a New York police precinct

It is one A.M. after the Fourth of July. Two low-life cops haul in two low-life crooks to interrogate them about a brutal murder. The younger crook, Jimmy Rosehips, is "a kid, that's all, pure punk but with the aspect of a choir boy." He is a drug addict. So is one of the cops, Jack, who gives him a fix to speed his confession. The second crook, Simon Cohn (a.k.a. Sean de Kahn), is a "weird." Bearded and lean, he calls Jimmy Rosehips his "daughter" and himself Jimmy's "teacher" of "a way of life . . . eclectic spiritualism." He has an extensive police record.

Both cops are cynical rule-breakers. In private, they make a cash bet on which crook pulled the trigger, and talk about whether to go with the good cop/bad cop "psychological crap" or "hurt 'em a little, physically." The older cop, Kelly, wants to "knock 'em around" and get a quick conviction. His crazy daughter Margie has called him and threatened to kill herself, and Kelly wants to "straighten her." He is mentally and physically exhausted; as he puts it, "fuckin' fucked out." The two cops split up and go one-on-one with their interrogations.

Monologue One: Jack is taking his turn with Sean. Sean has agreed to turn Jimmy in, but Jack is not satisfied. He asks Sean, "Is he Sunshine?" The usually calm and icy Sean explodes, "How the fuck do you know so much?" Jack tells Sean it's all in his file, and starts singing "You Are My Sunshine" to bait him.

Thomas Babe comments: "Sean's story is the purest version I've ever done of a man getting completely lost in the point he wanted to make. He starts out trying to tell Jack that we (all of us men) are basically the same kind of people, and he ends up telling the same Jack that we are all different and unknowable. What makes him shift his course, as I saw it, was to relive again in the telling an enigmatic event in his life he thought he understood and which turns out to be even more enigmatic than he imagined—not because this soldier attracted him, but because he still doesn't know exactly what it means to him and how to deal with it. Never was this meant to be a pitch or sermon; Sean would not allow that. It's an untoward miracle (to him) that he's been this open, which is why he retreats into sarcasm in the last line."

• • •

Monologue Two: Kelly strip-searches Jimmy and Jimmy refuses to put his clothes back on. He has overhead Margie's phone call, and now he asks Kelly about her. Initially, Kelly is hostile, but his exhaustion takes over and he confides in Jimmy, finally taking the naked man into his arms. He is surprised to find himself sexually aroused. While they embrace, Jimmy steals Kelly's gun from its holster. He's so high on junk that he doesn't know quite what to do with it and accidentally shoots Kelly, hitting him square in his rear-pocket wallet. The sound of the shot brings in Jack and Sean. Jimmy holds them at gunpoint. The phone rings. Jack answers and finds out that Margie went through with her suicide threat; she is dead. Too numb to respond, Kelly only asks Jack if he got a confession from Sean. Jimmy explodes at him.

Thomas Babe comments: "Jimmy's speech started out in my mind as a recreation similar to Sean's—some signal even that he feels shaped his life and defines what he is right now. What altered its final form in the play was that he is trying, with all the moxie he has, to convince the fucked-out, boozed, hopped-up skeptics around him that this very private epiphany of his has some central meaning. He may lose track of himself momentarily, but he is still—in his own mind—more feelingly a part of the world that he imagines his listeners to be. There's something arrogant about this, and naive, and those qualities shouldn't be lost. Jimmy's status as a loser in the whole play hinges on his sentimentality, and here he gets a chance to go at it without fear of contradiction. (He's holding the gun.)"

1

SEAN

A while ago, in Vietnam, in actual fact, I saw something, a man, and he was a soldier, well, everybody was a soldier but me, and I ignored them, I figured it was better not to know a single one of them personally because I might have to save his life and the pressure would've been wrong on me to save the life of a man I knew or maybe loved so I didn't. But there was this one man I didn't know, had never even ever seen before, sitting under a tree; he had his shirt off, he was all bloody and dirty from a firefight, and he was doing nothing, just smoking a joint, and I was watching him the way I sometimes watched the men, thinking the dumbest crap, like how much I wanted to touch his shoulder, and he was nobody special at all and suddenly he turned toward me and waved and I thought, he must be waving at somebody behind me, so I turned around and saw there was nobody else but the two of us, and he waved again, and I started to be sort of pleased because I could see his eyes were intelligent and kind, and then he pointed right at me, and I thought, what is this, does he like me, this stranger, and then he said something that I couldn't hear, and I think I smiled and made the I-can't-hear-you gesture, so he stood up and started to shout and I still couldn't hear, but I wanted to, so then he stood all the way up and that's when I heard the shot and he was nailed in the neck by a sniper and dropped like a ton of bricks, and of course, the shooting started again and me, by instinct, crawled on my belly to him, to where I stuck a wad in his neck and turned him over and cradled his head in my lap and wiped the shit off his forehead, because I always comforted the men I knew I couldn't help who were going to die and then I realized, Christ on the bloody cross, you shitbucket, you know you're going to weep, and so it was, for the first time ever, I opened my kit and gave myself a short of morphine, and I sat there I'm told, for twelve hours, with his head in my lap, and he seemed to me to be an angel and every time I came out of it I fixed again. The sergeant said to me afterwards: shit, son, you were holdin' onto that stiff so dear, goddamn if we didn't think we were gonna have to stuff the *both* of you in the body bag. *(Pause.)* Give me a hit, officer. Just a little hit, please. *(SEAN gets his hit.)* What's wrong is, I should've taken that beating he gave me better, it shouldn't've hurt so much, I should've ignored it, or been able to, but that's what's wrong, this thing is getting through to me again. *(Pause.)* You know how many times I didn't say a thing and didn't do a thing, not one goddamn thing, and I know you'll find that hard to believe, considering my package, but I was good a long time a very long time until I was overwhelmed with it. *(Pause; a different tone; sad.)* There's a woman inside me, officer, and she aches for the men she has known. She flirts with them and cries for them when they have to go in the morning; she likes to please them but she likes to have her cigarette lit, at least when I used to smoke . . . and I hate her so much that most often I want to kill her, because she loves her men so completely that it terrifies me . . . and she says to me, whenever I think there is no woman in me, that I am a liar and a fool, and she is the one who makes me cry and she's the one who makes me sing goddamn songs to men . . . live men, dead men, it doesn't matter. *(Pause.)* And he was her first, my woman, her first man.

Nothing came of it but that I ran my fingers through his hair for, they tell me, twelve hours, and I sang:
You are my so forth
My only so forth
You make me so forth
(*Pause.* SEAN's *tone changes slightly back to its old crispness.*) Does a word of this make the least little sense to you?

2

JIMMY

(*Enraged.*) I wanna say something and if you don't go over there and sit down, I mean, like now, I'm gonna blow your fuckin' brains out. I mean it. All right, I said to myself, Jimmy, sweetheart, you may haul dog-do for the rest of your life, and uphill, but you and this woman of yours, blown up like a balloon, you've both come to this sacred place and you are about to have a son. Well, I was, you can laugh, but I was going to, and she thought so, too, she said, I'm that good—what is that kind of good?—she said, I'll deliver you a son, and we were ready, and he says, Here, excuse me, I am in transit between births and smoke cigars to get the fetal fluid off my hands, and I said, Great, Doc, just awful great, but be good and at your level best, and we ended up in a room that was just about as bad a room as you would ever want to be in, yeah, it was like a men's room, and everybody was all smiles, even Lisa, because it had crowned—my first look was peach fuzz on the cranium, damp as September rain, peeking through her mommy's opening, and at first I said, No thank you, but the nurses are making me ashamed, they say the father is so important, and Lisa's saying, We got up for this together so don't chicken on me, Jimmy, and I'm crying, thinking, whatever it is, it's alive, it's got wet hair on it. So I donned the blue suit and the blue booties and the blue mask and the blue hat and I waited, and I was saying, James, you are a progenitor, and Lisa, you are the other thing—I'm thinking, what's it, what's it, the progenetrix, and we neither of us know, we don't fuckin' know, but we hope it works, and it was coming, man, was it ever coming, and then it got stuck: and there was panic everywhere except for Lisa, I mean, she didn't know, and the doctors looked at each other, back and forth, and they heated up the vacuum cleaners and the scalpels and they said, everybody, put your hands on her, altogether, and push, let's gather together and push, and this male doctor said push, and this male intern said push, and this male father said push, and this male whatever-the-hell-he-was said push, and we helped her, we pushed while she pushed, and the only other woman in the room, who was the nurse, didn't push but listened with a stethoscope to see if it was alive, what we were pushing at and just like suddenly, one last push, and Bingo! a baby appeared, all covered completely in some shitstorm of cold cream and tied by a cord to her mommy, and I said, thanks, yeah, I said that, and it's likely more than thanks . . . and I noticed, well, I mean what can I say, yes, it was a little girl, right there, dressed in cream and a little poopy, stuck in the tubes like she was when I didn't even know the lady was a lady, and I thought only, Not fuck off little person, you are not the man I wanted to come from there, I didn't think at all how bad my disappointment was. I didn't think anything, okay? Okay, I thought, just, you are my daughter and those people will wash the cream off you and in a while, I'm afraid, daughter, you'll be mine— and this is on a two-minute acquaintance in a delivery room—I thought, daughter, fuck it, from now till I die, I'll have to answer to you. When she popped out, whole and perfect, I mean, a little pooped, too long in the birth canal, all the light I ever had ran to her, all what I hoped, and in the bar around the corner from the hospital I told the keeper there, I'm glad I didn't have a son, but what else could I say? *(Pause.)* What could I say? Somebody's got to tell *me*. *(Pause.)* I mean, did you ever think, Sergeant, when you saw your daughter the first time, that some part of you—was in her? Did you ever feel that, looking at Margie? Do you know what I mean? I mean, do you feel nothin' at all, anyway at all, now she's dead? Say something!

The Primary English Class

Israel Horovitz

Premiere: Circle in the Square Theatre, New York City, 1976

Setting: A classroom on the sixth floor of a walk-up

A Polish janitor sings "I Can't Give You Anything But Love, Baby" in Polish as he sweeps out the classroom. One by one, students arrive: a dashing Italian, a tiny Frenchman, a nearsighted German, an elderly Chinese woman, a giggly Japanese girl. All of their surnames mean "wastebasket" in their native languages—a fact they establish by pantomime, since nobody speaks one word of anyone else's language. (Two offstage translators interpret for the audience.) Finally, the Primary English teacher comes in, introducing herself as Debbie Wastba ("Odd name, huh? Dates all the way back to Mesopotamia. My great-grandfather shortened it after his . . . uh . . . trouble.") This is her first day of teaching, and she is hilariously incompetent at speaking to non-English speakers. It takes her ten minutes to get the students to sit down. Now that she's finally gotten them into their chairs, she smiles and starts over.

WASTBA

(From her desk.) Listen, now, I'll just go really slow. *(Pauses, smiles.)* My name is Debbie Wastba. *(She writes her name on blackboard. Each takes notebook and copies down name.)* W-A-S-T-B-A. That's pronounced Wass-tah-bah: Wastba.

(She links each of the three syllables together on board, in the following way: WA ST BA.) Think of *Wah* as in wah-tah. Splash. Splash. *Stah* as in stah-bility. And *Bah* as in Bah-dum . . . as in *(Sings "Dragnet" theme.)* Bum-tah-bum-bum. Well, listen. It was literally double its length in its ancient, biblical form. *(Pauses.)* Actually, that tune was wrong. It would be much more like . . . *(Sings again, to tune of "My Funny Valentine.")* Bum bum-bum bum-bum-bum . . . bum bum-bum bum-bum-bum . . . bum bum-bum baaahhhmmmmmmmm . . . *(Pauses: sees they are confused.)* Well, anyway, really, you can easily check your Bibles if you want. *(Rummages through stack of papers on desk, holds up lesson plan.)* This is our lesson plan. That's *lesson . . . plan.* Lesson plan. We're going to be together for several hours and I thought it would be highly professional and competent for me to make a plan. And I did. And here it is: *(She reads, smiling confidently.)* One. A pleasant welcome and normal chatter. For two, I've planned your basic salutations, such as the goods—good morning, good afternoon, good night, good luck and good grief. *(She laughs.)* That was a mildly amusing joke: "good grief." Later in the night—after we've learned a bit of English—you'll be able to, well, get the joke. *(Pauses.)* Let's move along. Three will be basic customs: ours here. *(Reading again.)* Four will be a short history of our English language. *(As the students take their notes, they, as we, begin to realize that Wastba is only writing the numbers one through six on to the blackboard—no words. They raise their hands in question, but she waves them away, barging ahead.)* Five will be the primary lesson of the primary English class, according to the book. And six will be the very essential verb "to be." At some point, we shall also inspect the very basic concept of silence. *(Smiles.)* Now then, as you can see, there are only six points to cover and hours and hours ahead in which to cover them. *(All stare blankly at her smiling face.)* *Now* then: Questions?

The Real Thing

Tom Stoppard

Premiere: Plymouth Theatre, New York City, 1984
Setting: London. A stage set, a living room

Henry is a man of letters, a celebrated playwright, and an ardent Monkees fan. He is next week's "castaway" on a classical music program called "Desert Island Discs," for which the guest prepares a list of ten indispensable recordings. Henry knows nothing about classical music; his personal Ten Best begins with The Righteous Brothers' "You've Lost That Lovin' Feeling."

Henry is obsessed with language, to the point where mixed metaphors cause him physical pain. He writes deft, witty plays about adultery. This subject matter comes closer to home when he leaves his wife for his actress lover Annie, marries Annie, then suffers the pain of her affair with a fellow actor. Finally the wit and the words don't help. Here he talks to his precocious daughter Debbie about love.

HENRY

It's to do with knowing and being known. I remember how it stopped seeming odd that in biblical Greek, knowing was used for making love. Whosit knew so-and-so. Carnal knowledge. It's what lovers trust each other with. Knowledge of each other, not of the flesh but through the flesh, knowledge of self, the real him, the real her, *in extremis*, the mask slipped from the face. Every other version of oneself is on offer to the public. We share our vivacity, grief, sulks, anger, joy . . . we hand it out to anybody who happens to be standing around, to friends and family with a momentary sense of indecency perhaps, to strangers without hesitation. Our lovers share us with the passing trade. But in pairs we insist that we give ourselves to each other. What selves? What's left? What else is there that hasn't been dealt out like a deck of cards? Carnal knowledge.

Personal, final, uncompromised. Knowing, being known. I revere that. Having that is being rich, you can be generous about what's shared—she walks, she talks, she laughs, she lends a sympathetic ear, she kicks off her shoes and dances on the tables, she's everybody's and it don't mean a thing, let them eat cake; knowledge is something else, the undealt card, and while it's held it makes you free-and-easy and nice to know, and when it's gone everything is pain. Every single thing. Every object that meets the eye, a pencil, a tangerine, a travel poster. As if the physical world has been wired up to pass a current back to the part of your brain where imagination glows like a filament in a lobe no bigger than a torch bulb. Pain. *(Pause.)*

Reckless

Craig Lucas

Premiere: The Production Company, New York City, 1983
Setting: Various Springfields in various states

It is Christmas Eve. Tom and Rachel Fitzsimmons are in bed, the TV blinking silently and lovely, deep snowdrifts outside.

Monologue One: Rachel's monologue opens the play.

Monologue Two: Immediately after Rachel's euphoric outpouring, Tom bursts into tears and tells her he's taken out a contract on her life. A hit man is coming to kill her; the whole thing has been staged to look like an accidental shooting during a burglary. At first Rachel doesn't believe him, but when she hears glass break downstairs, she takes Tom's advice and flees. As she stands at a pay phone in bathrobe and slippers, a man named Lloyd Bophtelophti offers to give her a lift. He ends up inviting her back to his home to share Christmas with him and his deaf, paraplegic wife Pooty. Pooty and Lloyd take charge of Rachel's uprooted life, finding her a job at Hands Across the Sea, the slightly suspicious charity group where the two of them work. Lloyd has just gone to chop wood, and Pooty surprises Rachel by answering one of her questions aloud.

———— 1 ————

RACHEL

I think I'm more excited than they are. I really do. I think we just have kids so we can tell them all about Santa Claus and have an excuse to believe it ourselves again. I really do. They are so excited. I remember that feeling so clearly. I didn't think I could ever sleep. And I remember pinching myself and pinching myself to stay awake so I could hear the reindeers' footsteps, you know? I wanted to believe it so badly. I think that was the last year I did . . . Oh god . . . Is it still snowing? Why don't you turn the sound up? Oh, it's coming down like crazy. You can hear it, can't you? When it gets deep like this? It just swallows up all the sound and you feel like you've been wrapped up in the hands of a big, sweet, giant, white . . . monster. Good monster. He's going to carry us away into a dream. My family always had champagne first thing before we opened our presents—I mean in the morning, you know: I always loved that. I felt like such an adult having champagne and I remember saying to my mother the bubbles in the champagne looked like snow if you turned your head upside down. I remember thinking that I wanted to live in Alaska because it always snowed and Santa was up there, so it must always be Christmas if it always snowed . . . You're my Santa Claus. And our two elves. I'm having one of my euphoria attacks. I think I'm going to be terminally happy, you'd better watch out, it's catching. Highly contagious . . . What's the matter? Just sleepy? Can we listen for a second, I won't stay up all night, I promise. (*Switches on TV.*)

————— 2 —————

POOTY

If you've ever worked with needy people, it doesn't matter
what their particular handicap, they can be blind, they can
be mentally ill, they can be disabled . . . I used to work
with the hearing impaired, teaching sign language. Almost
immediately you realize how easy it is to take their infirmity
for granted in the sea of so much need. Abnormality becomes normality. When I lost the use of my legs, a friend
drove me up here to Springfield to take a look at this place
where you work with the handicapped. I watched the various physical therapists work with the patients and there
was one: I remember he was working with a quadraplegic.
I thought he was the most beautiful man I'd ever seen. A
light shining out through his skin. And I thought if I couldn't
be with him I'd die. But I knew I would just be one more
crippled dame as far as he was concerned, so my friend
helped to get me registered as deaf and disabled. I thought
if I were somehow needier than the rest I would get special
attention. I realized soon enough—everyone gets special
attention where Lloyd is concerned, but by then it was too
late. He was in love with me, with my honesty. He learned
to sign; he told me how he'd run away from a bad marriage
and changed his name so he wouldn't have to pay child
support. He got me a job at Hands Across the Sea. I couldn't
bring myself to tell him I had another name and another
life, that I'd run away too, because I owed the government
so much money and wasn't able to pay after the accident . . . I believe in honesty. I believe in total honesty.
And I need him and he needs me to be the person he thinks
I am and I am that person, I really am that person. I'm a
crippled deaf girl—"Short and stout. Here is my wheelchair, here is my mouth."

[RACHEL: I'm not judging you.]

When he goes out I scream and scream just to hear my
voice. Noise. I recite poetry I remember from grade school,

I babble, I talk back to the television, I even call people on the phone and say it's a wrong number just to have a conversation. I'm afraid I'm going to open my mouth to scream one day and . . . *(She does: no sound.)*

Reunion

David Mamet

Premiere: St. Nicholas Theatre Company, Chicago, 1976
Setting: Bernie Cary's apartment, Boston
Carol Mindler, a young married woman, has looked up the father she hasn't seen since she was a little girl. Bernie Cary, her father, describes himself to her: "What's to tell? You see it all here. Have a look. Fifty-three years old. Ex-alcoholic. Ex-this. Ex-that. Democrat." Bernie served in the Army Air Force as a tail gunner. Later he worked in a San Francisco body shop, for the phone company on Cape Cod, and as a cross-country mover for Allied Van Lines. Here he tells Carol how he got that job, and missed his brother's funeral.

BERNIE

I'll tell you a story. So I'd been drunk at the time for several years and was walking down Tremont Street one evening around nine and here's this big van in front of a warehouse and the driver is ringing the bell in the shipping dock trying to get in (which he won't do, because they moved a couple of weeks ago and the warehouse is deserted. But he doesn't know that.)

So I say, "Hey, you looking for Hub City Transport?" And he says yeah, and I tell him they're over in Lechmere. So he says "Where?" So I tell him I don't know the address but I can take him there. Which was, of course, a bunch

of shit, but I figured maybe I could make a couple of bucks
on the deal.

And why not.

So I ride over to Lechmere.

I find the warehouse.

You ever been to Lechmere?

[CAROL: Just passing through.]

Very depressing. So, anyway. He's in Lechmere to pick up
a load. And he offers me ten bucks to help me load the
van.

So fine. Later we go across the street for a cup of coffee
and he gives me this story. He just fired his partner, he
likes the way I handle furniture, and do I want a job?

Hey, what the hell.

We finish the coffee and we go.

And for one year I didn't get home, never shaved, wore
the same goddamn clothes, slept in the cab, made some
money, spent some money, saw the country. Alex died,
and I missed his funeral.

Which, of course, is why Lorraine won't talk to me.

Because I got back in September and I'm back a day or
so and I go over to Alex's.

Lorraine answers the door and I tell her,

"Lorraine, tell your fat-ass husband to grab his coat because we are going to the track." He loved the track.

And she says: "If I ever catch you in my sight again,
drunk or sober, I'm going to punch your fucking heart out."

Which were harsh words for her.

And to this day—she believed I was in town and drunk
at the time of the funeral—not once have I seen or spoken
to her in ten years. . . .

And we were very close at one time.

She was a good woman.

Very loyal. . . .

Alex fought in the war.

What the hell. How's your mother?

Savage in Limbo

John Patrick Shanley

Premiere: Double Image Theatre, New York City, 1985
Setting: Scales, a bar in the Bronx

A bartender and four of his neighborhood patrons, all thirty-two years old, spend a Monday night at Scales. Shanley calls this a "concert play . . . more a series of related emotional and intellectual events than a conventional story." There are many long personal speeches which might be thought of as arias.

Monologue One: Linda Rotunda is "a done-up, attractive, overripe Italian girl." Monday is usually her night out with her boyfriend, Tony Aronica, but tonight she's crying in the bar because Tony's "gone crazy. . . . He says, 'Linda, I wanna see ugly girls.' "

Monologue Two: Tony Aronica is "a streamlined Italian stud with a streak of self-doubt and a yearning sweetness." He has come to the bar to explain his decision to Linda.

Monologue Three: The title character, Denise Savage, is a thirty-two-year-old virgin. She is "small, wild-haired, strong, belligerent, determined, dissatisfied, and scared. She is in pain, paranoid, and full of hunger. She has hungry ears."

--------- 1 ---------

LINDA

What are you tellin' me? You're tellin' me nothin'. I tell you what's goin' on, and you tell me it ain't goin' on. It's goin' on. Anthony wants to see ugly girls 'cause I don't know why, but that's the fuckin' news and don't tell me otherwise. Every Monday night I go to his place and we spend time together, and this night I go and he's got this look in his eye. Like he knows somethin', and like he never seen me before. I got a scared feelin' right away. I touch him but he puts my hand away. He says he wants to talk.

What's he wanna talk about before we go to bed? What's there to talk about? When a woman wants to talk to a man, it's 'cause she wants the man to see her better. When it's the other way, when the man stops you from touchin' to talk, what's there to talk about? It's gotta be bad. I tried to keep him from talkin'. I turned myself on. But there was somethin' in his mind. Even my mother sees what Anthony's got. Even my mother. She'd like a taste. She knows where I'm goin' on Monday nights. I don't come home till late, the mornin' sometimes, but she don't say anything. Any other time she would. But she knows where I go, and she wants it for me. Once I was goin', and she whispered to me so's my father wouldn't hear, Take it, Linda. That's all. Take it, Linda. And I did. And now he don't wanna see me 'cause he wants to see ugly women. I said I'd be ugly for him, but he said no. It didn't work that way. I'm so ashamed. I feel ugly. I feel fat. Anthony don't want me no more.

——— **2** ———

TONY

I was in my car outside this place over the weekend. I hadda couple a drinks and I was a little fuzzy, so I was waitin' till I cleared. It was dark. I was sittin' there. And this unknown girl got in. She just got in the car. And she started talkin' to me. She started rappin' to me about the Soviet Union. Yeah. 'Bout their economy. Housin'. How they feel about China bein' right there. Everything. Everything about the Soviet Union. She musta talked for two hours. Russian paranoia. *Tass.* The Gulag. I'm sittin' there an' I'm takin' this in. The Trans-Siberian Railroad. What kinda tanks they got in Eastern Europe. Why they need American wheat. And then she was finished. She'd told me everything she knew. So I took her in the back seat and I banged her. And do you know something? It was the best. It was the best I ever had. And it whadn't 'cause she knew a lotta tricks or like that. It was 'cause she'd told me about the Soviet Union. And then she left. Now here's the thing. She was very ugly. I don't even wanna talk about how she looked. Mucho ugly. I didn't think I could ever be with a woman like that. But it came about outta whatever, happenstance, and I was. And it turned out to be better than what I went after. Do you see what I mean? Do you see what I'm comin' towards? I always went for the girl like you. And what finally fuckin' come to me, what finally fuckin' penetrated the wall here, was there was somethin' else. Somethin' I never even thought about, didn't have a clue about. When I talked to you, I called it ugly girls. I don't know what to call it. There's other people. Like in science fiction. Another dimension right there but you can't see it. I got into it for a minute by accident. Through a crack. I caught a flash. The dimension a ugly girls. I'm like one a those guys inna factory and they bring in all new machines. That's what I feel like. Like I gotta retrain or I'm gonna lose my place. Some girls you look at, some girls you don't. I wanna see the things I didn't see before an' let the stuff I was lookin' at go by. I've done the fuckin' thing we're in, Linda. I've been with you, I talked to you. I know what that is. That's what I meant when I said you didn't know nothin', but I whadn't sayin' it right. You look at what I look at. You know what I know. I wanna look at somethin' else. I wanna know somethin' else. I'm thirty-two years old. I wanna change.

_____ 3 _____

SAVAGE

I don't care. I don't care how you think about me. What d'you want? You want me to act like somebody on TV? This one got this one way an' that's how they are? I don't know how I am, who I am. I don't know what I believe. I don't know where to go to find out. I don't know what to do to be the one person that somewhere inside I wanna be. I

don't know nothin' but the one thing: I gotta move. And
you, too. This whole world I'm in's gotta break up an' move.
[MURK: Get out.

SAVAGE: I gotta drink in fronta me I ain't finished.]
We're on the cliff. We were born here. Well, do you wanna
die on the cliff? Do you wanna die in bed? Do you think
you're gonna live forever? They told us if you jump off the
cliff, you die. And you probably do, but fuck it. Fuck it.
We don't know that. You don't know nothin' you ain't done,
an' nobody can tell you nothin'. Ain't you tired a livin' if
this is all livin' is? And you know it's not. I may be an
asshole and I may not know what to do, but you hear what
I'm sayin' to you, dammit you do. In your heart you do.
This is not life. This is not life. This is not life. Ugly women,
right, Tony? Somethin' else. I don't care what. God, gimme
somethin' else 'cause this is definitely not it. New eyes new
ears new hands. Gimme back my soul from where you took
it, gimme back my friends, gimme back my priests an' my
father, and take this goddamn virginity from off my life.
HUNGER HUNGER HUNGER. If somebody don't gimme
somethin', I'm gonna die. I wanna play pool. (*Picks up the
pool cue and uses it as a spear or a wand.*) Somebody play
pool with me? (*No one moves.*) I come in here a lotta nights,
a lotta nights, an' I play pool by myself. I like the game.
You hit the white ball, and that ball hits another, and it
goes somewhere. When I first started, I didn't mind playin'
alone. But you get tired of it. The balls don't do nothin'
unless you make 'em do it. It's all you. They're just like
stones. It's like I'm some woman lives inna cave and plays
with stones. Somebody play pool with me. You be the cue
ball. Hit me and I'll fly. You don't wanna jump yourself,
push me off. You can't keep up your courage alone, playin'
with stones.

Say Goodnight, Gracie

Ralph Pape

Premiere: Actors Playhouse, New York City, 1979
Setting: Jerry and Ginny's East Village apartment, New
York City

Jerry is an out-of-work actor, Steve is an out-of-work writer,
and Bobby is a barely working rock singer. Tonight is their
tenth high school reunion. They are meeting at the apartment Jerry shares with his girlfriend Ginny, to steel themselves for the big event. Steve arrives first, coming in before
Jerry and scaring him with a gorilla mask. Jerry, who's just
had a rotten audition, announces that he's going to skip the
reunion. Ginny and Steve try to change his mind. Then
Bobby arrives with his stewardess girlfriend Catherine ("Is
she beautiful, or what?"). They get very stoned and talk
about high school.

CATHERINE

I was in high school during the Cuban missile crisis. When
the blockade went into effect, they led us downstairs into
the basement, and the nuns stood around and everyone
had to say the rosary because people really believed that
a nuclear war could have broken out that morning. I didn't
want to stay there. I didn't want to die like that. I was near
a flight of steps that led upstairs and when no one was
looking, I snuck out. I just . . . wanted to be outside. I had
never been disobedient or questioned authority before that
moment.

[BOBBY: (*Appreciatively.*) All right . . . !]
It was cold outside and there was an incredible blue sky
and no wind. There were no people. I walked around the
empty schoolyard. I was so afraid. There were tears in my
eyes because I really believed I was looking at everything
for the last time. It was so beautiful. I felt like a little girl.
I began to touch things. The brick wall of the school. The

iron railing of the fence that ran around the yard. The bicycle rack. Everything was so cold and yet so beautiful. I filled my lungs with air. I was alive. I had never admitted to myself how much I loved just being alive. And I knew if I survived, I would never forget that morning when I had wanted to touch and feel everything around me. I was sixteen at this time. A virgin . . . After the crisis had passed, I still felt like I was moving through a very beautiful dream. I had a date with Greg Sutton, the captain of the basketball team, very soon after. That night, without even realizing that I was saying the words, I begged Greg to fuck me. He couldn't believe it. He was probably a virgin, too. I said, Greg, all of us are on this earth for only a short while, and we can't be afraid, we have to open ourselves up to every moment . . . so Greg fucked me in the back seat of his car that cold winter's night at the drive-in. Moonlight shone through the windows. I can't begin to describe what it was like. I can only ask you to imagine it. In and out. In and out. In and out. I wrapped my legs around him and I remembered how beautiful and precious the world had seemed to me that morning and I grabbed at him repeatedly and plunged my tongue deep inside his mouth. My breasts were heaving up and down. I was so hot and wet. It was indescribable . . . I can only ask you to try and imagine this. Anyway, after that night, Greg must have done some bragging to his friends, because the next week I was literally besieged with requests for dates. All of which I accepted. Greg became jealous, but I explained to him that I needed to reach out and touch everyone for myself, just as, that morning, I had wanted to touch every leaf on the big oak tree outside the school when I thought the world would perish in a fiery holocaust. Before the term was over, I had gone to bed with over twenty different boys. And my geometry teacher, Mr. Handfield. That summer, I took a house with some girls down at the Jersey shore. College boys were in and out of that house every night, and I denied myself nothing. At long last, I became a stewardess and traveled all over the world and had innumerable sexual experiences with men of every race and culture imaginable . . . also, I was able to see the clouds close up, which I had always wanted to do. I wanted to reach out and touch them. I still do. Perhaps someday I will . . . But I have never lost the joy of just being alive ever since that morning in 1962. Bobby always tells me I'm the most passionate person he knows, in or out of bed, and he understands why, although I love him, I have to have the freedom to reach out and touch and commune with my fellow human creatures. Because we are all on this earth for only a very short while . . . And I just can't get depressed by that . . .

Scooter Thomas Makes It to the Top of the World

Peter Parnell

Premiere: Eugene O'Neill Playwrights Conference, Waterford, Connecticut, 1977

Setting: Bare stage

Dennis's boyhood friend Scooter has died in a mountain-climbing accident in California. Scooter may have "slipped," as he did with so many things in his life, or he may have died in "a perfect swan dive, right out to the center!" As Dennis prepares to go to the funeral, he relives his memories of friendship with Scooter—idyllic beginnings, strained growing-apart. Here Dennis remembers a scene from their college days, sharing a joint while Dennis told "Scoots" about his grandmother's death.

DENNIS

I was alone in the house with her when it—she died at the kitchen table, while sipping a cup of tea. Lapsang Souchong. Her favorite blend. I haven't been able to look at an old lady or drink a cup of Twinings since. Every time I see someone hunched over asleep on a park bench, in the subway—I have this uncontrollable urge to you know go and—just to make sure they haven't . . . (Laughs.) Isn't that crazy? (Brief pause.) The doctor asked me to help move the body from the kitchen to the bedroom. I mean, she was beginning to turn blue, and. So I grabbed one end, and he the other—she was incredibly heavy, dead-weight by now—and the doctor had a very bad back, and once or twice he practically—and I remember this terrible thought flashed through my mind that he might have a heart attack also, and then I'd be stuck with two of them there on the living room carpet. "Gott in Himmel, dot vass a heavy voman," he said as we tucked her in. "I vill not forget her for ze rest of my life . . ."

[SCOOTER: (Laughs.) Sorry, it's just.]

No. (Beat.) I wanted them to scatter the ashes. To the four winds off Montauk Point. So that parts of her could end up in London, Nantucket, Atlanta, and somewhere past Idaho. She always said she wanted to travel. But they didn't do that. They—placed her in an urn and put her in the earth. Just in case it was what she'd wanted. They hadn't known what she'd—so first they did one thing, and then they did the other. So they wound up doing neither, really. They— I don't know what they did. (Beat.) The dying wasn't the worst part. It was the sense of obligation I couldn't stand. The dying was just, one minute I was talking to her and the next minute I was still talking to her but she was dead. I found that to be, somehow, very, well, somehow, sort of, funny . . .

The Sea Horse

Edward J. Moore

Premiere: West Side Theatre, New York City, 1974
Setting: The Sea Horse, a dockside bar in California

The Sea Horse is run by Gertrude "Dirty Gertie" Blum, a tough, earthy woman who weighs about 200 pounds. It is past closing time on a sopping wet night when Harry Bales pounds on her door. Harry is Gertrude's lover, a big, well-built sailor. He's soaked to the skin, but Gertrude cold-shoulders him. She heard that Harry's boat docked at six P.M., and thinks he has spent the time in between with one of his "broads." Harry swears that he hasn't. He wanted to wait and see Gertrude alone.

Monologue One: Harry tells Gertrude he's "different this trip," and why he has changed. (*Note:* Hank is a local fisherman. He is selling a shrimp boat which Harry is thinking of buying.)

Monologue Two: Gertrude mistrusts Harry's tenderness and tells him he's "full of shit." When he tells her he loves her, she's livid. She thinks all men are like Frank, the man she married when she was eighteen: "You're all bastards. . . . I see what ya do to those simple bitches, you wind 'em around your finger, get 'em to marry ya, then you start usin' 'em, beating 'em, like he did, he beat me, he beat me bad, look at me!!!" The one kind man in Gertrude's past was her father. She tells how she lost him.

1

HARRY

A while back . . . I get relieved off the midwatch, and I come topside out of that stinking hot engine room . . . I open the hatch . . . and I feel strange . . . (*Laughs.*) it's hard to explain . . . I remember the sea was so calm that night, I mean, not a ripple. It doesn't happen too often, the sight is unbelievable if you've never seen it be-

fore . . . can you imagine . . . an ocean, an ocean! As far
as you can see, that looks like a sheet of glass, like you
could walk out on it. The moon up full . . . the sky, not a
cloud . . . just all freckled up, with tiny little diamonds . . . all the years I been steaming I never seen anything like it . . . not like that night . . . well, I walked aft
and I sat down on number four davit . . . I could feel the
screw humming under me . . . *(Makes humming noise.)*
and I sat there, watching our wake cutting through this
glazed sheet of ice . . . And I started thinking of a kid . . . ya
see. I imagined myself sitting there with a little boy next
to me . . . and he was my son . . . and it was so real I could
see him. He had a tiny pair of nonskids on, and khakis, and
a little striped sweater, I remember it was blue. And he
had on one of my old watch caps, it was cut down and
pulled over his ears to keep out the night cold. And he was
sitting on a cushion next to me and I had my arm around
him and I was tellin' him all about the sea and everything . . . you know I must have sat there for over an hour
just talkin' to him . . . and that's when I started making my
plans . . . ya see, I want that kid! And I want my own boat,
that's why it's so important I talk to Hank, so I don't have
to be away from him so long. And I'd like to get an old
beat-up house somewhere, that way it would be cheap, and
I could fix it up. And when he gets old enough, I want him
to go out with me . . . on the boat, and his old man will
teach him how to be the best damn little salt! *(He leans
toward her. Smiles.)* And he'll have a great mom! *(A moment.)* Well . . . what do ya think?!

----------- **2** -----------

GERTRUDE

I was sitting on the pier one day, doing my homework with
some friends . . . waiting for my dad to take me home. I
heard all this shouting coming from the Horse. I saw my
dad throw this man out, a couple of other men came out

too. This man was trying to hit my dad . . . I got up and started running towards him . . . crying "Daddy, Daddy!" My dad turned to me, and the man stabbed him . . . he died . . . I held him, and he died. *(She gets up and crosses, stands near downstage center table. Without emotion.)* You know I couldn't remember my name . . . For the longest time after, I just couldn't think of it, isn't that strange? . . . Daddy has a sister, so I stayed with her . . . they had a terrible time with me . . . I could remember everything that happened that night, all the questions everyone asked me, I would answer everything right . . . but I couldn't remember my name. My teacher had to come up and touch me . . . "Gertrude? Why don't you answer me?" *(A beat, then starts crossing stage left.)* I was okay after a while . . . finished school . . . then I started coming down here again, to watch my ships . . . but I would never go near the Horse . . . Frank . . . he knew what happened . . . but thought it was stupid letting this place rot away . . . When he walked out on me, we owed everyone! I thought I could make a go of it for a while . . . *just* . . . to get things squared away . . . it was bad! *(Sits on bar stool, left.)* Bums wouldn't pay, just walk out . . . rest of 'em were no better either, gave me a bad time . . . one day this swab *grabbed* me . . . I let him have it with a bottle, right in the face! . . . After that I got respect! . . . Money! *(Turns, looks at* HARRY.*)* . . . And I didn't *need* . . . *anyone* . . . *anymore.*

Serenading Louie

Lanford Wilson

Premiere: Circle Repertory Company, New York City, 1976
Setting: North Chicago suburbs
Two married couples, friends since college days, are facing

disillusionment as they creep toward middle age. Gabby and Alex's marriage is crumbling; as Gabby says plaintively, "When you're home you spend every waking hour asleep. Of course you're never home." Eventually she learns that her husband has fallen in love with the seventeen-year-old girl from whom he buys pot.

Carl was the golden boy of their set, a college football legend who became in Alex's phrase, a "millionaire construction developer magnate jock, minored in nineteenth-century Romantic Lit." He has known for a long time that his wife Mary is having an affair with his CPA and, much to his surprise, he has said and done nothing. At first he tells Alex, "I can't galvanize any concern. Nothing anyone says is real, how am I supposed to relate to it?" But finally his feelings flood out in a desperate outcry, "WHAT'S SHE TRYING TO DO? I DON'T KNOW WHAT TO SAY. I DON'T KNOW HOW TO FEEL, ALEX. I DON'T KNOW HOW TO FEEL; I WANT IT BACK—LIKE IT WAS." By the end of the evening, he will murder his wife, his daughter, himself. This speech is addressed to the audience.

(*Note: Serenading Louie* was revised by Lanford Wilson in 1984, and this monologue was altered. It appears here as published in the 1976 edition [Dramatists Play Service]. See "A Conversation with Lanford Wilson" on page 339 for his comments on both versions.)

CARL

I'm not what you'd call particularly religious. I wouldn't want to misrepresent myself. Like everyone else who sits up for the last late show—I jump up to turn off the sermonette before the Rabbi from the Cicero precinct can tell me I'm not saved. I've only been terribly religious—passionately religious once. When I was fourteen. Mom was to have an operation— (*Crosses down center.*) I don't think it was terribly serious but operations scared hell out of me

anyway and I became the most zealously religious little boy
in town. I prayed and cried and bartered with God—I
promised to quit smoking—I'd been smoking already about
three years by then—and to never again masturbate and
never swear if he would spare Mom's life. This was for an
operation like—well, I won't guess—minor, in any case.
And when she recovered—quite easily—I was positive it
was a direct result of my prayers. Dreamed of being can-
onized—we were Baptist, remember—nevertheless. I broke
my promise gradually, so I wouldn't notice or so *God* wouldn't
notice. I didn't actually *buy* a package of cigarettes for over
a year. *(Crosses to fireplace.)* By then I had managed to
convince myself that she would have recovered anyway.
*(Crosses to sofa, gets glass. Crosses to desk, lights ciga-
rette.)* It's very odd. About prayer. I don't just quit because
I've thirty some years invested in it. When the sky suddenly
splits wide open one day and angels sing—you look up and
say—thank God, I kept up my praying. *(Crosses to dining
room. Beat. Not too seriously, but down.)* But I don't think—
a paradox here—I don't think I ever quite forgave Mom
for causing me to make a solemn promise I wasn't strong
enough to keep.

Shivaree

William Mastrosimone

Premiere: Seattle Repertory Theatre, 1983
Setting: Chandler's apartment, the South
Chandler is a hemophiliac. He lives in a carefully padded
white room maintained by his mother, a cabdriver obsessed
with protecting her son from any possible injury. The room
reflects Chandler's interests in astronomy, science, Botti-
celli. On this moonlit night, he has bribed his neighbor
Scagg with the ice-cream allowance he's hoarded all year

to buy him a whore, wine, and candles. The "date" is a
disaster. First, Chandler's mother comes home, then he
cuts himself on the cheap wine's metal cap and needs a
transfusion. The whore takes his year's savings anyway.
("You pay for the time, not the ride, babe.") Chandler is
desolate—until his new neighbor comes out on her balcony.

Shivaree is a bellydancer. She is dressed in traditional
garb—harem pants, coin bra, veils—playing zills (finger
cymbals). Moonstruck, Chandler invites her over "for tea
sometime." Shivaree responds, "Sometime's for dreamers.
I'm up for it right now. . . . But not for tea. You got beer?"
Chandler tells her he has some wine, and she bridges the
gap between balconies with her ironing board. He asks her
about bellydancing.

_____

SHIVAREE

Well, sport, you can dance for dance and get a flat rate, or
you can dance for tips and get what you get. Like after
dancin' at the Hyatt last night, seven sheiks from Dubai
approach me and said they was throwin' some highbrow
shindig up in their suite, would I grace their company with
the dance, salam alekum, the whole bit, and I says, Hell
yeah, and I walks in and it looks like a sheet sale, all kinds
of Mideastern folk jabberin' and the musicians go big for
some Guazi tune and I let loose my stuff. I do veil work
where I put myself in this envelope like a little chrysalis
in a gossamer cocoon listenin' to the beat of my heart, and
then I break out with hip shimmies and shoulder rolls and
belly flutters, mad swirls, Byzantine smiles and half-closed
eyes, and my hands are cobras slitherin' on air, hoods open
and I'm Little Egypt, Theodora, Nefertiti, and Salome, all
in one skin, and these before me was Solomon and Herod
and Caeser and Tutankhamen shoutin' Ayawah, Shivaree,
Ayawah, which roughly means, Go for it, little darlin'—
and this young sheik he's clappin hands to my zills, and he

rolls up this hundred dollar bill and tries to slip it in my
clothes, which makes me stop dancin', which makes the
musicians stop, and there's this hush when I fling that
hundred dollar bill on the rug, and it gets so quiet you
could hear a rat tiptoe on cotton, and I says, Look here,
sucker, I'm a dancer, and I'm moved by Ishtar, Aphrodite,
Venus, Isis, Astarte, and Rickie Lee Jones, all them sultry
ladies of the East. I am the goddess of the feathery foot,
and I only take orders from the moon. Direct. I have turned
dives into temples, cadavers into footstompers, drunks into
believers, and Tuesday night into Sunday mornin' gospel-
time, and I don't take tips. It ain't proper to tip a goddess.
And I starts to leave in a huff, and the young sheik comes
to 'pologize, asks me to Arabia, he would take care o' everything, and then I know he's talkin about the even more
ancient horizontal-dance of the harem girl, and I says, Tell
me, sheik, you got biscuits 'n gravy over there? And he
says, What's biscuits and gravy? And I walked out sayin',
See there, sheik, you're living a deprived life,—And that's
m'story bub, now where's the wine?

Short Eyes

Miguel Piñero

Premiere: New York Shakespeare Festival, New York City,
1974
Setting: Prison dayroom
Most of the men in this prison are black and Hispanic.
Clark Davis, a young, frightened white man, is ushered
onto the cell block. It is Clark's first time in the "joint,"
and an older white convict named Longshoe befriends him
and shows him the ropes. Minutes later, a prison guard
comes to the gate and lays into Clark, calling him
"filth . . . sick fucking degenerate . . . I got a eight-year-

old daughter who was molested by one of those bastards
and I just as well pretend that he was you, Davis, do you
understand that?" Clark is a "short eyes," a child molester.
The attitude in the day room changes immediately to men-
ace and contempt. Longshoe walks up to Clark and spits
in his face. In the rigid hierarchies of prison, the "short
eyes" is the lowest of the low.

Monologue One: Clark's crime has just been revealed.
The men have all left except Juan, who is mopping the
floor. He asks Clark if he really did it.

Monologue Two: Juan has just come back from a visit
with his girlfriend. The men talk about women. A black
con named Ice tells a story about an upstate prison where
he once did time.

----- 1 -----

CLARK

You know, somehow it seems like there's no beginning.
Seems like I've always been in there all my life. I have like
little picture incidents running across my mind . . . I remember being . . . fifteen or sixteen years old (JUAN *crosses
upstage center to clean toilet.*) or something around that
age, waking up to the sound of voices coming from the
living room . . . cartoons on the TV . . . They were watching cartoons on the TV, two little girls. One was my
sister, and her friend . . . And you know how it is when
you get up in the morning, the inevitable hard-on is getting up with you. I draped the sheet around my shoulders . . . Everyone else was sleeping . . . The girl watching TV with my sister . . . yes . . . Hispanic . . . pale-
looking skin . . . She was eight . . . nine . . . ten . . . what
the difference, she was a child . . . She was very pretty—
high cheekbones, flashing black eyes . . . She was wearing
blue short pants . . . tight-fitting . . . A white blouse, or
shirt . . . My sister . . . she left to do number two . . . (JUAN
returns to stage right.) She told her friend wait for me, I'm

going to do number two, and they laughed about it. I sneaked in standing a little behind her . . . She felt me standing there and turned to me . . . She smiled such a pretty little smile . . . I told her I was a vampire and she laughed . . . I spread the sheets apart and she suddenly stopped laughing . . . She just stood there staring at me . . . Shocked? surprised? intrigued? Don't know . . . don't know . . . She just stood and stared . . . (JUAN *crosses to downstage left.*) I came closer like a vampire . . . She started backing away . . . ran toward the door . . . stopped, looked at me again. Never at my face . . . my body . . . I couldn't really tell whether or not the look on her face was one of fear . . . but I'll never forget that look. (BROWN *crosses on catwalk from left to right with a banana. Stands at right.*)

I was really scared that she'd tell her parents. Weeks passed without confrontation . . . and I was feeling less and less afraid . . . But that's not my thing, showing myself naked to little girls in schoolyards. (JUAN *crosses to downstage right corner and begins to mop from downstage right to downstage left.*) One time . . . no, it was the first time . . . the very first time. I was alone watching TV . . . Was I in school or out . . . And there was this little Puerto Rican girl from next door . . . Her father was the new janitor . . . I had seen her before . . . many times . . . sliding down the banister . . . Always her panties looked dirty . . . She was . . . oh, why do I always try to make their age higher than it really was . . . even to myself. She was young, much too young . . . Why did she come there? For who? Hundred questions. Not one small answer . . . not even a lie flickers across my brain.

[OFFSTAGE VOICE: All right, listen up. The following inmates report for sanitation duty: Smalls, Gary; Medena, James; Pfeifer, Willis; Martinez, Raul. Report to C.O. grounds for sanitation duty.]

How did I get to the bathroom with her? Don't know. I was standing there with her, I was combing her hair. I was combing her hair. Her curly reddish hair . . . (JUAN *crosses*

upstage right, starts to mop upstage right to upstage left.)
I was naked . . . naked . . . except for these flowerprinted
cotton underwears . . . No slippers, barefooted . . . Suddenly I get this feeling over me . . . like a flash fever . . .
and I'm hard . . . I placed my hands on her small shoulders . . . and pressed her hand and placed it on my penis
. . . Did she know what to do? Or did I coerce her? I pulled
down my drawers . . . But then I felt too naked, so I put
them back on . . . My eyes were closed . . . but I felt as
if there was this giant eye off in space staring at me . . . *(JUAN
stops upstage left and listens to CLARK, who is unaware
JUAN is in back of him.)*

I opened them and saw her staring at me in the cabinet
mirror. I pulled her back away from the view of the mirror . . . My hands up her dress, feeling her under-devel-
oped body . . . I . . . I . . . I began pulling her underwear
down on the bowl . . . She resisted . . . slightly, just a moment . . . I sat on the bowl . . . She turned and threw her
arms around my neck and kissed me on the lips . . . She
gave a small nervous giggle . . . I couldn't look at her . . . I
closed my eyes . . . turned her body . . . to face away from
me . . . I lubricated myself . . . and . . . I hear a scream,
my own . . . there was a spot of blood on my drawers . . . I
took them off right then and there . . . ripped them up and
flushed them down the toilet . . . She had dressed herself
up and asked me if we could do it again tomorrow . . . and
was I her boyfriend now . . . I said yes, yes . . . *(JUAN goes
to center stage, starts mopping center stage right to stage
left. BROWN exits from catwalk above right.)* I couldn't sit
still that whole morning, I just couldn't relax. I dressed and
took a walk . . . Next thing I know I was running—out of
breath . . . I had run over twenty blocks . . . twenty blocks
blind . . . without knowing . . . I was running . . . Juan,
was it my conscious or subconscious that my rest stop was
a children's playground . . . Coincidence perhaps . . . But
why did I run in that direction, no, better still, why did I
start walking in that direction . . . Coincidence? Why didn't

my breath give out elsewhere . . . Coincidence? (JUAN *moves to downstage left,* CLARK *moves to upstage center and sits on window ledge.*) I sat on the park bench and watched the little girls swing . . . slide . . . run . . . jump rope . . . Fat . . . skinny . . . black . . . white . . . Chinese . . . I sat there until the next morning . . . The next day I went home and met the little Puerto Rican girl again . . . Almost three times a week . . . The rest of the time I would be in the playground or in the children's section of the movies . . . But you know something?

[Er, er . . . (CLARK *moves toward* JUAN, *who is in downstage left corner.*)

JUAN: Juan.

CLARK: Yes, Juan . . . Juan the listener . . . the compassionate]

. . . you know something, Juan . . . I soon became . . . became . . . what? A pro? A professional degenerate? (*The sound of garbage cans banging together is heard offstage.*) I don't know if you can call it a second insight on children. But . . . I would go to the park . . . and sit there for hours and talk with a little girl and know if I would do it or not with her . . . Just a few words was all I needed . . . Talk stupid things they consider grown-up talk . . . Soon my hand would hold hers, then I would caress her face . . . Next her thighs . . . under their dress . . . I never took any of them home or drove away with them in my car . . . I always told them to meet me in the very same building they lived in . . .

[OFFSTAGE VOICE: On the sanitation gate. (*Sound of gate opening.*)]

On the roof or their basements under the stairs . . . Sometimes in their own home if the parents were out . . . The easiest ones were the Puerto Ricans and the black girls . . . Little white ones would masturbate you right there in the park for a dollar or a quarter . . . depending on how much emphasis their parents put in their heads on making money . . . I felt ashamed at first . . . But then I would rehearse at nights what to do the next time . . . planning . . . I (JUAN *starts moving slowly from downstage left to upstage left.*) couldn't help myself . . . I couldn't help myself . . . Something drove me to it . . . I thought of killing myself . . . but I just couldn't go through with it . . . I don't really wanna die . . . I wanted to stop, really I did . . . I just didn't know how. I thought maybe I was crazy . . . but I read all types of psychology books . . . I heard or read somewhere that crazy people can't distinguish right from wrong . . . Yet I can . . . I know what's right and I know what I'm doing is wrong, yet I can't stop myself . . .

——— 2 ———

ICE

Dig this . . . I was in my cell . . . like this is where they have all those French Canadian bigots. Let me tell you I was raised in Georgia for a while, but like I swear to God I never seen anybody as racist as a French Canadian. Anyway, like I was in my cell about nine, dig. I was reading this short-heist book. Brother man, this was a smoker. S . . M . . . O . . . K . . E . . . R. Just after a few pages . . . I had to put down the damn book because my Johnson Ronson was ripping through my cheap underwears. So I put the book down . . . jumped out my bed . . . stick the mirrors out the cell . . . to see if anybody was coming down the gallery . . . Coast clear . . . Like upstate you know ain't like down here. You ain't got no cellies, Cupcakes . . . you be by yourself. So I would really stretch out in doing up my wood . . . I got this picture of Jane Fonda. 'Cause you can't have nothing on the walls. She's got this black silk satin bikini. Man, I could almost touch those fine white tits of hers. And that cute round butt sticking out and all. Dig. I strip naked . . . and started rolling. She was looking good on my mind.

[OMAR: Why a white girl?]

ICE: 'Cause, sucker, we weren't allow to have short-

heist pictures . . . and how many black girls have taken
short-heist flicks.

JUAN: Hundreds of them. And hundreds of Puerto Rican
girls too.

ICE: Yeah, well . . . I guess I wanted a white girl.

EL RAHEEM: You wanted a girl so bad . . . made him
no different if it was just imagination.

ICE: Hey, man, you guys gonna let me tell this thing
or what?

OMAR: Ain't nobody stopping you. Run it. Juan's listenin'.]

Yeah, she was sure looking good on my mind . . .
Jesus . . . So I started calling out her name real softly . . .
"Jane . . . Jane . . . Janeeee . . . oooo Janeee baby. Oooooo,
Janneeee baby . . ." (LONGSHOE *shows short-heist book to*
ICE. *Inmates gather around table.*)

[OMAR: Goddamn! Will you look at the gash on that girl.
That's pure polyunsaturated pussy.]

Wesson Oil never had it so good. "Oh, Jane baby. Oh, Jane
mama. Ooooo Jane. Come here, get a part of some reallll
downnnn home gut-stomped black buck fucking . . ." Man,
I was really running. Wow. She was in front of me. Dancing, spreading her legs wider and wider . . . Till I could
see her throatmmm. Them white thighs crushing me to
death. Wiggling and crawling on the floor. Calling her name
out, "Janneee babyyyyy . . . ooooo, Janeee baby . . . This
is black power. Git honey, git honey, git git
git . . . ununhahahaha . . . mmmmm," calling her name
out faster, a little bit louder. A little bit faster, a little bit
louder . . . And I'm whipping my Johnson to the
bone . . . Soon everybody on the tier knew I was working
out cause soon everybody's voices is with me. And we're
all tryin' to get this one last big nut together. . . . "Git it,
git it. Janneeee . . . baby . . . Get it, get it, get it, get it,
get it, get it, get it." I scream, my knees buckle . . . and
I'm kneeling there, beat as a son of a bitch, because that's
the way I felt, beat as a son of a bitch. I really burnt Jane

that night. You know if I ever meet that broad, Jane Fonda . . . (BROWN *and* CLARK *appear at gate.*)

[BROWN: On the gate . . . (CLARK *enters,* BROWN *closes gate,* BROWN *exits.*)]

I'm going to ask her if she ever felt a strange sensation that night. Anyway, brother man . . . I turn my head and bang. (CLARK *walks over to* JUAN.)

[CLARK: Can I see you, please. I need to talk to you, please.

JUAN: Later.

CLARK: Please.

ICE: The man said later. You're interrupting me . . . creep.

PACO: Go to your place, maricón. You know . . . go on, man, bang, then what happened.

ICE: Oh yeah, bang.]

I happened to look up and there's these two redneck . . . peckerwood big-foot country honkies . . . looking and grinning at me . . . I don't know how they was there cause I had my eyes close all the time I was gitting my rocks off, better for the imagination. Helps the concentration, dig. They weren't saying a word, just standing there grinning . . . grinning these two big grins . . . these two real big grins on the faces that reach from one ear to the other. So I started grinning back. Grinning that old nigger grin we give to Charlie . . . We stood there grinning at each other for about five minutes . . . them grinning at my Johnson . . . me grinning at them grinning at my Johnson . . . just grinning . . . Hold it, no really, just grinning. It's weird. Freaky kinda thing. Somebody stops to watch you masturbate, then stands there grinning at you. I mean, like, what can you say. Really, what can you say to them? To anybody. All of a sudden the biggest one with the biggest grin gives out a groan. "Hey, Harry, this fucking face has been pulling his pecker on a white woman." So Harry comes over and said very intelligently, "Da . . . da . . . this ain't no white woman, Joey. I mean, no real white woman. She's a Communist, Joey, she really is, da . . . da . . . she's white trash, Joey. Take my word for it, she's white trash. The *Daily News* said so." So Joey runs this down on Harry: "Harry, I know what she is . . . I read the papers, too, you know. But she is a white woman. And this nigger has been thinking about . . . having screwed her. Now you know that's un-American. Harry, open up the dead lock." So Harry runs to open up the dead lock. Now Joey got the nigger knocker wrapped around his hand real tight, dig. I know he about to correct me on some honky rules. I know what's about to jump off . . . I'm in my cell . . . And I'm cool . . . That's my name . . . Ice . . . The lames roll in front of my cell and I go into my Antarctic frigid position . . . you can see the frost all over my cell. But before Harry could open the dead lock . . . I told him, "Joey baby" . . . now, I'm locking up on the third tier . . . I said, "Joey baby . . . I sure hope you can fly." He said, "What you talking about, nigger boy?" I said, "Fly like a bird. You know F-L-Y. 'Cause once you open this gate . . . I ain't about to let you whip me with that stick." I stood up on my toes. Pointed over the rail and said, "Both of us are going, Joey." He yelled out, "Harry, don't up the gate. This nigger crazy." Now I'm a crazy nigger 'cause I wouldn't let them come in here and kick me in my ass.

Sister Mary Ignatius Explains It All for You

Christopher Durang

Premiere: Ensemble Studio Theatre, New York City, 1979
Setting: Blank stage with lectern and easel

Sister Mary Ignatius is the nun to end all nuns. The play begins with a lengthy lecture on Catholic doctrine, delivered by Sister Mary with the support of her seven-year-old pupil Thomas.

Monologue One: Sister Mary explains it all for the audience. (*Note:* She has many similar monologues throughout the play.)

Monologue Two: Sister Mary's lecture is interrupted by four people dressed as the Blessed Mother, St. Joseph, and two humps of a camel. They introduce themselves as four students from her fifth grade class of 1959. They have come to perform a Christmas pageant written by Sister Mary's prize student. They do so, and afterward they tell Sister Mary about their lives since her tutelage. Philomena is an unwed mother, Aloysius is an alcoholic wife-beater, Gary is gay, and Diane has had two abortions. She tells Sister Mary that they have come here today to embarrass her. When Sister Mary asks why, Diane tells her simply, "Because I believed you. I believed how you said the world worked, and that God loved us, and the story of the Good Shepherd and the lost sheep; and I don't think you should lie to people." She continues.

_____ 1 _____

SISTER

(*Crossing herself.*) In the name of the Father, and of the Son, and of the Holy Ghost, Amen. (*Shows the next drawing on the easel, which is a neat if childlike picture of the planet earth, the sun, and moon.*) First there is the earth. Near the earth is the sun, and also nearby is the moon. (*Goes to next picture which, split in three, shows the gates of heaven amid clouds, some sort of murky area of paths, or some other image that might suggest waiting, wandering, and a third area of people burning up in flames, with little devils with little pitchforks, poking them.*) Outside the universe, where we go after death, is heaven, hell, and purgatory. Heaven is where we live in eternal bliss with our Lord Jesus Christ. (*Bows her head.*) Hell is where we are eternally deprived of the presence of our Lord Jesus Christ *(Bows her head.)*, and are thus miserable. This is the greatest agony of hell, but there are also unspeakable physical torments, which we shall nonetheless speak of later. Purgatory is the middle area where we go after death to suffer if we have not been perfect in our lives and are thus not ready for heaven, or if we have not received the sacraments and made a good confession to a priest right before our death. Purgatory, depending on our sins, can go on for a very, *very* long time and is fairly unpleasant. Though we do not yet know whether there is any physical torment in purgatory, we do know that there is much psychological torment because we are being delayed from being in the presence of our Lord Jesus Christ. *(Bows her head.)* For those non-Catholics present, I bow my head to show respect for our Savior when I say His Name. Our Lord Jesus Christ. *(Bows head.)* Our Lord Jesus Christ. *(Bows head.)* Our Lord Jesus Christ. *(Bows head.)* You can expect to be in purgatory for anywhere from three hundred years to seven hundred billion years. This may sound like forever, but don't forget in terms of eternity seven hundred billion years does come to an end. All things come to an end except our Lord Jesus Christ. *(Bows head. Points to the drawing again, reviewing her point.)* Heaven, hell, purgatory. *(Smiles. Goes to the next drawing which, like that of purgatory, is of a murky area, perhaps with a prisonlike fence, and which has unhappy babylike creatures floating about in it.)* There is also limbo, which is where unbaptized babies were sent for eternity before the Ecumenical Council and Pope John XXIII. The unbaptized babies sent to limbo never leave limbo and so never get to heaven. *Now* unbaptized babies are sent straight to purgatory where, presumably, someone baptizes them and then they are sent on to heaven. The unbaptized babies who died before the Ecumenical Council, however, remain in limbo and will never be admitted to heaven. Limbo is not all that unpleasant, it's just that it isn't heaven and you never leave there. I want to be very

clear about the Immaculate Conception. It does not mean
that the Blessed Mother gave birth to Christ without the
prior unpleasantness of physical intimacy. That is true but
it is not called the Immaculate Conception; that is called
the Virgin Birth. The Immaculate Conception means that
the Blessed Mother was herself born without original sin.
Everyone makes this error, it makes me lose my patience.
That Mary's conception was immaculate is an infallible
statement. A lot of fault-finding non-Catholics run around
saying that Catholics believe that the Pope is infallible
whenever he speaks. This is untrue. The Pope is infallible
only on certain occasions, when he speaks "ex cathedra,"
which is Latin for "out of the cathedral." When he speaks
ex cathedra, we must accept what he says at that moment
as dogma, or risk hell fire; or, now that things are becoming
more liberal, many, many years in purgatory. I would now
like a glass of water.

2

DIANE

When I was sixteen, my mother got breast cancer, which
spread. I prayed to God to let her suffering be small, but
her suffering seemed to me quite extreme. She was in bad
pain for half a year, and then terrible pain for much of a
full year. The ulcerations on her body were horrifying to
her and to me. Her last few weeks she slipped into a semi-
conscious state, which allowed her, unfortunately, to wake
up for a few minutes at a time and to have a full awareness
of her pain and her fear of death. She was able to recognize
me, and she would try to cry, but she was unable to; and
to speak, but she was unable to. I think she wanted me to
get her new doctors; she never really accepted that her
disease was going to kill her, and she thought in her panic
that her doctors must be incompetent and that new ones
could magically cure her. Then, thank goodness, she went
into a full coma. A nurse who I knew to be Catholic assured

me that everything would be done to keep her alive—a dubious comfort. Happily, the doctor was not Catholic, or if he was, not doctrinaire, and they didn't use extraordinary means to keep her alive; and she finally died after several more weeks in her coma. Now there are, I'm sure, far worse deaths—terrible burnings, tortures, plague, pestilence, famine; Christ on the cross even, as Sister likes to say. But I thought my mother's death was bad enough, and I got confused as to why I had been praying and to whom. I mean, if prayer was really this sort of button you pressed—admit you need the Lord, then He stops your suffering—then why didn't it always work? Or ever work? And when it worked, so-called, and our prayers were supposedly answered, wasn't it as likely to be chance as God? God always answers our prayers, you said, He just sometimes says no. But why would He say no to stopping my mother's suffering? I wasn't even asking that she live, just that He end her suffering. And it can't be that He was letting her suffer because she'd been bad, because she hadn't been bad and besides suffering doesn't seem to work that way, considering the suffering of children who've obviously done nothing wrong. So why was He letting her suffer? Spite? Was the Lord God actually malicious? That seemed possible, but farfetched. Maybe He had no control over it, maybe He wasn't omnipotent as you taught us He was. Maybe He created the world sort of by accident by belching one morning or getting the hiccups, and maybe He had no idea how the whole thing worked. In which case, He wouldn't be malicious, just useless. Or, of course, more likely than that, He didn't exist at all, the universe was hiccupped or belched into existence all on its own, and my mother's suffering just existed like rain or wind or humidity. I became angry at myself, and by extension at you, for ever having expected anything beyond randomness from the world. And while I was thinking these things, the day that my mother died, I was raped. Now I know that's really too much, one really loses all sympathy for me because I sound like I'm making it up or something. But bad things sometimes happen all at once, and this particular day on my return from the hospital I was raped by some maniac who broke into the house. He had a knife and cut me up some. Anyway, I don't really want to go on about the experience, but I got very depressed for about five years. Somehow the utter randomness of things—my mother's suffering, my attack by a lunatic who was either born a lunatic or made one by cruel parents or perhaps by an imbalance of hormones or whatever, etc. etc.—*this randomness seemed intolerable*. I found I grew to hate you, Sister, for making me once expect everything to be ordered and to make sense. My psychiatrist said he thought my hatred of you was obsessive, that I just was looking for someone to blame. Then he seduced me, and he was the father of my second abortion.

[SISTER: I think she's making all this up.]

He said I seduced him. And maybe that's so. But he could be lying just to make himself feel better. (*To* SISTER) And of course your idea that I should have had this baby, either baby, is preposterous. Have you any idea what a terrible mother I'd be? I'm a nervous wreck.

[SISTER: God would have given you the strength.]

I suppose it is childish to look for blame, part of the randomness of things is that there is no one to blame; but basically I think everything is your fault, Sister.

Small Craft Warnings
Tennessee Williams

Premiere: Truck & Warehouse Theatre, New York City, 1972

Setting: Monk's Place, a beachfront bar on the Southern California coast

Monk's Place is the kind of bar where certain locals drink

night after night, bottle after bottle. On this foggy night, the regular barflies are Doc, who lost his medical license for drinking too much, but practices illegally; Violet, a tentative, hazy-eyed nymphomaniac; Bill McCorkle, a professional stud; and Bill's current meal ticket, Leona Dawson.

Leona is an itinerant hairdresser. She enters the bar "like a small bull making his charge into the ring. . . . On her head of dyed corkscrew curls is a sailor's hat which she occasionally whips off her head to slap something with— the bar, a tabletop, somebody's back—to emphasize a point." Today was the "death-day" anniversary of her cherished young brother, who died of pernicious anemia. Leona has spent the day in the mobile home she shares with Bill, cooking a fancy "memorial dinner," knocking back whisky, and crying her her eyes out. She is angry enough at Bill for sneaking out of the trailer without a word, but her fury explodes when she finds out that Violet is groping him under the table. She busts up the bar, kicks Bill out, and resolves to leave town before morning.

Monologue One: Leona tells Bill why she's leaving.

Monologue Two: Two strangers have entered the bar. Quentin is a homosexual screenwriter, so jaded he only gets sexual pleasure from "straight trade." He has picked up a young cyclist named Bobby, but loses all interest when he finds out that this clean-cut, All-American boy is already gay. Bobby is riding his bike from Iowa to Mexico. He has just seen the ocean for the first time in his life and is full of the joy of the road. His youthful innocence reminds Leona of her angelic brother. A self-proclaimed "faggot's moll," she asks Bobby to travel with her. Bobby talks about Quentin.

———— 1 ————

LEONA

When I pass out I wake up in a chair or on the floor, oh, no, the floor was good enough for me in your opinion, and

sometimes you stepped on me even, yeah, like I was a rug
or a bug, because your nature is selfish. You think because
you've lived off one woman after another woman after eight
or ten women you're something superior, special. Well,
you're special but not superior, baby. I'm going to worry
about you after I've gone and I'm sure as hell leaving tonight, fog or no fog on the highway, but I'll worry about
you because you refuse to grow up and that's a mistake that
you make, because you can only refuse to grow up for a
limited period in your lifetime and get by with it . . . I
loved you! . . . I'm not going to cry. It's only being so tired
that makes me cry.

  [VIOLET *(Starts weeping for her.)* Bill, get up and tell
    Leona good-bye. She's a lonely girl without a soul in
    the world.]

I've got the world in the world, and McCorkle don't have
to make the effort to get himself or any part of him up, it's
easier to stay down. And as for being lonely, listen, ducks,
that applies to every mother's son and daughter of us alive,
we were given warning of that before we were born almost,
and yet . . . When I come to a new place, it takes me two
or three weeks, that's all it takes me, to find somebody to
live with in my home on wheels and to find a night spot to
hang out in. Those first two or three weeks are rough,
sometimes I wish I'd stayed where I was before, but I know
from experience that I'll find somebody and locate a night
spot to booze in, and get acquainted with . . . friends . . .
*(The light has focused on her. She moves downstage with
her hands in her pockets, her face and voice very grave as
if she were less confident that things will be as she says.)*
And then, all at once, something wonderful happens. All
the past disappointments in people I left behind me, just
disappear, evaporate from my mind, and I just remember
the good things, such as their sleeping faces, and . . . Life!
Life! I never just said, "Oh, well," I've always said "Life!"
to life, like a song to God, too, because I've lived in my
lifetime and not been afraid of . . . changes . . . *(She goes*

back to the bar.) . . . However, y'see, I've got this pride in my nature. When I live with a person I love and care for in my life, I expect his respect, and when I see I've lost it, I GO, GO! . . . So a home on wheels is the only right home for me.

———— 2 ————

BOBBY

In Goldenfield, Iowa, there was a man like that, ran a flower shop with a back room, decorated Chinese, with incense and naked pictures, which he invited boys into. I heard about it. Well, things like that aren't tolerated for long in towns like Goldenfield. There's suspicion and talk and then public outrage and action, and he had to leave so quick he didn't clear out the shop. *(The bar lights have faded out, and the special spot illuminates* BOBBY.*)* A bunch of us entered one night. The drying-up flowers rattled in the wind and the wind chimes tinkled and the . . . naked pictures were just . . . pathetic, y'know. Except for a sketch of Michelangelo's *David.* I don't think anyone noticed me snatch it off the wall and stuff it into my pocket. Dreams . . . images . . . nights . . . On the plains of Nebraska I passed a night with a group of runaway kids my age and it got cold after sunset. A lovely wild young girl invited me under a blanket with just a smile, and then a boy, me between, and both of them kept saying "love," one of 'em in one ear and one in the other, till I didn't know which was which "love" in which ear or which . . . touch . . . The plain was high and the night air . . . exhilarating and the touches not heavy . . . The man with the hangup has set my bike by the door. *(Extends his hand to* LEONA. *The bar is relighted.)* It's been a pleasure to meet a lady like you. Oh, I've got a lot of new adventures, experiences, to think over alone on my speed iron. I think I'll drive all night, I don't feel tired. *(*BOBBY *smiles as he opens the door and nods good-bye to Monk's Place.)*

Soap Opera
Ralph Pape

Premiere: Commissioned by Actors Theatre of Louisville, 1982

Setting: Bare stage

Three actors sit on stools and tell their story to the audience in alternating monologues. The "soap opera" of the title is a romantic triangle which finally explodes into violence. These two monologues open the play.

Monologue One: Ralph Pape writes, "When Lucy talks, it's as if she were telling her story to a roomful of girlfriends."

Monologue Two: Ralph Pape writes, "Johnny treats the audience one-on-one, as if telling his story to a psychiatrist or a confessor."

1

LUCY

I can have just about any man I want these days. It's great. But for a long time, I used to think of myself as being unattractive and couldn't get many men at all. I hated that period in my life, and I hated myself too. Until I met this guy, Johnny. Johnny really dug me. He told me he used to think of himself as being unattractive to women, or something like that, and for a long time went around hating himself also. But he was *so* attracted to me that he just threw all his inhibitions right out the window. He pursued me constantly until I agreed to go out with him—he worshipped me—he adored me. I couldn't *believe* that a man was paying this much attention to me. You have to understand: I was, like, incredibly shy. (*Beat. She smiles at this memory of herself.*) But Johnny changed all that. He would say things to me, things that an intelligent person would consider sentimental or corny, about my eyes, my lips, my hair. And at first I thought: oh come on, *Jesus*— (*Beat.*

Very thoughtful.) But I'll tell you something: when someone really believes what he's saying, you believe it, too.
When someone tells you, over and over, that he loves you,
that you're the most precious thing in his whole life, you
lay awake at night beside him, crying, trying to find within
yourself the qualities that he seems able to see so clearly,
and at last you see them, too. And it's like: *well, of course.*
(Beat.) And you know that you can inspire love in a man.
(Beat.) Or he would say things to me that at first embarrassed me like crazy. Him too, I could tell. But Johnny was
just so head over heels in love that embarrassment flew
right out the window, and the next thing I know, we're in
this dark restaurant. With wine and candlelight. With beautiful thick red napkins spread over our laps. Holding hands
under the table. And Johnny's leaning over the flame and
whispering things to me about . . . my cunt. And he's saying the word: cunt. And I just couldn't *believe* it. He's
telling me what he loves about it, how it feels and how it
tastes. *(Beat.)* O.K., but you want to know something?
When a man talks like that to you, I don't care what your
upbringing is, how shocked you are at first, when you can
see in his eyes that he really means it, that he's not playing
a game, and not trying to be this supercool stud, you just
nearly die with the desire that pours all through you. You
just think about him wanting you so much that he can *say*
such things to you, and *his* desire for you becomes *your*
desire for him. *(Beat.)* Well, by the time the waiter came
with our food, I had to keep my head down and bite my
lip, because I was trembling so hard. I could feel myself
wanting to burst free for the first time in my life, and
Johnny, that bastard, just squeezed my hand under the
table and smiled. He knew, he knew. *(Beat.)* Oh let me
tell you, that was some night. From that night on, the sex
between us, which had been good, became *incredible.* Johnny
couldn't believe that I had ever considered myself unattractive to men, and for the first time in my life, I couldn't
either. And right about then, other guys started to pay

attention to me at the office, the same guys who would just shove papers in my tray and tell me to take them to so and so. At first I was baffled, but then I took a good look at myself in the mirror in the ladies' room, and I thought: well, Lucy . . . *of course.* Because the face that looked back at me knew two things so clearly that any guy who looked into it would also know it right away and would have to deal with it. And the two things were, one: that I could inspire love in a man, and two: that I could drive that same man mad with physical desire. *(Beat.)* It never ceases to amaze me how when you truly see yourself in a certain way, others see you that way too.

2

JOHNNY

The thing about Lucy was how she could make me feel like I could say or do anything to her when we were alone. She could take the whole world and just put it away somewhere, on the other side of the door, and the world didn't matter anymore. The world could not touch us or tell us what to do or make us feel guilty about what we said or what we did. It was just us, only us. And that suited me fine, because what had the world ever done for me but bring me sorrow and pain? I had accepted, long ago, the truth which came with the pain—which are two words for the same thing, as I see it—and this made me different from other people right off, who think that *pain* is one thing and *the truth* another. That's their problem and not mine, although I'm sure they don't see it that way. Most people don't really *see* things at all, because most people are so *stupid* that it never dawns on them what life really is: just a word for something which we are all part of, which doesn't care that *we* are a part of *it;* which doesn't care about our dreams, or give two shits about our chances for finding beauty or happiness. *(Beat.)* When I was ten years old, I stood in my pajamas in the grass, about an hour before sunrise, and watched our house go up in flames. Through the smoke, the sky was so lovely I could never describe it, filled with soft stars fading into the blue. I thought: it's like another world. Which is a pretty obvious and stupid way of putting it, but I was in shock so they told me, so I guess it was not so stupid after all. Even after the funeral, off by myself at night, all I could think was how impossible the heavens looked, too beautiful to be true, all lit up and quiet and so endless. . . . I wanted to die, in that moment of silence, not like my brother and sisters in the fire, but peacefully, sweetly. I wanted to turn into a vapor, into a mist, and be pulled upward, stretched so thin that there would be nothing left of me, just swirling dust, soft and bright. . . . After a while, I could hear the screaming again, but far away, where it couldn't hurt me. I could hear the roaring of the water in the hoses: it was soothing. It made me smile and feel sleepy. I stood still and closed my eyes and floated away, off the face of this earth. There was a cooler and cooler breeze the higher I got, higher than the birds and the planets, and with my eyes shut tight, I saw it all again, from a heavenly distance: my mother, naked, her body black with soot, held back by neighbors, clawing and digging her fingers into the air like it was a living thing she could rip apart; my father, naked, his arms wrapped around himself, the nails of his fingers digging into the flesh of his sides, his legs rooted to the earth like a tree. . . . The way he bellowed before he fell to his knees and pitched forward into the earth . . . into the flowers my mother had planted years before. (*Beat.*) The thing about Lucy, the thing that made me want to fuck her endlessly, that made me want to enter her as no man has ever entered a woman before was how she could take the whole world and just put it away somewhere, and the world didn't matter anymore. And how, with every move our bodies made together in the night, it was only us, it was only us, Lucy and Johnny, Lucy and Johnny, only us.

A Soldier's Play

Charles Fuller

Premiere: Negro Ensemble Company, New York City, 1981
Setting: Fort Neal, Louisiana, 1944

A black drill sergeant has been murdered at Fort Neal, where a platoon of black soldiers is waiting to go overseas to fight in World War II. Suspicion immediately falls upon two white officers, and when the captain assigned by the Army to investigate the murder turns out to be a black man, the case seems cut-and-dried. But as Captain Davenport interviews the soldiers about their murdered sergeant, the story becomes more complex.

Sergeant Waters, whom we see in flashbacks, was a difficult man with a pathological loathing for "geechies . . . singin', clownin', yas-sah-bossin' Niggahs." He singled out C.J. Memphis, a gentle, guitar-strumming country boy, as the object of his hatred, ultimately driving him to suicide. Finally, it was Sergeant Waters's own brand of self-hating racism that led to his murder—by a fellow black. This flashback portrayal of Sergeant Waters occurs when Captain Davenport interviews one of the soldiers, Private Wilkie, about the sergeant's reaction to C.J. Memphis.

WATERS

He's the kinda' boy seems innocent, Wilkie. Got everybody around the post thinking he's a strong, black buck! Hits home runs—white boys envy his strength—his speed, the power in his swing. Then this colored champion lets those same white boys call him "Shine"—or "Sambo" at the Officers' Club. They laugh at his blues songs, and he just smiles—can't talk, barely read or write his own name—and don't care! He'll tell you they like him—or that colored folks ain't supposed to have but so much sense. (*Intense.*) Do you know the damage one ignorant *Negro* can do? (*Remembering,* WATERS *crosses limbo area.*) We were in France during the First War, Wilkie. We had won decorations, but the white boys had told all the French gals we had tails. And they found this ignorant colored soldier. Paid him to tie a tail to his ass and parade around naked making monkey sounds. *(Shakes his head.)* They sat him on a big round table in the Café Napoleon, put a reed in his hand, a crown on his head, a blanket on his shoulders and made him eat bananas in front of them Frenchies. And ohhh, the white boys danced that night—passed out leaflets with that boy's picture on them—called him "Moonshine, King of the Monkeys." And when we slit his throat, you know that fool asked us what he had done wrong? *(Pause.)* My daddy told me, we got to turn our backs on his kind, Wilkie. Close our ranks to the chittlin's, the collard greens—the corn-bread style. We are men—soldiers, and I don't intend to have our race cheated out of its place of honor and respect in *this* war because of fools like C.J.! You watch everything he does— *Everything!*

Still Life

Emily Mann

Premiere: American Place Theatre, New York City, 1981
Setting: The stage is set up as a panel or conference room: a long table with ashtrays and water glasses, a screen for projected slides

Mann describes her play as a documentary "about three people the author met in Minnesota. . . . The rhythms are real people's speech, but often in the playing may have the sense of improvisation as with the best jazz musicians, the monologues sometimes sounding like extended riffs."

There are three characters. Mark is a Vietnam vet, Cheryl is his wife, and Nadine is his lover. Though the characters' speeches are often intercut, there is no interaction among them: no "scenes." Each tells the audience his or her story.

Monologue One: Mark is "twenty-eight, ex-Marine, Vietnam vet, husband, artist, lover, father." He is haunted by his memories of the war, including an incident in which his best buddy R.J. shot a wounded woman in the face. Mark's own words and Nadine and Cheryl's stories about him form a portrait of a complex, disturbed, and disturbing man, capable of incredible gentleness and twisted cruelty.

Monologue Two: Cheryl is Mark's wife and the mother of his son. She is six months pregnant, frightened, and stuck. At various times Mark has beaten her badly and used her image for a series of artworks about mutilation. For all Cheryl's victimization, she is a woman who was strong enough to deliver her own baby and shrug it off as "no big deal."

Monologue Three: Nadine is "forty-three years old, artist, mother of three, divorcée, a woman with many jobs and many lives." She and her ex-husband, both alcoholics, battered each other. About herself, she says, "I guess I could possibly be the most vulnerable person of all of us. But I've also built up all these other devices which will overrule that."

——————— 1 ———————

MARK

I don't know. I just don't know. Sometimes I look at a news story, I look at something someone goes to prison for here, I think about it. There's no difference. It's just a different place. This country had all these rules and regulations and then all of a sudden they removed these things. Then you come back and try to make your life in that society where you had to deal with them. You find that if you violate them, which I found, you go to jail, which I did. I sit back here sometimes and watch the news, watch my mother, watch my father. My parents watch the news and say: "Oh my God, somebody did that! Somebody went in there . . . and started shooting . . . and killed all those people. They ought to execute him." I look at them. I want to say, "Hell, what the fuck, why didn't you ever listen . . . you want to hear what I did?" It's real confusion. I'm guilty and I'm not guilty. I still want to tell my folks. I need to tell them what I did.

[CHERYL: There was a time when a man would confess to me "I'm a jerk" at a private moment and I would smile sweetly and try to comfort him. Now I believe him.]

I . . . I killed three children, a mother and father in cold blood. *(Crying.)*

[CHERYL: Don't.]

I killed three children, a mother and father . . . *(Long pause.)*

[NADINE: Mark.]

I killed them with a pistol in front of a lot of people. I demanded something from the parents and then systematically destroyed them. And that's . . . that's the heaviest part of what I'm carrying around. You know about it now, a few other people know about it, my wife knows about it, Nadine knows about it, and nobody else knows about it. For the rest of my life . . . I have a son . . . He's going to die for what I've done. This is what I'm carrying around; that's what this logic is about with my children. A friend hit a booby-trap. And these people knew about it. I knew they knew. I knew that they were working with the VC infrastructure. I demanded that they tell me. They wouldn't say anything. I just wanted them to confess before I killed them. And they wouldn't. So I killed their children and then I killed them. I was angry. I was angry with all the power I had. I couldn't beat them. They beat me. *(Crying.)* I lost friends in my unit . . . I did wrong. People in the unit watched me kill them. Some of them tried to stop me. I don't know. I can't . . . oh, God . . . a certain amount of stink went all the way back to the rear. I almost got into a certain amount of trouble. It was all rationalized, that there was a logic behind it. But they knew. And everybody who knew had a part in it. There was enough evidence, but it

wasn't a very good image to put out in terms of . . . the
Marines overseas, so nothing happened. I have a child . . . a
child who passed through the age that the little child was.
My son . . . my son wouldn't know the difference between
a VC and a Marine. The children were so little. I suppose
I could find a rationalization. All that a person can do is try
and find words to try and excuse me, but I know it's the
same damn thing as lining Jews up. It's no different than
what the Nazis did. It's the same thing. I know that I'm
not alone. I know that other people did it, too. More people
went through more hell than I did . . . but they didn't do
this. I don't know . . . I don't know . . . if it's a terrible
flaw of *mine,* then I guess deep down I'm just everything
that's bad. I guess there is a rationale that says anyone who
wants to live that bad and gets in that situation . . . *(Long
pause.)* but I should have done better. I mean, I really
strove to be good. I had a whole set of values. I had 'em
and I didn't. I don't know. I want to come to the point
where I tell myself that I've punished myself enough. In
spite of it all, I don't want to punish myself anymore. I
knew I would want to censor myself for you. I didn't want
you to say: what kind of a nut, what kind of a bad person
is he? And yet, it's all right. I'm not gonna lie. My wife
tries to censor me . . . from people, from certain things. I
can't watch war shows. I can't drive. Certain things I can't
deal with. She has to deal with the situation, us sitting
around, a car backfires, and I hit the deck. She knows about
the graveyards, and R.J. and the woman. She lives with all
this still hanging out. I'm shell-shocked.

2

CHERYL

I hate to cook. Probably because he likes to cook. I hate
to cook. I don't know how to cook, and I hate it. Mark does
this spaghetti dinner once a year. Has he ever told you
about that? Holy Christ!

[MARK: Excuse me. (*Leaves.*)]

Every day before Thanksgiving Mark does a spaghetti dinner, and this is a traditional thing. This is the one traditional
bone Mark has in his body, and I'd like to break it. He has
twenty to forty-five people come to this thing. He makes
ravioli, lasagne, spaghetti, meatballs, three different kinds
of spaghetti sauces: shrimp, plain, meat sauce. Oh, he makes
gnocci! He makes his own noodles! And it's good. He's a
damn good cook for Italian food. But you can imagine what
I go through for three weeks for that party to feed forty
people. Sit-down dinner. He insists it's a sit-down dinner.
So here I am running around with no time to cook with
him. I'm trying to get enough shit in my house to feed forty
people sit-down dinner. We heated the porch last year
because we did not have enough room to seat forty people.
And I run around serving all these slobs, and this is the
first year he's really charged anyone. And we lose on it
every year. I mean, we lose, first year we lost $300. This
dinner is a $500 deal. I'm having a baby this November,
and if he thinks he's having any kind of spaghetti dinner,
he can get his butt out of here. I can't take it.

Pizzas! He makes homemade pizzas. You should see my
oven. Oh my God! There's pizza shit everywhere. Baked
on. And when it's over with, he just gets up and walks out.
He's just done. The cleanup is no big deal to him. He won't
even help. He rolls up the carpets for this dinner. People
get smashed! He's got wine everywhere, red wine. It has
to be red so if it gets on my rugs, my rugs are ruined and
my couch is ruined. I've just said it so many times I hate
it. He knows I hate it. My brother brought over some speed
to get me through that night. My brother, Jack, who is a
capitalist—intelligent—makes me sick. Never got into drugs.
Was too old. Missed that whole scene. But he now has
speed occasionally on his bad day, you know, drink, two
drinks one night, speed to get him through the day. Businessman. He brought me some speed to get me through
the night cause he knew what a basket case I'd be. And

then Mark goes and invites my family. And they're the last people I want to see at this. Sure, they love it. I mean, they all sit around and they stuff themselves to death. I'm not kidding! It is one big stuffing feast. The first time, the first spaghetti dinner we had was right after Danny was born. Danny's baby book got torn up. I had to start a whole new one. Mark's crazy friends. Drunk. Broken dishes everywhere. I'm not kidding. It's just a disaster. Spaghetti on the walls. Spaghetti pots dropped in the kitchen. Spaghetti all over the sink. That's why I ask him. I go, "Why?" "It's traditional. I have to do this every year." It was three years ago he started. Tradition my ass. I'm telling you. I mean, he wonders why I can't sleep with him sometimes. Because I just work up such a hate for him inside that (MARK *re-enters*) I'm a perfectionist. My house has to be this way, and before I go to sleep, I'll pick up after him. I'm constantly picking up after him. Christ Almighty! In the morning, if he comes in late, he's read the newspaper and there's newspaper all over the room. He *throws* it when he's done with it. I've broken toes on his shoes. I broke *this* toe on his shoe. He always leaves his shoes right out in walking space. Every morning I trip on either his tennis or his good shoes. Whichever pair he doesn't have on. He's so inconsiderate of other people. He's so selfish, he's so self-centered. And this is what I tell him. I'm just tired of it. He's so selfish. Because this spaghetti dinner just ruins me. Baby or no baby, it just completely ruins me. And he's showing off his, his wonderful cooking that he does once a year. And I suppose this is why I hate cooking.

——— **3** ———

NADINE

Men are stripped.

[MARK: It's shooting fireworks off, the Fourth of July.] We took away all their toys . . . their armor. When I was younger, I'd see a man in uniform and I'd think: what a hunk. Something would thrill in me. Now we look at a man in uniform—a Green Beret, a Marine—and we're embarrassed somehow. We don't know who they are anymore. What's a man? Where's the model? All they had left was being Provider. And now with the economics, they're losing it all. My father is a farmer. This year, my mother learned to plow. I talked to my father on the phone the other night and I said: "Hey, Dad, I hear Mom's learning how to plow." "Well, sure," he said. "She's been a farmer's wife for forty-fifty years." "Yes. But she's just learning to plow now." And there was a silence and then he said: "That's a feminist issue I'd rather not discuss at the moment." So. We don't want them to be the Provider, because we want to do that ourselves. We don't want them to be heroes, and we don't want them to be knights in shining armor, John Wayne—so what's left for them to be, huh? Oh, I'm worried about men. They're not coming through. (My husband.) How could I have ever gotten married? They were programmed to fuck, now they have to make love. And they can't do it. It all comes down to fucking versus loving. We don't like them in the old way anymore. And I don't think they like us, much. Now that's a war, huh?

Strange Snow

Steve Metcalfe

Premiere: Manhattan Theatre Club, New York City, 1982
Setting: The Flanagans' house

Martha Flanagan is a shy high school teacher who spends her Friday nights at home correcting papers and her Saturday mornings cleaning up the beer cans emptied by her brother David, a moody Vietnam vet who makes his living as a trucker. Big-boned and formerly fat, Martha still sees herself as "a battleship. With the face of an icebreaker." She has given up on romance . . . or so she thinks.

It's well before dawn when a boisterous stranger leaps onto Martha and David's front porch and starts hollering. Martha runs downstairs brandishing a golf club and threatens to call the police. The man on the porch is Joseph "Megs" Megessey, a fast-talking, rowdy mechanic and Vietnam buddy of David's. It's opening day of trout season, and Megs has come by to fetch David. Infectiously cheerful, he grabs the contemptuous Martha and dances her around the kitchen, crooning about trout. She's half shocked and half charmed. When a hungover David staggers downstairs, she surprises them both by downing a beer and agreeing to come on the fishing trip.

The trip is a fiasco. Nobody catches any fish, Martha gets soaked to the skin, and David, who's not at all thrilled by his sister's attraction to "crazy" Megs, gets so drunk that Megs has to carry him into the house. Martha changes to warm clothes and heats up some soup. Megs gushes with praise, but she fends off his compliments.

MARTHA

Look, I'm not one of those pieces of fluff you see in men's magazines. Does that make me less a woman? It does not. (*Pause.*) And I'm a fool because for some stupid reason I think it does. And so I buy contact lenses and clothes I can't really afford. You think I'd of learned by now. You think I'd have learned at the start. (*Pause.*) The soup is almost hot. (*Pause.*) David had to even get me a date for my high school formal. I was on the decorations committee, the tickets committee. I put together the whole thing. Nobody asked me to go. David rounded up his friends and told them one of them had to invite me or he'd beat them all up. I think perhaps they drew straws. I didn't know. Suddenly I was invited, that's all that mattered. I was so happy. Well, it was something that couldn't be kept quiet,

(MARTHA *crosses downstage stage right of table.*) David's
blackmail. I heard rumors. I confronted David. He wouldn't
admit what he'd done but I knew. *(Pause.)*

[MEGS: You go? *(Pause.)*]

I got very sick the night of the prom. A twenty-four-hour
thing. David meant well.

Streamers

David Rabe

Premiere: Long Wharf Theatre, New Haven, 1976
Setting: Army barracks
Streamers takes its title from Army slang for parachutes
that don't open, an image of senseless and violent death
that pervades the play. A diverse group of Army draftees
waits to be shipped out to Vietnam. Martin hates the Army
so much that he tries to slit his wrists. Three other draftees
are sharing a barracks room. Roger is a streetwise black
man, Richie is openly gay, and Billy is a homophobic college
dropout from Wisconsin. One night, after lights out, he
tells his roommates the following story. (*Note:* Somewhat
later, Richie asks Billy if "Frankie" is Billy himself. Billy
flies into a violent rage, which may or may not be a cover.)

BILLY

I . . . had a buddy, Rog . . . and this is the whole thing,
this is the whole point, a kid I grew up with, played ball
with in high school, and he was a tough little cat, a real
bad man sometimes. Used to have gangster pictures, up in
his room. Anyway, we got into this deal, where we'd drive
on down to the big city, man, you know, hit the bad spots,
let some queer pick us up . . . sort of . . . long enough to
buy us some good stuff. It was kinda the thing to do for

awhile, and we all did it, the whole gang of us. So we'd let
these cats pick us up, most of 'em old guys, and they were
hurtin' and happy as hell to have us, and we'd get alot of
free booze, maybe a meal and we'd turn 'em on. Then pretty
soon they's ask us—did we want to go over to their place.
"Sure," we'd say and order one more drink, and then when
we hit the street, we'd tell 'em to kiss off. We'd call 'em
fag and queer and jazz like that and tell 'em to kiss off. And
Frankie, the kid I'm tellin' you about, he had a mean streak
in him and if they gave us a bad time at all, he'd put 'em
down. That's the way he was. So that kinda jazz went on
and on for sort of a long time and it was a good deal if we
were low on cash or needed a laugh and it went on for a
while. And then Frankie—one day he come up to me—
and he says he was goin' home with the guy he was with.
He said, "What the hell, what did it matter?" And he's
sayin', Frankie's sayin'—Why don't I tag along? "What the
hell," he's sayin', "what does it matter who does it to you,
some broad or some old guy, you close your eyes, a mouth's
a mouth, it don't matter"—that's what he's sayin'. I tried
to talk him out of it but he wasn't hearin' anything I was
sayin'. So, the next day, see, he calls me up to tell me
about it. "Okay, okay," he says, it was a cool scene, he
says; they played poker—a buck minimum and he made a
fortune. Frankie was eatin' it up, man. It was a pretty way
to live, he says. So he stayed at it, and he had this nice
little girl he was goin' with at the time—you know the way
a real bad cat can sometimes do that, have a good little girl
who's crazy about him and he is for her, too, and he's a
different cat when he's with her?

[ROGER: Uh-huh. *(The hall light slants across* BILLY'S
face.)]

Well, that was him and Linda, and then one day he dropped
her, he cut her loose. He was hooked, man. He was into
it with no way he knew out—you understand what I'm
sayin'? He had got his ass hooked. He had never thought
he would and then one day he woke up and he was on it.

He just hadn't been told, that's the way I figure it; somebody didn't tell him somethin' he shoulda been told and
he come to me wailin' one day, man, all broke up and
wailin', my boy Frankie, my main man, and he was a fag.
He was faggot, black Roger, and I'm not lyin'. I am not
lyin' to you.

The Sun Always Shines for the Cool

Miguel Piñero

Premiere: BMC Production Company, New York City, 1979
Setting: An after-hours bar in a large city
An ex-con named Justice runs a bar where the hustlers,
players, and prostitutes of the city come to drink and hang
out. The players' code is rigid: If you disrespect the place
by leaning your back on the bar, you buy drinks for the
house. If you cross someone's line, you die.

Monologue One: The legendary hustler Viejo has just
been released from prison. He talks to a flashy young pimp
who calls himself Cat Eyes, warning him that he's outside
the players' circle. Cat Eyes responds, "Look, man, I don't
care what them motherfuckers think about me and my game,
I'm getting over. That's what counts. I pay my bills and eat
good food . . . and I fuck every night." (*Note:* Cat Eyes
doesn't know it, but the "Chile" he is planning to pimp for
is Viejo's daughter.)

Monologue Two: Willie Bodega is a "heist kid." He is
white, and the other players call him "the talking gringo . . . a
whitey that raps like a nigger." Willie got his name because
of his wheeling and dealing in prison. ("Bodega" is Spanish
for a small market; a corner store.) Viejo taught him and
his brother Billy the rules of the street. Now Willy tells
Viejo about Billy's death.

——————— 1 ———————

CAT EYES

You see them dudes? They think they got it made.

[VIEJO: Don't you?]

They got some of it made, but not all of it. They got themselves years ahead of me in the game . . . plenty of time
in the life to learn much experience. But me, I came fast,
Viejo, faster than any of them. That's why they don't like
me, cuz they all know that I'm swifter than any of them
were at my age, man. I am a young blood fresh off the
doctor's mitts. You know I still have the smell of the afterbirth hanging about me . . . but I'm swifter than those people who call themselves "folks," and have the smell of death
in the breath. Me? I am new life, Viejo, I am new life. You
think I don't know they are jealous of me and my fast talking
self. Man. I know that. Shit, that is why I talk to them the
way I do cuz I know that. You think I may be wrong, but
I'm not . . . I'm not . . . Viejo, my rap is strong and my
words are never wrong. I'm young and faster than a streak
of lightning and a ball of heat . . . and I always land on my
feet . . . ever since I could remember I never touched the
floor with my knees. You see that girl, Chile, they all wanted
her but they all fear Justice and Lefty Gorilla, but not me
cuz their time is up on the earth. I know that his is a jungle
law . . . (*Enter* BAM-BAM *and* SATISFACTION.) and I'm
steaking my name to that game. She is gonna make me a
very wealthy man, my man. She is gonna put me on the
mack map of the year . . . every year until doomsday.

——————— 2 ———————

WILLIE BODEGA

Yeah man, I was there, but there was nothing that I could
have done, man. You know, like he gave me the out, man.
He would've been really sore at me if I would have fucked
around and blew it. You know how Billy was, man. Let me

tell you something, Viejo. I'm sorry he dead, dig, but I'm proud at the way he went, man, real proud at the way he went. Like that's the way we should all go when the time comes that we have to say it's a game of cards . . . holding court in the streets . . . guns smoking, man, that's the way to do it when you got to do it. Becuz when you play it that way, and you don't want to end the game that way, then you should never had played anyway, right? . . . Right! Like, that what's it all about, ain't it, man? Going with your head held high and your trigger fingers aching . . . man. Viejo, you know that I would have stayed with him if he wanted me to. I would have gone with him to shake hands with Satan. Shit, I bet he lonely down there . . . get all the heat . . . man that's what he always got a lot of, fucking heat. Ever since I could remember, man, our old man played it to the bitter end with us. He played it so tough that we never learn what it meant to be a little warm inside ourselves. But, man, the time were like hard candy in a cheap soda shop. But like that day, man, like that day, I should have remember, "When a cross-eyed mark gets in your way, don't play," cuz it's bad luck . . . when you speak like you ain't ever gonna see daylight again, man, that's the time to spend in bed with pussy-smelling pillows in your face. You know that the time to hit the invisible man in the life scene, man, but he knew all that too . . . he knew all that too, but he went anyway, man. Viejo, he knew that too. You taught both of us that shit way back then. You remember, right? . . . the rooftop, shootin' coke bottles off the edge. Man I was mean with a pistol and so was he . . . but that day he spoke like he wasn't gonna enjoy the bread from the sting no matter how much it was. It was like he knew that there was a jinx in the air for him that day, but he went. He insisted in making the hit anyway . . . it was like he had what you call a bad ju ju, there was like no wind in the air . . . man, no taste in our mouth, no feeling in our pulse, no beating in our hearts, man. The train didn't even make noise for us that day. The lights were all red in every corner that we came to, but he wanted to go to the hit anyway . . . He was going for broke, man. He was tired, I guess, like so many of us get tired with this whole thing out here. Remember the way he held his guns in his holsters, real close to his heart, man? But that day he held them down around his waist like if he wanted to put his head and heart out there for the buzzard in blue. He wanted to die, man. Viejo, he wanted to die and I didn't want him to . . . but like that his right to go if he wanted to. I see him running, man. He was running. The first cap was booked into his leg, man. He fell, got up and booked a cap into the man . . . they came out of nowhere, man. They came out of nowhere blasting them .38s his way. He was next to the building. They blew right through the door, and he came out as they walked his way where he was suppose to have been laying dead. He came out blasting caps into their asses, man. They ran, they ran and those that didn't lay down and play dead on the streets, were laid down dead. They laid down and played dead and I laugh cuz I knew that he was badder than all of them in the shining blue uniforms looking like semigods. He was a rebel. He was Satan in heaven fighting God for a piece of the action man. That's who he was, Lucifer, fighting God for a piece of the action. That's what he looked like. He looked like a young god taking his anger out on the fucking world. And he was mean-looking in his walk, in the bullets that flew out of his power. That was his power. That's why they had to kill him three times over after he was dead . . . but they should have known, man, that he was alive . . . he was more alive than they will ever be, cuz he was a rebel in the middle of them all, and he would have never hanged up his gloves . . . they were on his mitts for good and he wore them tight . . .

Table Settings

James Lapine

Premiere: Playwrights Horizons, New York City, 1980
Setting: A dining table

This comedy features three generations of an archetypal Jewish family at various meals. The same dining table is reset for restaurant or home scenes, and every scene has a title announced by a voice-over. The family includes the matriarchal Jewish Mother, in her late sixties and "proudly from Minsk"; the Older Son, a martini-swilling divorce lawyer; his WASPy Wife and two children (Granddaughter and Grandson); the Younger Son, "a mess in his late twenties"; and his social worker Girlfriend. After one nerve-wracking, ear-splitting dinner, the Wife—described as "the ultimate shiksa"—clears the table. The scene is entitled "Sunnyside Up."

WIFE

(*Commercial music comes up in the background.* WIFE *picks the napkins off the table and begins doing her deep yoga breathing. The breathing exercise turns her grimace to a smile. She gives this speech as she clears the table.*) I've always been happy. Always. Oh, sure, there was a time when even I gàve into depression. But really, there's no question about it. I'm just a happy person by nature. Now that can threaten some people. (*She looks around the space to indicate the "some people" as her family.*) Sometimes when I have a smile on my face they ask me, "What's the matter?" Like if I'm just in a merry mood, there has to be a reason. I'm just simpleminded! Now there's a lot to be said for simplicity. I don't claim to feel less than anyone else. Sure, I have my bad days, but I let go. I get angry, and that's that. I don't make things complex when they can be simple and easy. I feel pain, but I don't dwell on it. I think of things that make me happy. Unlike some people

I know, I count my blessings and not my problems. Take my mother-in-law, for instance. All that woman seems to talk about is this one's stomach cancer, and that one's cataract operation and who's divorcing who. (*She takes the plastic glasses, the last item to be cleared, and throws them through the open dutch door in a fit. She then grabs a coffee cup and without losing a beat or her smile continues her speech.*) And my husband is forever glued to his newspaper—sometimes I think that man would rather read about political unrest and crime than be with his own family. And the kids. Children, our one hope for the future—last night I joined them in the TV room. They were watching this gruesome program about starving people, in Indo-Asia—or somewhere! Well, I just shut that television off and said, "For crying out loud can't you kids watch something a little cheerier? Whatever happened to 'Ozzie and Harriet?' " Well, those kids looked at me like I was nuts. Listen, I just try to smile and bring a little happiness into this family. I mean we're all going to end up with six feet of ground on top of us, let's have a few laughs. But you know, some people see the cup of life as half empty. I see it as half full. And if those half empties won't let us half full be happy. (*Angry.*) FUCK 'EM.

Taken in Marriage

Thomas Babe

Premiere: New York Shakespeare Festival, New York City, 1979

Setting: Assembly hall of a church in a New Hampshire college town

The church hall is set for Hank and Annie's wedding reception. The wedding is tomorrow; today is the rehearsal. The first to arrive is Dixie Avalon, a singer and cocktail waitress at a nearby ski lodge. She has been hired by one of the men to perform at the wedding. The bride's family doesn't want music, but Dixie won't leave until she's paid for her trouble. The men stay out late at a pub and miss the rehearsal, while Dixie becomes a confessional ear for the women of the bridal party. These include Annie, the nervous bride; Andy, her tough older sister, married five times and currently sleeping with Annie's fiancée; the girls' mother Ruth and her "hockle-faced" sister, Aunt Helen, a spinster who "married" a female stunt pilot.

Monologue One: Annie remembers her father as "a lovely man." Andy calls him "a monster." She advises her naive little sister against getting married. Ruth, now a widow, contributes her two cents.

* * *

Thomas Babe comments: "Ruth starts out giving a lecture about fidelity and ends up remembering Harry, and how much she loved him and how much he hurt her. Though she's not willing to show it, she gets lost in what her homily invokes. Harry becomes, in the course of her ruminations, vivid to her as the thing she cared for most in the world, and the only model of caring she ever knew. It's not a big deal; it's an inward progress for the character."

Monologue Two: Finally the men have shown up. They are bombed drunk and sleeping it off in the church upstairs. Annie is having serious second thoughts about marrying Hank. Dixie correctly suspects that she's pining for somebody else. Annie denies it, then tells her about an old boyfriend named Michael, who "had a little of the saint about him." They broke up many years before, but Annie misses him and still feels guilty for hurting him.

* * *

Thomas Babe comments: "The only thing Annie knows are the facts, not the reason why she wants to tell the facts. She's telling the facts to see if those facts make sense to anyone else. Perhaps she knows the answer, lo, these many years later—that the guy she is talking about was just a bastard. But it is her peculiar dilemma that making such judgments is foreign to her; putting this guy in a bag is wrong. She was a part of everything she did, and what she tells us about it all is still a question."

1

RUTH

It was a small point. I may seem the smallest part of a fool, and Anne and Andrea may think worse, but I'm not. I'm shrewd, after my fashion, and I got that way from living with Harry, day in and day out, for low those, and high those, twenty-five years. We merely ran together, into each other, back and forth, for twenty-five years, so that you could not have separated us if you tried, it was not even the distance of a feather. We began in an intimacy of a rare sort, and ended that way, or would've, if I had been able to make it to the hospital before he made his departure from this world. Now, what I am saying will not make much sense, or be of much importance, if you believe that all these marriages that are performed in tunics and on fields or aboard ferries going around Manhattan island, or where they read John Donne and Rod McKuen and make up vows about sharing the housekeeping and bearing analysts' bills mutually . . . if you believe those ceremonies, as they are still called, are ought more than contracts of employment for a certain period to be terminated at the will of one or the other of the mutual contractors, or by consent, or when it ain't fun no mo', then I will seem worse than a fool, I will be your village idiot. But there were times when I breathed when he breathed, when he couldn't have been more than about a thousand miles away and he had that pain he got behind his forehead or his knee went out and I would know it. Just the same way I knew, that thousand miles away, when he was shacked up with some dear little thing and I'd know. He'd come home and wouldn't even feel it necessary to be ashamed or whistle a lot, I'd know, he'd know I knew, I knew he knew I knew, and we'd have a good laugh anyway. It was, and it is, always, more important to be loyal than anything else in the world because love, romantic love, fresh lust, I prefer to call it, is transitory, convertible, strenuous, expensive, a little vacuous and evacuating, thrilling and oh so fragile, so unlikely, so unlike anything that feels like a place to put one's head down. He was cruel to me, Harry, indifferent, profane mostly . . . at the worst, cold, and sometimes, out of contempt or indifference, he simply screwed me, without concern, and my body might just as well have been his own hand in the john, poring over those magazines he kept in the desk that I found when I had to clean up after he passed on so suddenly. But there was, over all, at the beginning always, in glorious bursts, sometimes in sustained long lento times, all we, each of us, could have ever cared for or wanted, so much so that to be bitter about the bad parts is to be, well, I think, downright shitty. (*Pause.*) I want you to remember that, Anne.

2

ANNIE

I lived with him eighteen months, the first man I ever lived with. I was in school and he was in school. He came and he went, and I came and I went, and it had all the feeling of a real life. You do the laundry, you make love, you have breakfast, you fight. And all the time, there was a pair of handcuffs on the doorknob of the bedroom. I never said, "What are these handcuffs doing here?" and he never said, "You may wonder what these handcuffs are doing here?" They were just there. What was most odd of all, though, was that it wasn't very long before I knew him, that I knew that I didn't really love him, not in the same way he seemed to love me, but I could never tell him that, because of all

the habits we shared, and because, if you must know, I
was afraid to hurt him and to lose him. So one thing lead
to another: and there were the handcuffs on the doorknob.
There was something I didn't know about him and me, and
I was scared silly. . . . It was in Hanover, New Hampshire,
in January, in the snow, in twilight, very cold, very somber,
that Michael said to me, "You can't go now." He said, "I
appreciate your feelings, I appreciate you're being honest
with me, but you can't leave just yet," and I said, "Sure as
hell I can." And he said, "This will hurt me, and I think it
will hurt you, because I know that you love me, and you
know I love you, and you know you love me, so this finding
yourself," he said, "this finding yourself, as you call it, I
can appreciate, but don't go. Let's find together." And I
said, what could I say, I'm pretty unhappy here, right now,
and you're swell, you're super, but . . . And he said, "No
buts, not now." He cried and I cried, it was fourteen below
and we held on to each other just to keep warm, and when
I put my arms around him, I could feel the handcuffs in
his pocket. He said to me: "If anything happens, you know,
to me you might be a little to blame." I said, "You're so
full of shit, honey, you're full up to the top." I walked
away—and thought he'd probably lie down in the snow and
die. (Pause.) Well, he didn't die, but he stood there long
enough to get frost bite, anyway.

Talking with . . .

Jane Martin

Premiere: Actors Theatre of Louisville/Manhattan Theatre
  Club, 1982
Setting: Bare stage
Talking with . . . is a gold mine for actresses: an evening
of eleven short one-woman plays. The characters include

a rodeo rider, two actresses, a Pentecostal snake handler, a tattooed woman, and a housewife who dresses as "Patches" of Oz. Their monologues range in style from wildly comic to starkly dramatic.

Monologue One: *French Fries*

Monologue Two: *Twirler*

_____ 1 _____

ANNA MAE

(She is an old woman in a straight-back chair holding a McDonald's cup. She is surrounded by several bundles of newspapers. She wears thick glasses that distort her eyes to the viewer.) If I had one wish in my life, why I'd like to live in McDonald's. Right there in the restaurant. 'Stead of in this old place. I'll come up to the brow of the hill, bowed down with my troubles, hurtin' under my load and I'll see that yellow horseshoe, sort of like part of a rainbow, and it gives my old spirit a lift. Lord, I can sit in a McDonald's all day. I've done it too. Walked the seven miles with the sun just on its way, and then sat on the curb till five minutes of seven. First one there and the last to leave. Just like some ol' french fry they forgot.

I like the young people workin' there. Like a team of fine young horses when I was growin' up. All smilin'. Tell you what I really like though is the plastic. God gave us plastic so there wouldn't be no stains on his world. See, in the human world of the earth it all gets scratched, stained, tore up, faded down. Loses its shine. All of it does. In time. Well, God he gave us the idea of plastic so we'd know what the everlasting really was. See if there's plastic then there's surely eternity. It's God's hint.

You ever watch folks when they come on in the McDonald's? They always speed up, almost run the last few steps. You see if they don't. Old Dobbin with the barn in sight. They know it's safe in there and it ain't safe outside. Now it ain't safe outside and you know it.

I've seen a man healed by a Big Mac. I have. I was just sittin' there. Last summer it was. Oh, they don't never move you on. It's a sacred law in McDonald's, you can sit for a hundred years. Only place in this world. Anyway, a fella, maybe thirty-five, maybe forty, come on in there dressed real nice, real bright tie, bran' new baseball cap, nice white socks and he had him that disease. You know the one I mean, Cerebral Walrus they call it. Anyway, he had him a cock leg. His poor old body had it two speeds at the same time. Now he got him some coffee, with a lid on, and sat him down and Jimmy the tow-head cook knew him, see, and he brought over a Big Mac. Well, the sick fella ate maybe half of it and then he was just sittin', you know, suffering those tremors, when a couple of *ants* come right out of the burger. Now there ain't no ants in McDonald's no way. Lord sent those ants, and the sick fella he looked real sharp at the burger and a bunch *more* ants marched on out nice as you please and his head lolled right over and he pitched himself out of that chair and banged his head on the floor, loud. Thwack! Like a bowling ball dropping. Made you half sick to hear it. We jump up and run over but he was cold out. Well those servin' kids, so cute, they watered him, stuck a touch pepper up his nostril, slapped him right smart, and bang, up he got. Standin' an' blinkin'. "Well, how are you?," we say. An' he looks us over, looks right in our eyes, and he say, "I'm fine." And he was. He was fine! Tipped his Cincinnati Reds baseball cap, big "jus'-swallowed-the-canary" grin, paraded out of there clean, straight like a polebean poplar, walked him a plumb line without no trace of the "walrus." Got outside, jumped up, whooped, hollered, sang him the National Anthem, flagged down a Circle Line bus, an' rode off up Muhammad Ali Boulevard wavin' an' smilin' like the King of the Pharoahs. Healed by a Big Mac. I saw it.

McDonald's. You ever see anybody die in a McDonald's? No sir. No way. Nobody ever has died in one. Shoot, they die in Burger Kings all the time. Kentucky Fried Chicken's

got their own damn ambulances. Noooooooooo, you can't
die in a McDonald's no matter how hard you try. It's the
spices. Seals you safe in this life like it seals in the flavor.
Yesssssss, yes!

I asked Jarrell could I live there. See they close up
around ten, and there ain't a thing goin' on in 'em till seven
A.M. I'd just sit in those nice swingy chairs and lean forward.
Rest my head on those cool, cool, smooth tables, sing me
a hymn and sleep like a baby. Jarrell, he said he'd write
him a letter up the chain of command and see would they
let me. Oh, I got my bid in. Peaceful and clean.

Sometimes I see it like the last of a movie. You know
how they start the picture up real close and then back it
off steady and far? Well, that's how I dream it. I'm living
in McDonald's and it's real late at night and you see me
up close, smiling, and then you see the whole McDonald's
from the outside, lit up and friendly. And I get smaller and
smaller, like they do, and then it's just a light in the darkness, like a star, and I'm in it. I'm part of that light, part
of the whole sky, and it's all McDonald's, but part of something even bigger, something fixed and shiny . . . like plastic.

I know. I know. It's just a dream. Just a beacon in the
storm. But you got to have a dream. It's our dreams make
us what we are.

— 2 —

APRIL

*(She is a young woman, stands center stage. She is dressed
in a spangled, single-piece swimsuit, the kind that is specially made for baton twirlers. She holds a shining, silver
baton in her hand.)* I started when I was six. Momma sawed
off a broom handle, and Uncle Carbo slapped some sort of
silver paint, well, gray really, on it and I went down in the
basement and twirled. Later on, Momma hit the daily double on horses named Spin Dry and Silver Revolver and she

said that was a sign so she gave me lessons at the Dainty Deb Dance Studio where the lady, Miss Aurelia, taught some twirling on the side.

I won the Ohio Juniors title when I was six and the Midwest Young Adult Division three years later and then in high school I finished fourth in the nationals. Momma and I wore look-alike Statue of Liberty costumes that she had to send clear to Nebraska to get and Daddy was there in a T-shirt with my name, April. My first name is April and my last name is March. There were four thousand people there, and when they yelled my name golden balloons fell out of the ceiling. Nobody, not even Charlene Ann Morrison, ever finished fourth at my age.

Oh, I've flown high and known tragedy both. My daddy says it's put spirit in my soul and steel in my heart. My left hand was crushed in a riding accident by a horse named Big Blood Red, and though I came back to twirl I couldn't do it at the highest level. That was denied me by Big Blood Red, who clipped my wings. You mustn't pity me though. Oh, by no means! Being denied showed me the way, showed me the glory that sits inside life where you can't see it.

People think you're a twit if you twirl. It's a prejudice of the unknowing. Twirlers are the niggers of a white university. Yes, they are. One time I was doing fire batons at a night game, and all of a sudden I see this guy walk out of the stands. I was doing triples and he walks right out past the half-time marshalls, comes up to me, he had this blue-bead headband, I can still see it. Walks right up, and when I come front after a back reverse he spits in my face. That's the only, single time I ever dropped a baton, dropped 'em both in front of sixty thousand people and he smiles, see, and he says this thing I won't repeat. He called me a bodily part in front of half of Ohio. It was like being raped. It shows that beauty inspires hate and that hating beauty is Satan. (*Breaks focus, identifies person in audience; focus, pause, line.*)

You haven't twirled, have you? I can see that by your

hands. Would you like to hold my silver baton? Here, hold
it.

You can't imagine what it feels like to have that baton
up in the air. I used to twirl with this girl who called it
blue-collar Zen. The "tons" catch the sun when they're up,
and when they go up, you go up too. You can't twirl if
you're not *inside* the "ton." When you've got 'em up over
twenty feet it's like flying or gliding. Your hands are still
down, but your insides spin and rise and leave the ground.
Only a twirler knows that—so we're not niggers.

The secret for a twirler is the light. You live or die with
the light. It's your fate. The best is a February sky clouded
right over in the late afternoon. It's all background then,
and what happens is that the "tons" leave tracks, traces,
they etch the air, and if you're hot, if your hands have it,
you can draw on the sky. Charlene Ann Morrison, God,
Charlene Ann! She was inspired by something beyond man.
She won the nationals nine years in a row. Unparalleled
and unrepeatable. Last two years she had leukemia, and at
the end you could see through her hands when she twirled.
Charlene Ann died with a "ton" thirty feet up, her momma
swears on that. I did speed with Charlene at a regional in
Fargo and she may be fibbin' but she says there was a day
when her "tons" erased while they turned. Like the sky
was a sheet of rain and the "tons" were car wipers and when
she had erased this certain part of the sky you could see
the face of the Lord God Jesus, and his hair was all rhine-
stones and he was doing this incredible singing like the
sound of a piccolo. The people who said Charlene was crazy
probably never twirled a day in their life.

Twirling is the physical parallel of revelation. You can't
know that. Twirling is the throwing of yourself up to God.
It's a pure gift, hidden from Satan because it is wrapped
and disguised in the midst of football. It is God throwing,
spirit fire, and very few come to it. You have to grow eyes
in your heart to understand its message, and when it opens
to you it becomes your path to suffer ridicule, to be crucified

by misunderstanding, and to be spit upon. I need my baton now.

There is one twirling no one sees. At the winter solstice we go to a meadow God showed us just outside of Green Bay. The God-throwers come there on December twenty-first. There's snow, sometimes deep snow, and our clothes fall away and we stand unprotected while acolytes bring the "tons." They are ebony "tons" with razors set all along the shaft. They are three feet long. One by one the twirlers throw, two "tons" each, thirty feet up, and as they fall back they cut your hands. The razors arch into the air and find God and then fly down to take your blood in a crucifixion, and the red drops draw God on the ground and if you are up with the batons you can look down and see him revealed. Red on white. Red on white. You can't imagine. You can't imagine how wonderful that is.

I started twirling when I was six but I never really twirled until my hand was crushed by the horse named Big Blood Red. I have seen God's face from thirty feet up in the air and I know him.

Listen. I will leave my silver baton here for you. Lying here as if I forgot it, and when the people file out, you can wait back and pick it up, it can be yours, it can be your burden. It is the eye of the needle. I leave it for you.

Teeth 'n' Smiles
David Hare

Premiere: Royal Court Theatre, London, 1975
Setting: Rock concert at Cambridge University, 1969
A drugged, drunk, wasted rock band arrives at Cambridge University to play an outdoor concert at the Jesus College Ball. The lead singer, Maggie, is carried in over a porter's shoulder and dumped in a bathtub. The roadies amuse

themselves with a trivia game called Pope's Balls ("the most borin' and useless piece of information you can think of"), and it takes a good hour for them to plug in one plug.

Somehow, the band makes it through the first set, but during the second, Maggie stops singing, addresses the audience confessionally, and passes out. Saraffian, the band's manager, slaps her back to consciousness and fires her. He also tells her that her songwriter lover is leaving. At which point the whole band gets busted.

It seems that Peyote, the drugged-out bass player, has been keeping his stash in Maggie's luggage and she's going to take the rap. Maggie reacts rather calmly and then sets the tent on fire. Saraffian bursts out laughing: "Bless you, my dear. . . . You've totally restored my faith in the young." Now in his fifties, Saraffian made his fortunes importing American soul groups to England—"except when they arrive they aren't quite the same people they are in the States. They're just five guys he met in a bar. . . . And in England nobody knows the difference. Seeing how they're black." This is the story Saraffian tells while the tent burns.

SARAFFIAN

I'll tell you of my evening at the Café de Paris. March 9th, 1941. (NASH *crosses with a bucket of water.*)

[ARTHUR: You won't put it out with that.

NASH: This ain't for the fire. It's for Peyote. (*He laughs and goes into the dark.*)]

I was with this girl. She's related to a Marquis on her mother's side and me a boy from Tottenham whose dad ran a spieler in his own back room. So I'm something of a toy, a bauble on her arm. And she said, please can we go to the Café de Paris, I think because she wants to shock her pals by being seen with me, but also because she does genuinely want to dance to the music of Snakehips Johnson and his Caribbean band. (LAURA *picks up as much equipment as she can manage and goes out*. SARAFFIAN, MAGGIE *and*

ARTHUR *left alone with the piano.*) So I say fine, off to
Piccadilly Circus, Coventry Street, under the Rialto cinema, the poshest . . . the jeweled heart of London where
young officers danced before scattering across four conti-
nents to fight in Hitler's war. You won't believe this but
you went downstairs into a perfect reproduction of the ball-
room on the *Titanic.* I should have been warned. And there
they are. A thousand young blades and a thousand young
girls with Marcel waves in their hair. So out of chronic
social unease, I became obstreperous, asking loudly for
brown ale, and which way to the pisshouse, showing off,
which gave me a lot of pleasure, I remember they enjoyed
me, thinking me amusing. And I was pretty pleased with
myself. The glittering heart of the empire, the waiter leaning over me to pick up the champagne. And then nothing.
As if acid has been thrown in my face. The waiter is dead
at my feet. And the champagne rises of its own accord in
the bottle and overflows. Two fifty-kilo bombs have fallen
through the cinema above and Snakehips Johnson is dead
and thirty-two others. I look at the waiter. He has just one
sliver of glass in his back from a shattered mirror. That's
all. (MAGGIE *gets up and moves away to sit on the stage.*)
So we're all lying there. A man lights a match and I can
see that my girl friend's clothes have been completely blown
off by the blast. She is twenty-one and her champagne is
now covered in a gray dust. A man is staring at his mother
whose head is almost totally severed. Another man is trying
to wash the wounded, he is pouring champagne over the
raw stump of a girl's thigh to soothe her. Then somebody
yells put the match out, we'll die if there's gas about, and
indeed there was a smell, a yellow smell.

I looked up. I could see the sky. It's as if we are in a
huge pit and above at the edges of the pit from milk bars
all over Leicester Square people are gathering to look down
the hole at the mess below. And we can't get out. There
are no stairs. Just people gaping. And us bleeding.

Then suddenly I realized that somebody, somehow, God

knows how, had got down and come among us. I just saw two men flitting through the shadows. I close my eyes. One comes near. I can smell his breath. He touches my hand. He then removes the ring from my finger. He goes.

He is looting the dead.

And my first thought is: I'm with you, pal.

I cannot help it, that was my first thought. Even here, even now, even in fire, even in blood, I am with you in your scarf and cap, slipping the jewels from the hands of the corpses. I'm with you.

So then a ladder came down and the work began. And we climbed out. There we are, an obscene parade, the rich in tatters, slipping back to our homes, the evening rather . . . spoilt . . . and how low, how low can men get stealing from the dead and dying?

And I just brush myself down and feel lightheaded, for the first time in my life totally sure of what I feel. I climb the ladder to the street, push my way through the crowd. My arm is grazed and bleeding. I hail a taxi. The man is a cockney. He stares hard at the exploded wealth. He stares at me in my dinner jacket. He says, "I don't want blood all over my fucking taxi." And he drives away.

There is a war going on. All the time. A war of attrition. (*He smiles.*)

Good luck.

Thieves

Herb Gardner

Premiere: Broadhurst Theatre, New York City, 1974
Setting: Upper East Side of Manhattan

It's a warm night in June, and all the crazies are out in Manhattan: bums on the streets, neurotics on the terraces. Martin Cramer is playing the flute on the terrace outside

266

THIEVES

his empty apartment. His wife Sally, who left him eight
days ago, has come back to discuss the divorce—over
candlelight and a bottle of wine. She is pregnant, but has
not told Martin yet.

Monologue One: Martin and Sally have just made love.
Sally asks her husband what happened to them. Martin
responds.

Monologue Two: Sally tells Martin where she sent their
furniture: to the very first apartment they shared, "the one-
room roach festival" at 78 Orchard Street.

———— 1 ————

MARTIN

First, Sally . . . First, I want you to know how much I
appreciate the wonderful work you've done on our apartment here. How you've managed to capture, in only five
short weeks, the subtle, elusive, yet classic mood previously found only in the Port Authority Bus Terminal. (*Pac-
ing about the room.*) In addition, Sally, you have, somewhat
mystically, lost or forgotten the name of the moving and
storage company with whom you placed nearly fifty-five
thousand dollars' worth of our furniture.

[SALLY: It's an Italian name, I know that. I'm working
on that . . .]

This, coupled with the fact that you disappeared eight days
ago on what was ostensibly a trip to Gristede Brothers to
buy some strawberry yogurt, and did not return until this
evening, has led to a certain amount of confusion for me . . .

[SALLY: I went to Gloria's place to think things out, to—
]

(*Opens crumpled letter.*) All confusion, of course, vanished
with the arrival last week of this simple, touching, yet con-
cise note from the Misters Morris, Klein, Fishback and
Fishback . . . (*Reads, only the slightest tremor in his voice.*)
"We have been retained by your wife, Sally Jane Cramer,
hereinafter referred to as 'Wife,' to represent her in the

matter of your divorce. Said wife having requested that her whereabouts remain unknown to you at present, we therefore . . ." *(Carefully folding letter into paper airplane.)* After eight days of staring into the air conditioner, wondering which Santini Brother had my furniture, which Gristede Brother had my wife, and which Fishback owned my soul, a light began to dawn . . . or maybe one went out . . . and I realized that nobody was hiding you from me, that your whereabouts, said wife, have been unknown to me for years . . . that you make a fine letter-writer, a great decorator, and a perfect stranger. *(Going to terrace doorway.)* You said you came back tonight to talk about the divorce. You didn't mention it. Neither did I. And the habit, the habit of being together, began again. *(Turns to her.)* But I couldn't sleep. I couldn't sleep and I thought about it and tonight, Sally, I have decided to retire from the games. The Olympics are over, lady, the torch is out . . . and you are free. *(He tosses the paper airplane through the terrace doorway, it sails into the street.)* Said husband, hereinafter referred as "gone," has had it.

2

SALLY

(Goes quickly to him.) Four B, Marty—*(Holds his arm.)* We made terrific promises and gorgeous love there. And we had nice, loud fights and threw inexpensive things at each other and hugged a lot and . . . *(Sees his blank, unremembering face.)* Well, you had to be there. *(Moving about the large, bare room.)* I woke up in the middle of the night last week and I didn't know who we were. This empty room woke me like an alarm bell and for a minute I didn't know. Without our coffee table, I didn't know. Without our couch . . . And then I remembered. We're the Cramers. We're this couple. And we're staying together because we're expected to dinner next Friday by some other couples; and the next Friday we're expecting them.

We're the Cramers. We don't love each other so we love other couples, and they love us. Held together by other couples, married to other marriages, traveling in fours, sixes, eights, shoulder to shoulder at each other's tables, boy, girl, boy, girl, boy, girl, close, close, so nobody slips away . . . (*She stands quite still.*) We're this couple; I remembered and I fell asleep . . . The next morning I heard somebody scream in the subway. Rush hour, the train stopped dead between Union Square and Canal and somebody blew. It was this high, nutsy scream, like somebody certain they're gonna die right there under the city. It scared the hell outa me and I put my hand to my throat and I felt it throbbing and I saw everybody looking and I knew it was me. It was me screaming, and I couldn't stop. And that night I went to Gristede Brothers and kept on walking. (*Silence for a moment.*) If you want to visit your furniture, the keys to the apartment are in the bookcase.

Tracers

Conceived by John DiFusco and written by the original cast

Premiere: Odyssey Theatre Company, Los Angeles, 1980
Setting: Multiple
Tracers was created by an acting/writing ensemble of eight Vietnam veterans, based on their personal experiences during and after the war. It is a theatrical collage of scenes, solo speeches, and music by Huey Lewis, the Doors, Country Joe and the Fish, and Bruce Springsteen.

Monologue One: Baby San, *Sense of Judgement.* Baby San is a new draftee, runtish and wet behind the ears.

Monologue Two: Little John, *In the Rear with the Beer and the Gear.* Little John is the team leader, a strong, tough guy who drinks. Before signing up for the Army, he spent two years in medical school.

————— 1 —————

BABY SAN

Look at this fuckin' belt buckle, Little John. *(He notices
audience for the first time and begins to deliver the following to them.)* I lost my sense of judgment yesterday. I killed
someone. Who? I don't know, we've never met. You think
you have to know someone to kill them. After all, it's just
you and him, and it's a very important part of both of your
lives. But I'm still here. Where? In the land of Buddha—
and banyan trees, and Cao Dai temples and South China
seas. Hey, papasan, I'll have another peppermint schnapps,
please. Gee, isn't Saigon beautiful?! I feel like I'm in Paris.
This is an outdoor café. Those are boulevards, statues, taxi-
cabs, and barbed wire. I lost my sense of judgment yesterday, I traded two cartons of Salem cigarettes for something
I should have traded one for. Now the guys are laughing
at me. But it's good pot, though. And that little mamasan's
face, so brown, so sincere. *"Chao, babysan, mon yoi, ong
mua den to toi, cho ong so mot com sai.* You buy from me,
I give you number-one *com sai."* Her? No, she's not hump-
ing rockets for the VC. Hey, do you think I killed her baby?
I lost my sense of judgment yesterday. You see, I sat down
in my bunker and I wrote a letter to my girlfriend and I
said, "Julie, I don't think that I love you anymore." She
hasn't written me back since. Since I only told the truth.
And the truth is . . . I don't know. I want to wake up now,
I would like to go home now. You see, we live in bunkers
here and we carry M-16s. She's nineteen, too. She goes to
college. She doesn't even know what a mortar round sounds
like. A couple of weeks ago I got a letter from her. She
wants my opinion on a wedding dress. *(Laughs.)* I lost my
sense of judgment yesterday, and Brooklyn seems like a
world away.

——————— 2 ———————

LITTLE JOHN

Well. Been out in the fuckin' bush for ten fuckin' days.
Fuckin' choppers picked us up outta a fuckin' rice paddy,
flew us back to fuckin' Charlie III fuckin' combat base.
Fuckin' six said we done fuckin' good. Fuckin' number one.
Gonna get us some Cinder-fuckin'-ella-fuckin' liberty. So
we went and got us a fuckin' shower and some clean fuckin'
fatigues, and hitched us a fuckin' ride into the fuckin' ville.
Found us a fuckin' bar and hoisted ourselves a fuckin' few.
After careful fuckin' consideration, we decided what we
really wanted to fuckin' do was get fuckin' laid. So we went
and found us a fuckin' massage parlor; talked to the fuckin'
mamasan; gave her some fuckin' P; she brought out her
fuckin' girls. Fuckin' number-one *sik lou* girls. I picked out
a fuckin' girl, we went behind the fuckin' curtains, took off
our fuckin' clean fuckin' fatigues, laid down on the fuckin'
mats—and we made love.

The Transfiguration of Benno Blimpie

Albert Innaurato

Premiere: Astor Place Theatre, New York City, 1977
Setting: Benno's room and various memory locations
Benno is twenty years old and weighs five hundred pounds.
He has barricaded himself in a room and is eating himself
to death. A sensitive boy from a working-class, Italian-
American family, Benno loves art and music and has tried
to find solace in beauty. But his life is grotesquely un-
beautiful. His parents are cruel and abusive, the boys in
the neighborhood taunt him and beat him, and his grandfather goes to the park to have sex with a thirteen-year-old
girl, who finally murders him in front of young Benno's

eyes. Benno sees no escape from a life he describes as "an oven. A fat roast burning in the oven."

Monologue One: Benno remembers his father from childhood: "in his early thirties or very late twenties, good-looking, a former athlete." Father is a blue-collar worker, Italian-American.

Monologue Two: Benno narrates his life to the audience.

Monologue Three: Benno's grandfather, "Pop-pop," has just been killed, and his parents are dressing to go to the wake. They fight and the father storms out, leaving Benno and his mother to follow. (*Note:* The "funeral" dress she is wearing is too tight and she feels ashamed.)

1

FATHER

Goddammit, Benno, quit followin' me. Where did she keep things, Benno? You know where that bitch, God forgive me, kept everything? Aw—how would you know? Sit down. How many eggs you want, Benno? Six enough? Benno, I make seven, that should fill us both. I hope she dies in that filthy Napolitan shack livin' with her virgin sister. Get the black pepper, Benno—don't spill it—watch out, don't spill it. Be careful, or you'll spill it; watch out . . . shit fire, you spilled it! Why are you so clumsy, my son? (*Stoop down as though picking black pepper up off the floor.*) Hey! I know what. I'll put pepperoni in the eggs. That's always good! (*Sings as he mimes adding the ingredients.*) "Pepperoni hits the spot, helps you shit because it's hot." Why didn't you fight back, Benno, hanh? Why didn't you fight back? I heard, I heard, Benno what them kids did to you. Why did you lay there like some queer? Hanh! I'll turn the heat up just a tidge. And maybe we better put some milk. Is there somethin' wrong with you my son? Are you a pansy, my son? Why ain't you out there in the street, playin' ball, roughin' up like I did? Why you always in here with you mama, like a girl? Shit, the eggs is stickin' to the pan, I'll stir them. We better put a tidge of sugar in. There. Why are you so fat, my son? Why don't you exercise? I'd never of let them kids near me when I was your age. I'll put some oregano in. Never. I'll tell you, I was a holy terror, a holy terror, geez. I'd have kicked them inna balls, like this. I'd have beat them with my fists, like this. I was no fatty, no pansy. I'd have punched them, I'd have beaten them sense-less. *(Dances around as though in a boxing ring.)* Left, right, left, right and a kick to the balls. *(Mimes a fight.)* Take that, motherfucker, take that and that! A right to the side of the head—pow! A left to the jaw and boop!—a knee between the legs! And another left and another right—he's down, he's bleedin'—my god!—he's out! Hey! Hey! *(Runs to the stove.)* Shit! Shit fire and save the matches! The eggs is burned.

2

BENNO

Benno grew up thinking that talent and sensitivity were things people took seriously. At least, that important people took seriously—artists, for instance, and teachers. Benno grew up hoping that looks and sex didn't matter. That paint-ings would satisfy any longing he'd ever have. And when that longing got too strong, a quick pulling with the palm would be enough. Benno was wrong. Benno has been heard to say that nothing matters save the taste of his own flesh. But since then, time has passed. For your benefit he has conjured up scenes better not remembered. And Benno realizes that he was guilty of oversimplification. There are things that matter: looks matter, sex matters. These are all that matter. Benno feels that those who deny this are par-ticipating in a huge joke. Benno has learned his lesson. Paintings, you see, aren't enough. When loneliness and emptiness and longing congeal like a jelly, nothing assuages the ache. Nothing, nothing, nothing. It was the end of spring, the traditional season of youth, renewal and young love. Benno returned to his old neighborhood, having celebrated his twentieth birthday. He found the poorest side street in his old neighborhood. Fitzgerald Street, by name. And he rented a room on the third floor of a row house on Fitzgerald Street. Benno nailed shut all the windows in that room, even though it was summer. Something about imbibing his own smell. Benno is not as isolated as you might think. He hears the horrible street noises. He hears the monster children screaming. He even allows himself to have his shade up one-half hour a day. Today at one P.M., Benno had his shade up. He stared out his nailed window, stared through the caked dirt that streaks the window's glass. He saw a wild circle flashing red across the street. He stared at that circle and was tempted to . . . never mind. He was tempted and stared and was tempted some more. And then he saw the agent of that circle. It was a little girl. A beautiful little girl. Oh yes, Benno knows beauty. He knows if he tells you. Once, when he saw something beautiful, it would flash across his eyes like a hot knife and he would peer, eyes stuck there until they ached. Once, he tells you, no longer. For beauty has lost his power over me, it has lost its power, no more beauty, no more longing to grasp it within me and smother it with my bulk, please God, no more beauty. (*He is almost weeping. He eats passionately and slowly pulls himself together.*)

3

MOTHER

Let's have some coffee, Benno. I need it. (*Heats coffee.*) Oh Jesus, Jesus, how'm I gonna face it? All them relatives of his: his sister Edith, that witch of a prune face, *faccia brutt', Virgine, ti conosci'*, Benno stop slobberin', and his brother, Basil—face like a rhinoceros' ass—how'm I gonna face them? They hate me. They look down on me—Mary the peasant, they call me. But it was me, the virgin knows, me, Mary the horse, put the old man up. Me! I hadda see him come and spit inna the sink every day. Me! And I hadda run the vacuum cleaner to get the scales from his sores. Those damn scales were everywhere, like fairy dust. I even found 'em on the window sill. How did they get on the window sill? What did he do, scratch them while watchin' some broad walk down the street? And do they thank me for cleanin' up afta him week afta friggin' week? Nah! Benno, why you puttin' five teaspoons of sugar in you coffee, hanh? Why can't you put two like a human being? Three, even three I could see, god knows, but five? Who do you take afta? Hanh? (Gets up and pours coffee for herself.) Take some coffee, Mary. Weep into them grounds. And them god damned lousy shits look down at me. My father, my friggin' father, god rest his soul, was eight times, nah, nine times the man theirs was! Nine times, you hear me? The day before he died I went a see him. Couldn't find him. Where was he, where? Then, suddenly, I hear this clang, this loud clang. CLANG! It come from the cellar. I run down. There he is, seventy-six, at least, chasin' rats with the shovel. He screamed: *Ecco! Ecco!* And then he smashes one with the shovel. CLANG!! It splattered all over the cellar. That was a real man. Not a ball-less bum like you no good bastard father. Well, have a cookie Mary, you deserve it. (*To Benno.*) No more for you, dinosaur, you've had seven. No more, I said. You shit, you! (*Pantomimes reaching over and slapping his hand. BENNO winces in place, as though fighting back tears.*) Cry baby! Looka him hold back the tears. No good sissy! Men don't cry. And looka! Just a big lump of lard. Jesus, I could store you up and cook with you. What did I do, oh virgin, to deserve all this suffering? Hanh? Looka them pimples. Don't scratch them you no good! If only you wasn't so flabby. If only you had some muscle on them monster arms and legs. But all you is, is a huge, flabby rat. You hear me? A rat; with them big, black dartin' eyes. I'm sick a you; and sick a that creep you no good bastard father. Who goes out and works like a dog? Me! Who comes home and cleans like a horse?

Hanh? I do! And who put that no good bum, your Pop-pop, God rest his soul, up for years and years and then he has to go out and let some nigger stab him with his own wine bottle and we don't even get his last check, god damn it all to hell, *I* did and *I* do, that's who! Mary! Mary the horse! Mary the horse, they call me—don't take another cookie, you pig—Mary the horse. *(She is becoming hysterical.)* They used a call me Bella, beautiful, you know that? Beautiful and I had red hair, flaming, and big boobs, almost as big as yours, you little queer, and a shape, Madone', what a shape! Old Joey Fercanti, I coulda married him, said my lips should be on the silver screen, that's how big they were and thick and red. Bella, Bella they called me. And when I danced they look at me and when I walked home from the market even with a dozen other girls, they looked at me and when I got married all the guys in the neighborhood got drunk. Bella! And look at me now—I'm almost as ugly as you, I'm a hag, a bitch! Got no shape no more and my hair's gray and fallin' out and your father, your father that no good lousy son of a bitch did this to me, worked at me and worked at me, a rat, chewin' at me, with big dartin' eyes and tearin' me to pieces! Look at me, look at me good. Oh my god, my god, how did I wind up like this, with the peelin' wallpaper and nothin' else, no furniture, no money, not a decent dress. What am I gonna wear to that wake? They'll laugh, you hear me, they'll laugh. *(She has reached a frenzy. And sobs for a moment and then slowly begins to calm down. Occasionally her chest heaves from sob. Benno stares wide-eyed. She has calmed down. Slowly she rises and pours herself another cup of coffee.)* Have some more coffee, Mary. That's all you got, caffeine, that's all you got in the whole world. *(To Benno.)* And you, monster, you with them big eyes, them big black eyes, what do you want now?

The Typists
Murray Schisgal

Premiere: Orpheum Theatre, New York City, 1963
Setting: An office

Paul Cunningham, a bright young man in his twenties, is
going to law school at night. Today is his first day of work
at an office job, typing addresses from the phone book onto
postcards. Paul's co-worker Sylvia Payton shows him the
ropes. She's Paul's age and is attracted to him. Between
postcards they chat, until suddenly both of them stop and
stare out at the audience. One after the other, they tell
their life stories. From this point, the play progresses surrealistically. As the two typists work toward the end of the
alphabet, they grow older and older. By the end of the
"workday," they're both in their sixties.

  Monologue One: Paul
  Monologue Two: Sylvia

. . .

Murray Schisgal comments: "The monologues in the play
were used to break the fourth-wall convention. More important, though, was the characters' need to justify their
lives to strangers, i.e., the audience. Monologue does not
permit of contradiction or interrogation. It is the ultimate
weapon of any character. 'Listen to me! Listen to me! I
have something to tell you!' And we must listen to him.
He doesn't give us a chance to talk.

  "The theatre started with the monologue and it will end
with a monologue. 'Listen to me! Listen to me!'"

1

PAUL

I was born in a poor section of Brooklyn. My parents were
at each other's throat most of the time. It was a miserable
childhood. I had no brothers or sisters; there was only the

three of us living in this old rundown house, with cats crying and screaming all night in the alley. Why my parents ever got married, I don't know, and why they stayed together for as long as they did I don't know that either. They're separated now. But it doesn't much matter any more. They were as unlike as any two people could be. All my father wanted was to be left alone to smoke his pipe and listen to the radio. My mother—she was a pretty woman, she knew how to dress, all right—she liked to go out and enjoy herself. I was stuck between the two of them and they pulled on both sides. I couldn't talk to one without the other accusing me of being ungrateful; I couldn't touch or kiss one of them without being afraid that the other one would see me and there would be a fight. I had to keep my thoughts to myself. I had to grow up wishing for some kind of miracle. I remember coming home from school one afternoon. I must have been twelve or thirteen. There was this man in the living room with my mother. They weren't doing anything; they were just sitting and talking. But I felt that something was going on. I seemed to stop breathing and I ran out of the house and threw up on the curbstone. Later on I swore to myself that I would make a miracle happen; that I wouldn't ever have to be where I didn't want to be and I wouldn't have to do what I didn't want to do; that I could be myself, without being afraid. But it's rough. With a background like mine you're always trying to catch up; it's as if you were born two steps behind the next fellow. *(They type, stop suddenly. They both stare at the audience,* SYLVIA *leaning forward,* PAUL *back in his chair, etc.)*

2

SYLVIA

My family never had money problems. In that respect we were very fortunate. My father made a good living, while he was alive, that is. He passed away when I was seventeen. You could say he and my mother had a fairly happy mar-

riage. At least we never knew when they were angry with
one another, and that's a good thing for children. I have a
sister. Charlotte. She's older than I am. She's married now
and we don't bother much with each other. But when we
were younger you wouldn't believe what went on. Every
time we quarreled, according to my parents she was right;
I was always wrong. She got everything she wanted, no
matter what, and I had to be content with the leftovers. It
was just unbearable. Anyway, my father was sick for a long
time before he passed away. He had this ring, it was a
beautiful ring, with a large onyx stone in it, and when I
was a girl I used to play with it. I'd close one eye and I'd
look inside of it and I'd see hundreds and hundreds of
beautiful red and blue stars. My father had always promised
me that ring; he always said it belonged to me. I thought
for certain he'd give it to me before he passed away, but
he didn't say anything about it; not a word. Well, afterward,
I saw it. You know where I saw it? On my sister's finger.
He had given it to her. Now I don't think that's a background that leaves many possibilities for development. I
don't forgive my father; definitely not. And I don't forgive
my sister. My mother, whom I now support with my hard
work, still says I'm wrong.

Uncommon Women and Others

Wendy Wasserstein

Premiere: Phoenix Theatre, New York City, 1977
Setting: A restaurant in the present, and six years earlier
   at a college for women
Five friends meet in a restaurant. They are all twenty-seven
and first met each other at college, where they were groomed
to be "Uncommon Women who as individuals have the
personal dignity that comes with intelligence, competence,

flexibility, maturity, and a sense of responsibility . . . without loss of gaiety, charm or femininity." They are finding this image a little bit hard to live up to, but cling to the hope that "when we're forty . . . *forty-five* . . . we can be pretty fucking amazing." As the five friends toast one another, the play flashes back to a series of scenes from their college years.

Holly Kaplan's father invented velveteen. She is "a relier for many years on the adage, 'If she lost twenty pounds, she'd be a very pretty girl, and if she worked, she'd do very well.' " Holly alternates between being a spectator and a spectacle. She has devised "a strong moral code of warmth to those you love and wit to those you're scared of." At twenty-seven, Holly is working toward her third graduate degree. Her parents call "three times a week at seven A.M. to ask me, "Are you thin, are you married to a root canal man, are *you* a root canal man?" In this flashback, the girls are approaching graduation. A late-night rap about penis envy (and penises) ends with an expedition to the candy machine to "see how much weight we can gain in one night." Holly stays home by herself. She lights a cigarette, puts on a James Taylor tape, picks up the phone, and covers herself with her raccoon coat "for comfort."

HOLLY

Operator, I'd like the phone number of a Dr. Mark Silverstein in Minneapolis, Minn. Could you connect me with that number, please? Thank you. Hello, can I speak to Mark? Oh, do you have his number in Philadelphia? Thank you. No, that's all right. I'll call him there. *(Dials again.)* Hello, may I please speak to Mark? Oh, Hi. My name is Holly Kaplan. I met you last summer at a museum with my friend Muffet. It was the Fogg Museum. Oh that's all right, I never remember who I meet at museums either. *(She giggles.)* What's new? I'm not quite certain what I'll be doing next year. I'm having trouble remembering what

I want. My friend Katie says I'm too diffuse. You'd like Katie. She's basing her life on Katharine Hepburn in *Adam's Rib*. She didn't tell me that but it's a good illustration. No, I haven't been back to the Fogg Museum this year. My brother goes to Harvard Medical, Business, and Law School. Maybe I'll move to Philadelphia. *(She giggles.)* I'm in North Stimson Hall, fourth floor, under my raccoon coat. I guess everything's all right here. I just like being under my coat. Last week when I was riding the bus back from Yale and covering myself with it I thought I had finally made it into a Salinger story. Only, I hated the bus, college, my boyfriend, and my parents. The only thing really nice was the coat. *(Pause.)* I take that back about my parents. Do you know what the expression "Good Ga Davened" means? It means someone who davened or prayed right. Girls who good ga davened did well. They marry doctors and go to Bermuda for Memorial Day weekends. These girls are also doctors, but they only work part-time because of their three musically inclined children, and weekly brownstone restorations. I think Mount Holyoke mothers have access to a "did well" list published annually, in New York, Winnetka, and Beverly Hills, and distributed on High Holy Days and Episcopal bake sales. I'm afraid I'm on the waiting list. *(Pause.)* You were on the waiting list for Johns Hopkins. I have a good memory for indecision. My mother says doctors take advantage unless you're thin. And then they want to marry you and place you among the good ga davened. She says girls who have their own apartments hang towels from the windows so the men on the street know when to come up. My friend Alice Harwitch is becoming a doctor and I've never seen her enter a strange building with towels in the windows. Of course, she's a radical lesbian. Sorry to have bothered you. Hey, maybe you'd like to visit here sometime, it's very pretty in the spring. We could see Emily Dickinson's house and buy doughnuts. I think about her a lot. And doughnuts, I think about them a lot, too. No, I don't write poetry, and I haven't read *The Bell Jar*. My friend Rita has. I don't know who Rita's basing her life on. Sometimes I think she'd like to be Katharine Hepburn, but Katie has the Katharine Hepburn market cornered and we're all allowed only one dominent characteristic. I'm holding a lottery for mine. (*She giggles again.*) Yes, I guess I do giggle a lot, and I am too cynical. I had my sarcastic summer when I was sixteen and somehow it exponentially progressed. Leilah, she's my nice friend who's merging with Margaret Mead, says sarcasm is a defense. Well, I couldn't very well call you up and tell you to move me to Minneapolis and let's have babies, could I? (*Her tone of voice changes.*) Well, sorry to have bothered you. Really, I'm fine. I find great comfort in "Lay Lady Lay," "One Bad Apple Don't Spoil the Whole Bunch Girl," and my raccoon coat. And I like my friends, I like them a lot. They're really exceptional. Uncommon women and all that drivel. Of course, they're not risky. I'm not frightened I'll ruin my relationship with them. Sometimes I think I'm happiest walking with my best. Katie always says she's my best, shredding leaves and bubble gum along the way and talking. Often I think I want a date or a relationship to be over so I can talk about it to Kate or Rita. I guess women are just not as scary as men and therefore they don't count as much. (HOLLY *begins to cry.*) I didn't mean that, I guess they just always make me feel worthwhile. (*Pause.*) Thank you, I'm sure you're worthwhile too. (*She is resigned.*) If it's all right, I'm not going to tell Muffet I called you. Muffet's the girl who was with me in the museum. Oh, that's all right. Well, thanks for talking to me. Goodbye, thank you. I guess so. (HOLLY *gets down on the bed. Turns the tape player back on. Slides the raccoon coat over her head. Music swells. Lights fade out.*)

The Wake of Jamey Foster

Beth Henley

Premiere: Eugene O'Neill Theatre, New York City, 1982
Setting: Marshael Foster's house and yard in Canton, Mississippi.

Marshael Foster's husband Jamey has died after being kicked in the head by a cow. The casket is brought to her house, and an outrageous crew of family and neighbors gathers for the viewing.

Monologue One: Brocker Slade is a neighboring pig farmer. At fifty-three, he is "big, tired, and worn-out. Yet sometimes when he smiles, he will look like a confused child." Marshael is not happy to see him. After she leaves, her kid brother Leon asks Brocker why.

Monologue Two: It is late at night and Marshael can't sleep. ("It's not like my nerves are raw, you know. It's like they've been stripped, leaving nothing but cold, cold bones.") Restless, she starts to pack Jamey's clothes into a sack. Marshael has distinctly mixed feelings about Jamey's death. Her husband had dreams of becoming "a great worldwide historian," but ended up as an unsuccessful real estate salesman. When Marshael tried to help him by sending his historical manuscript out to a publisher, he left her for a twenty-two-year-old pie baker. Still, it is clear that she loved him—or loved what he could have been.

----- 1 -----

BROCKER

(He takes pictures through the following.)

She, ah, called me to come pick her up from the hospital Tuesday night. We were driving home. It was raining. She was upset, but, ah, but she still looked, you know, good. And for some reason, I started telling her how the first time I'd seen her was, when she was playing her violin at the pancake supper. I said she looked like some sort of wild, frightened angel, ripping up that violin with her black eyes blazing. Then, ah, she started crying. She told me to pull the car over. I did. Well, I don't know. Nothing had ever happened, that way, between us before, and I felt funny with my tongue down her throat holding onto her hair. You know, with her husband there paralyzed in the hospital and with her all in distress. Seemed like maybe I was taking advantage of a situation or something; and so I left. I just took off. Walked home in the storm. Stepped in some god-damn horseshit, leaving her there in the car—alone—wanting somebody; needing something. God. What an asshole. Jesus, no wonder she hates me. (*Upstairs*, MARSHAEL *walks out onto the balcony.*) I leave the one woman I love alone in a great, unrelenting deluge. I give her nothing. Nothing. Not one thing. God, help us all. Listen, Leon; I gotta go. (*He heads for the front door.*)

———— 2 ————

MARSHAEL

All these ties. You never wore even half of 'em. Wasted ties. God, loose change. Always pockets full of loose change. And your Spearmint chewing gum sticks. Damn, and look— your lost car keys. Oh, well, the car's gone now. Damn you, leaving me alone with your mess. Leaving me again with all your goddamn, gruesome mess t'clean up. Damn, you, wait! You wait! You're not leaving me here like this. You're gonna face me! I won't survive! You cheat! I've got t'have something . . . redemption . . . something. (*She leaves the room, goes down to the parlor and walks in. The coffin is closed. She begins to circle it.*) There you are. Coward. Hiding. Away from me. Hiding. (*Moving in on him.*) Look, I know I hurt you something bad, but why did you have to hold her fat, little hand like that? Huh? Treating me like nothing! I'm not . . . nothing. Hey, I'm talking. I'm talking to you. You'd better look at me. I mean it, you bastard! (*She pulls the lid off the coffin.*) Jamey. God, your face. Jamey, I'm scared. I'm so scared. I'm scared not to be loved. I'm scared for our life not to work out. It didn't, did it? Jamey? Damn you, where are you? Are you down in Mobile, baby? Have you taken a spin t'Mobile? I'm asking you—shit—Crystal Springs? How 'bout Scotland? You wanted to go there . . . your grandfather was from there. You shit! You're not . . . I know you're not . . . I love you! God. Stupid thing to say. I love you!! Okay; okay. You're gone. You're gone. You're not laughing. You're not . . . nothing. *(She moves away from the coffin, realizing it contains nothing of value.)* Still I gotta have something. Still something . . . *(As she runs out of the parlor then out the front door.)* The trees. Still have the trees. The purple, purple trees—*(The front door is left open. There is a moment of silence before Brocker appears in the side yard carrying wild flowers and a ladder. He is very drunk. He wears some of the flowers in his hair.)*

A Weekend Near Madison

Kathleen Tolan

Premiere: Actors Theatre of Louisville, 1983
Setting: A handbuilt home near Madison, Wisconsin, Autumn 1979

David is a Wisconsin psychiatrist and Doe, his wife, is a writer with writer's block. This weekend their old friend Nessa, a lesbian feminist singer, is coming through town with her band. She and her lover Samantha are staying with David and Doe. So is David's younger brother Jim, who has hitchhiked up in the pouring rain to see Nessa. He and Nessa were lovers a long time ago, before she "came out." Now Nessa and Sam want a baby, and Nessa would like Jim to father it.

Monologue One: A young female patient of David's keeps calling him up in distress. Nessa suggests a feminist women's collective. When David tells her brusquely that he finds "certain aspects of the women's movement to be a real turn-off," she lets him have it.

Monologue Two: Nessa and Sam have just left to perform their second concert. Jim is still trying to figure out how he feels about the fatherhood request. Doe finds him pondering and asks if he's okay. Jim tells her he's "kind of overwhelmed by . . . well, you know. Modern life. . . . And all this talk about women."

————— 1 —————

NESSA

So what if there are things that aren't, like, "tasteful." And any movement is gonna attract fucked-up people as well as strong, healthy, intelligent people, and some who would've been sympathetic are turned off. Well, so fucking what. They'll be part of the second wave. I mean, you know this, David, any movement is going to alienate people who are too lazy to look at the main intentions of the movement. And I'll tell you something. I came out because I was sick and tired of being a goddamn "sympathizer." *(Pause.)* It's the only way. I really believe that. Women have been oppressed for so long that nothing is going to change if we keep sleeping with our oppressors. I'm sorry, but it's true. Okay, just look at sex. Men fuck you, and the only way, this is true, think about it, the only way to really get off is to submit, I mean there has to be an element of that, of letting go, d'you know, to have it work. So if you're letting go with the people who are keeping you down. . . . And if it's one of those rare cases where the guy isn't an asshole, and he really cares about who you are, it's even harder. Because if the guy is that sensitive he's gotta be really fucked-up. *(Beat.)* Think about it. We have all been so programmed in so many ways to think of the woman as serving the man. The only way to change that is for women to return to the source. To each other. It's the only way.

_____ 2 _____

JIM

I have this memory of this one day when we were all living together?

[DOE. Yes.]

It was a Saturday afternoon in October. Everyone else had gone into Boston for the weekend, so it was just Nessa and you and David and me.

[DOE. Uh-huh.]

Chad Jackson had gotten a big load of wood earlier in the week, and we'd agreed to divide it between the two houses and help each other split the logs on Saturday.

[DOE. I remember that weekend.

JIM. Uh-huh.]

I'd been inside all week, bent over some overdue research paper . . .

[DOE. Uh-huh.]

That afternoon David retrieved me from my little cell and we walked down the road to Chad's. It was this incredible day—bright and windy and it smelled like snow—in fact they were forecasting the first storm, so Chad and David and I got into this kind of frenzy to beat the snow.

[DOE. Uh-huh.]

We were splitting and stacking and yelling and cursing and telling stories, and then the work itself—the physical labor— together with being out in that day—kind of overtook us. And we just kept going, lifting and splitting and lifting and splitting, in silence. Just our breath and the chopping and throwing and the sounds of the woods . . . And when we'd done half of it, we hopped into the truck and drove the rest up to our place and went at it there . . . And I was panting and aching and soaked with sweat—I had no idea where the strength was coming from to lift the ax. At one point I straightened up and just stood there. The light was fading, the sky was a pale yellow, cut with a thin string of charcoal clouds. A patch of the yard was washed with a golden light from the kitchen window. I looked up, and you and Nessa were standing there, looking out at us. And I waved. And you both waved. And, I felt this full-ness. . . . I've never felt so full . . . of life . . . as I did at that moment. *(Pause.)* And I felt like a man. A man. In some deep, ancient sense. *(Pause.)* I don't know. I mean, if I were honest, I guess I'd say that's all I really want. That kind of romantic, traditional thing. I mean, it did feel like we were continuing something . . . the men outside, split-ting wood for the long winter, the women in the kitchen cooking dinner. I mean, I mean, everything else seems so insignificant when I think of that moment.

The Woolgatherer

William Mastrosimone

Premiere: Rutgers Theatre Company, New Brunswick, New Jersey, 1979

Setting: Rose's efficiency apartment, South Philadelphia

Rose is a shy, grave, strange girl who works at the candy counter of a Five-and-Ten. Today she met Cliff, a boisterous truck driver passing through town. Impressed by a "beau-tiful" gesture he made at the store, gently wiping a finger-print off her glass counter, she invited him home with her. Cliff thinks it's an easy seduction. He picks up a six-pack and jauntily escorts Rose home. But Rose is no ordinary pickup. As soon as they walk through the door of her cheer-less apartment, she starts to tell Cliff about a girl who hanged herself "right here in this room." Rose lives in a closeted world of her own, full of leftover food scraps, dead houseplants, and stolen men's sweaters.

Monologue One: Cliff's bad language reminds Rose of "them kids at the zoo . . . radios up against their ears and wild ugly music and cursing! I hate that!" When Cliff asks, "What kids at the zoo?" Rose tells him about "those tall birds with the long thin necks . . . Derricks! No. Cranes."

Monologue Two: Cliff tells Rose about driving a truck. Rose, who has never gone anywhere, thinks it sounds "wonderful . . . free as a bird." Cliff responds.

—————— 1 ——————

ROSE

You may think it's funny but I was the last one to see them alive last summer. There was only seven of them in the world and the zoo had four of them. I used to walk there every night just to watch them stand so still in the water. And they walked so graceful, in slow motion. And they have legs as skinny as my little finger. Long legs. And there was only seven in the world because they killed them off for feathers for ladies hats or something. And one night a gang of boys came by with radios to their ears and cursing real bad, you know, F—, and everything. And I was, you know, ascared. And they started saying things to me, you know, dirty things, and laughing at the birds. And one kid threw a stone to see how close he could splash the birds, and then another kid tried to see how close he could splash the birds, and then they all started throwing stones to splash the birds, and then they started throwing stones *at* the birds, and I started screaming STOP IT! and a stone hit a bird's leg and it bended like a straw and the birds keeled over in the water, flapping wings in the water, and the kids kept laughing and throwing stones and I kept screaming STOP IT! STOP IT! but they couldn't hear me through that ugly music on the radios and kept laughing and cursing and throwing stones, and I ran and got the zoo guard and he got his club and we ran to the place of the birds but the kids were gone. And there was white feathers on the water. And the water was real still. And there was big swirls of blood. And the birds were real still. Their beaks a little open. Legs broke. Toes curled. Still. Like the world stopped. And the guard said something to me but I couldn't hear him. I just saw his mouth moving. And I started screaming. And the cops came and took me the hospital and they gave me a needle to make me stop screaming. And they never caught the gang. But even if they did, what good's that? They can't make the birds come alive again.

2

CLIFF

Free. What's free? Pushin' an eight-year-old played-out dog on retreads that drops a gear box when you get a little ahead of schedule? Free. You say free 'cause you're stuck behind a candy counter all day and a Five-and-Dime don't move. Free. When a dispatcher slips you an extra yard to overload your rig, you ain't free to turn it down, because it's your bread and butter. Without the butter. So now you got to sneak past the scale stations where these jerky little guys with clipboards and twenty-seven pens in their shirt pocket wait for you and your freedom to come eighteen-wheelin' down Primrose Pike. Flags you over. Weighs the rig. You get a fine that wipes out the bribe you just took. Click a button and you got a thousand good buddies who map you a snakepath on backroads that never heard of rules and regulations. But then, out of nowhere, a little yellow flasher comes up in the rearview. Motor Vehicle Inspector out looking for his afternoon quota. Pulls you over. You know he's gonna weigh the rig and slap another summons on you. You know he's gonna crank up his portable scales. Gets out his car like John Wayne with an A-bomb in his holster. Sunglasses so you can't see his eyes. Asks for your logbook, please. Always says please. Looks at it. Scans your

eyes that look more like roadmaps than roadmaps. Closes
it. Hands it back. Knows it's all faked up. Knows you wrote
"rest" every four hundred fifty miles even when you took
no rest because that's the law. But he can't prove it. So to
show his boss he wasn't strokin' the breeze, he gets you
for something else. Dead tail light. Missing mud flap. Dirty
license plate. He's a bonafide specialist in smallness.

"Take a seat in the back of the car, please."

"Hey, look, buddy, could you give me a break?"
He pretends he don't hear. And you got to sit there and
listen to his pen skip. And trucks are passing you. Trucks
with no tail lights. Trucks with no mud flaps. Trucks with
bond papers expired. Trucks with last year's license plates.
But he's got you. And you sit there. And you think. You
think of the money. You think of the doctor who said rattling
around in that bucket of clankity junk's giving you the blad-
der of a seventy-five-year-old. You think of your woman.
Wonder what she's doing. And who she's doing it with. For
a second you don't blame her. Then he hands you the
summons. Puts you in the hole half a yard. Gun the engine.
Pop a Benzedrine. Hit the road. You never turn around.
Never. Tires up on the curb on a narrow street in Baltimore.
Stacking the load on the curb. A rusty old man who's been
cheating death for ten years comes running out the store
waving his arms.

"Hey, buddy, could you bring it in that door for me?"

"Sorry, pal. Bill of lading says sidewalk delivery."

"But can't you just wheel it in for me, buddy. Take you
two seconds."

"I do what the order says, pal."
You really want to help the guy, but why should you? Hey,
sometimes you're the bird, and sometimes you're the windshield. Today, you get to be the bird.

"Sorry, pal. I go by the bill."
And he slips you a sawbuck. Stuff it in your shirt. And you
say:

"Where would you like it, sir?"

Score's even. Next stop, the docks. Pull in. Dispatcher stands there pencil and clipboard checking off unicorns. Pretends he don't see you. You snap on your smile:

"Hey, how ya doin', champ?"

"What can I do for you?"

"Look, buddy, I'm running a little late and I got to blow this town in an hour."

"You got an appointment?"

"Appointment? What're you? a frickin' dentist? Why can't I pull in that spot and unload?"

"No room."

"No room? What's that empty space there?"

"That docks reserved. You got to wait."

"How long?"

"Till there's room."

"How long's that about?"

"You tell me."

Here's another punk you want to bust in the snotbox. But, hey, you asked to get in the game, so play by the rules. You hand him the sawbuck the old man slipped you. And you get a little surprise. He hands it back and walks away. Slow. Now you want to rip his arm off and slap him across the face with it. But that ain't in Murphy's Law: You can't quit, you can't win, you can't break even. So you peel off a double saw. He takes it like he grabbed an ass. Like it never happened. Says like an old beer buddy:

"Back it in, Amigo. Have you truckin' in a snap."

You swear this is your last run. Breeze through the want ads. You're not "Accountant." "Dishwasher and gravedigger" don't appeal. Only thing you're really qualified for is "Plasma donor urgently needed." Next thing you know, you're upshifting through an amber light. And not to hear a personal question you're about to ask, you turn up the radio. But they don't play the good songs no more. They just play them new songs. "O baby o baby o baby o baby I want you o baby I need you o baby drop your laundry." They got shoemakers makin' songs. Fidgit on the CB. Talk ice patches. Radar traps. See a phone booth. Choke it with quarters, dimes, nickles. She's not there. Do a hundred miles. Blinking neon. Diner. Pull over. Coffee, danish, small talk. Do your little routine. Make a waitress laugh. Find out Johnny Blade fell asleep at the wheel out Nevada. Through a guardrail. Two hundred feet. Now he's truckin' in a wheelchair. Do a hundred miles. You think of that waitress in the last diner and sleep. And if you had a choice, you'd take sleep. But you don't. Drink black coffee till you can't taste nothin' but the hotness. You get used to your own stink. No bath, three days. Phone booth. Let it ring thirty times. She's not there. Four in the goddamn morning. Not home. You start talkin' to yourself. You argue with yourself. Whether she this, me that. Whether you should pull over and sleep or do another hundred miles. You argue, you lose, you win, you doze. Rig edges into the other lane. Guy in a Volkswagen beeps like crazy. You see his mouth moving behind the windshield. He's in the right, but you curse him, his family, his car, dog, kids that ain't born yet. Pull over. Lay on the front seat. Tell yourself you're just resting your eyes because the load's got to be in San Jose in six hours or they don't want it, and by rough calculations you can't make it in less than seven and a half. Lay your arm over your face to block out the sun. You see the veins in your wrist, red and blue, like roads on the map. And that question you been giving the slips for the last thousand miles catches up, and you whisper to nobody in particular, "What am I doing? What am I doing?" And you fade. Wonderful. It scares you. You spring up. You think you slept ten hours. It's only two minutes. The Volkswagen passing you. Other trucks passing you. Leap to the wheel. Pop a benny. Peel off. Insect hits the windshield. Leaves its soft green smear on top a thousand others. Count the white lines shooting past. Lose count. Lose touch. Lose yourself in the road. And you're caught. You move with the pack. Keep it between the lines. That's what it comes down to. Keep it movin' even though the road funnels into some

gigantic meatgrinder and every robot's over the limit to be
the first one inside where it's all mangled and mixed and
you holler, SLOW DOWN! but they only see your mouth
movin' behind the windshield. Bulldog tailgating, poundin'
foghorn to make you go faster into the grinder. Sign reads:
NO STOPPING OR STANDING. Radio's goin' "O baby o baby."
Three lanes merge into two. The broken white line becomes
a solid yellow line, and the solid fades and two lanes merge
into one. You floor it. Into the tunnel. Engine echoes off
the walls, drowns out your brain. Air goes rancid. Roll up
the window. Radio goes dead. Turn on the lights. Lights
dim out. Flying down into the tunnel. You look for a miracle. You see a diner ahead. You notice your right blinker
clicking.

Zooman and the Sign

Charles Fuller

Premiere: Negro Ensemble Company, New York City, 1980
Setting: A black urban family neighborhood, formerly safe
Zooman is a streetwise, contemptuous young black man.
In a revenge feud, one of his stray bullets hit an eleven-
year-old girl who was playing nearby. The murdered girl's
family is thrown into shock by the killing. Amid threats of
vengeance and violence, Reuben Tate, the grieving father,
raises a sign in front of the family's house. It reads: "THE
KILLERS OF OUR DAUGHTER JINNY ARE FREE ON THE STREETS
BECAUSE OUR NEIGHBORS WILL NOT IDENTIFY THEM."

The sign polarizes the neighborhood and puts the case
into the papers. Finally, Zooman can't take it. He jumps
onto the Tates' porch and starts slashing the sign with a
knife. At once he is killed by a shot fired by Reuben's
vigilante brother. The cycle of violence and loss continues.
A new sign goes up: "HERE, LESTER JOHNSON WAS KILLED.

HE WILL BE MISSED BY FAMILY AND FRIENDS. HE WAS
KNOWN AS ZOOMAN."

The following monologue opens the play. (*Note:* Zooman
has several monologues.)

ZOOMAN

Once upon a time, while the goose was drinkin' wine? Ole'
monkey robbed the people on the trolley car line. (*Laughs.*)
I carry a gun and a knife. A gun in this pocket—and ole'
"Magic" in this one! (*Takes out knife and flicks it open.*)
Now you see it—(*Makes a stabbing gesture.*) Now you
don't! (*Smiles.*) I cut a mothafucka' with this baby yesterday.
Ole' foreigner walking on the subway platform. (*He wad-
dles, amused.*) Arms swingin' all ova' everywhere—bum-
pin' into people—glasses, two, three inches thick standin'
out from his eyes, can't half see! And I'm trying to listen
to my music too? No-talking mothafucka' needed to get cut.
(*Smiles.*) "Magic" knicked him. "Magic" is sharp as a razor.
He ain't even know he was cut till he was halfway down
the platform, and the blood started runnin' down the ole'
punk's hand. (*Looks at the knife.*) Mothafucka' started
screamin'—dropped his newspapa'—jumpin' up and down,
pleadin' to everybody waitin' on the subway. Ain' nobody
do nothin'—ole' jive West Indian mothafucka' damn near
got hit by a train! (*Laughs.*) Fell all down on the ground
and shit—peed on hisself! Shiiit, he wasn't hurt that bad!
'Magic' only knicked the scared mothafucka'! (*To himself,
after a pause.*) Mothafucka' don't know what scared is!
(*Crosses stage left onto the stage right sidewalk area; dis-
tinct change of mood.*) They call me, Zoo-man! That's right.
Z-O-O-M-A-N! From the Bottom! I'm the runner' down
thea'. When I knuck with a dude, I fight like a panther.
Strike like a cobra! Stomp on mothafuckas' like a whole
herd of Bi-son! Zooman! (*Irritated.*) That ole' mothafucka'
yesterday coulda' put somebody's eye out. Swinging his
arms around like he owned the whole fuckin' platform.

Lotta' ole' people take advantage of you jes' cause they ole'. Movin' all slow and shit—mumblin' unda' they breath—*(Crosses stage right onto his platform.)* shufflin' down the street all bent ova and twisted up—skin hangin' off they faces—makes my stomach turn jes' to look at 'em! I got an Aunt like that. Me and Kenny useta' stay to that mean bitch's house sometimes. Evil ole' skunk walkin' down the avenue, one mile an hour and shit, useta hit us across the mouth with a fly swatter jes' for talkin' at the mothafuckin' table! I was glad when the "junkies" would steal her check. We useta' tell her, she was dumb for goin' down there— don't nobody with any sense walk on the "Avenue" with a social-security check in they hands! *(To himself.)* Lotta' times we'd be to that bitch's house, three—four days, wouldn't eat nothin'. *(Casually crosses stage left onto stage right sidewalk.)* What am I doing here now? I just killed somebody. Little girl, I think. Me and Stockholm turned the corner of this street?—and there's Gustav and them jive mothafuckas' from uptown, and this little bitch has to be sitting on her front steps playing jacks—or some ole' kid shit! But I had tol' Gustav if I eva' saw his ass around the 'Avenue,' I'd blow him away. *(Shrugs.)* So I started shootin' and she jes' got hit by one of the strays, that's all. She ain't had no business bein' out there. That street is a war zone—ain' nobody see her, we was runnin'—shit! And in that neighborhood you supposed to stay indoors, anyway! *(Pause.)* She was in the wrong place at the wrong time— how am I supposed to feel guilty over somethin' like that? Shiiit, I don't know the little bitch, anyway. *(ZOOMAN exits.)*

MONOLOGUE
REFERENCE CHART

Play	Role	Age
WOMEN—TEENS		
Coyote Ugly	Scarlet	12
Getting Out	Arlie	teen
Talking with . . .	April	teen

Play	Role	Age
WOMEN—YOUNG—*Comic*		
Between Daylight and Boonville	Marlene	35
'dentity Crisis	Jane	20s
Gloria and Esperanza	Gloria	young
Landscape of the Body	Rosalie	30s
Loose Ends	Janice	25–30
Lunchtime	Avis	25
Marco Polo Sings a Solo	Diane	20s–30s
The Primary English Class	Debbie Wastba	young
Say Goodnight, Gracie	Catherine	late 20s
Table Settings	Wife	mid-30s

Play	Role	Age
WOMEN—YOUNG—*Seriocomic*		
The Art of Dining	Elizabeth Barrow Colt	early 30s
Birdbath	Velma	26
Calm Down Mother	Sue	20
Come Back to the 5 & Dime, Jimmy Dean, Jimmy Dean	Mona	young
Cowboy Mouth	Cavale	young
Crimes of the Heart	Babe Botrelle	24
Danny and the Deep Blue Sea	Roberta	31
The Days and Nights of Beebee Fenstermaker	Beebee	20s
The Foreigner	Catherine	20s

Character Description	Original Actor	Publisher
trapper, healer & witch	Laurie Metcalf	Dramatists Play Svc.
juvenile delinquent	Pamela Reed	Avon Books
baton twirler	Lisa Goodman	Samuel French
trailer park housewife	Lorna Johnson	Samuel French
manic depressive	Katherine Clarke	Dramatists Play Svc.
showgirl	Julie Bovasso	Samuel French
porno actress	Peg Murray	Dramatists Play Svc.
urban flake	Patricia Richardson	Samuel French
housewife	Kathy Ruhl	Samuel French
retired child prodigy	Madeline Kahn	Dramatists Play Svc.
English teacher	Diane Keaton	Dramatists Play Svc.
airline stewardess	Carolyn Groves	Dramatists Play Svc.
"the ultimate shiksa"	Chris Weatherhead	Samuel French
nearsighted writer	Dianne Wiest	Avon Books
cafeteria worker, Bronx	Barbara Young	Samuel French
tenement dweller	Sharon Gans	Samuel French
five-and-dime worker, Texas	*Sandy Dennis	Samuel French
rock-and-roll kidnapper	Brenda Smiley	Winter House Ltd.
cracked Southern belle	*Mia Dillon	Dramatists Play Svc.
Bronx-Italian	June Stein	Dramatists Play Svc.
would-be novelist, Southern	Rose Gregorio	Dramatists Play Svc.
Southern debutante	Ellen Lauren	Dramatists Play Svc.

* = NYC cast, not original production

Play	Role	Age
The Great Nebula in Orion	Louise	early 30s
In the Boom Boom Room	Chrissy	20s
Jesse and the Bandit Queen	Belle Starr	30
The Lady and the Clarinet	Luba	30s
A Map of the World	Peggy Whitton	early 20s
The Marriage of Bette and Boo	Bette Brennan	20s–30s
Museum	Tink Solheim	20s
Painting Churches	Mags	early 30s
Reckless	Rachel	young
Reckless	Pooty	young
Savage in Limbo	Linda	32
Shivaree	Shivaree	young
Still Life	Cheryl	28
Strange Snow	Martha	30s
Uncommon Women and Others	Holly Kaplan	20s
A Weekend Near Madison	Nessa	early 30s

WOMEN—YOUNG—*Dramatic*

Play	Role	Age
Aunt Dan and Lemon	Aunt Dan	young
Blue Window	Libby	33
Blues for Mister Charlie	Juanita	20s
A Day in the Death of Joe Egg	Sheila	35
The Death of a Miner	Mary Alice Hagar	late 20s– 30s

Character Description	Original Actor	Publisher
fashion designer	Lisa Ross	Dramatists Play Svc.
go-go dancer, Philadelphia	Madeline Kahn	Samuel French
train robber, Western	Pamela Payton-Wright	Samuel French
wine merchant	*Stockard Channing	Dramatists Play Svc.
movie actress	*Elizabeth McGovern	Samuel French
wife and attempted mother	Joan Allen	Dramatists Play Svc.
art lover	Lisa Richards	Avon Books
portrait painter	Frances Conroy	Avon Books
escaped housewife	Lori Cardille	Dramatists Play Svc.
disabled charity worker	Maureen Silliman	Dramatist Play Svc.
Bronx-Italian	Mary McDonnell	Dramatists Play Svc.
bellydancer, Deep South	Maggie Baird	Samuel French
wife of Vietnam vet	Mary McDonnell	Dramatist Play Svc.
high school biology teacher	Kaiulani Lee	Samuel French
student at a women's college	Alma Cuervo	Dramatists Play Svc.
lesbian folksinger	Mary McDonnell	Samuel French
American tutor at Oxford	Linda Hunt	Dramatists Play Svc.
neurotic New Yorker	Randy Danson	Samuel French
student, Southern black	Diana Sands	Samuel French
housewife, British	Zena Walker	Faber & Faber
coal miner, Appalachian	Mary McDonnell	Samuel French

* = NYC cast, not original production

Play	Role	Age
F.O.B.	Grace	20s
Getting Out	Arlene	late 20s
In the Boom Boom Room	Susan	20s-30s
Kennedy's Children	Carla	26
Later	Kate	20s-30s
The Mound Builders	Jean Loggins	25
Passing Game	Julie	young
Savage in Limbo	Denise Savage	32
The Sea Horse	Gertrude Blum	late 30s
Sister Mary Ignatius Explains It All for You	Diane Symonds	28–30
Soap Opera	Lucy	mid-20s
Taken in Marriage	Annie	mid-20s
Thieves	Sally Cramer	mid-30s
The Transfiguration of Benno Blimpie	Mother	30s
The Typists	Sylvia	20s
The Wake of Jamey Foster	Marshael Foster	33
The Woolgatherer	Rose	20s-30s

WOMEN—MIDDLE-AGED—*Comic*

Death Comes to Us All, Mary Agnes	Vivien	45
Sister Mary Ignatius Explains It All for You	Sister	40-60

Character Description	Original Actor	Publisher
journalism student, Chinese-American	Hope Nakamura	Avon Books
ex-con, Kentucky	Susan Kingsley	Avon Books
m.c. in a go-go bar	Mary Woronov	Samuel French
actress/model/would-be sex goddess	Shirley Knight	Samuel French
office assistant	Patti Lupone	Dramatists Play Svc.
gynecologist	Trish Hawkins	Hill & Wang
actor's wife	Margaret Ladd	Samuel French
virgin from the Bronx	Deborah Hedwall	Dramatists Play Svc.
dockside bar owner	Conchata Farrell	Samuel French
ex-Catholic	Ann McDonough	Dramatists Play Svc.
office worker	N/A	Dramatists Play Svc.
bride-to-be	Kathleen Quinlan	Dramatists Play Svc.
sixth-grade teacher, NY	Marlo Thomas	Samuel French
working-class Italian mother	Rosemary de Angelis	Dramatists Play Svc.
office typist	Anne Jackson	Dramatists Play Svc.
seamstress and recent widow, Southern	Susan Kingsley	Dramatists Play Svc.
salesgirl at a candy counter, South Philadelphia	Mary Beth Fisher	Samuel French
heiress	Martha Gaylord	Dramatists Play Svc.
nun	Elizabeth Franz	Dramatists Play Svc.

N/A = not available

Play	Role	Age
WOMEN—MIDDLE-AGED—*Seriocomic*		
The House of Blue Leaves	Bananas Shaughnessy	44
A Midnight Moon at the Greasy Spoon	Zulma Samson	late 40s
Taken in Marriage	Ruth	mid-age
WOMEN—MIDDLE-AGED—*Dramatic*		
Cloud Nine	Betty	mid-age
Fences	Rose Maxson	43
The Effect of Gamma Rays on Man-in-the-Moon Marigolds	Beatrice	mid-age
Ma Rainey's Black Bottom	Ma Rainey	mid-age
Small Craft Warnings	Leona Dawson	mid-age
Still Life	Nadine	43
WOMEN—OLDER		
Bosoms and Neglect	Henny	83
Painting Churches	Fanny Church	60s
Talking with . . .	Anna Mae	old
MEN—TEENS		
Baby with the Bathwater	Young Man (Daisy)	17
Brontosaurus	Nephew	17-18
Curse of the Starving Class	Wesley	late teens
The Dance and the Railroad	Ma	18
Gemini	Herschel Weinberger	16

Character Description	Original Actor	Publisher
insane housewife	Katherine Helmond	Samuel French
out-of-work actress, black	Joan Turetzki	Arte Publico Press
New Hampshire matriarch	Colleen Dewhurst	Dramatists Play Svc.
mother of two, English	Julie Covington	Pluto Press
wife & mother, black	Mary Alice	New American Library
"a widow of confusion"	Sada Thompson	Colophon Books
legendary blues singer, Black	Theresa Merritt	New American Library
beautician and barfly	Helena Carroll	New Directions
artist, divorcée	Timothy Near	Dramatists Play Svc.
blind woman	Kate Reid	Dramatists Play Svc.
uppercrust Boston eccentric	Marian Seldes	Avon Books
McDonald's fan, Southern	Theresa Merritt	Samuel French
psychiatric patient	Keith Reddin	Dramatists Play Svc.
theology student	Jeff Daniels	Dramatists Play Service
California farmboy	Ebbe Roe Smith	Dramatists Play Svc.
Chinese railroad worker	Tzi Ma	Avon Books
public transit freak	Jonathan Hadary	Dramatists Play Svc.

Play	Role	Age
The House of Blue Leaves	Ronnie Shaughnessy	18
Life and Limb	Tod Cartmell	17
Oh Dad, Poor Dad . . .	Jonathan	17
Small Craft Warnings	Bobby	late teens

MEN—YOUNG—*Comic*

Play	Role	Age
The Actor's Nightmare	George Spelvin	20-30
Gloria and Esperanza	Psychiatrist	young
Grown Ups	Jake	30s
Kennedy's Children	Sparger	aging
Landscape of the Body	Raulito	30s
Little Footsteps	Ben	35
Little Murders	Rev. Henry Dupas	young

MEN—YOUNG—*Seriocomic*

Play	Role	Age
Angels Fall	Zappy	21
Christmas on Mars	Nissim	30
Daddies	George	30s
Danny and the Deep Blue Sea	Danny	29
The Fairy Garden	Mechanic	young
F.O.B.	Dale	20s
The Homecoming	Lenny	early 30s
The Lady and the Clarinet	Jack	young
Native Speech	Hungry Mother	early 30s

Character Description	Original Actor	Publisher
Army draftee	William Atherton	Samuel French
black marketeer	*Patrick Breen	Dramatists Play Svc.
stamp collector, stutterer	Austin Pendleton	Hill & Wang
gay teenager from Iowa	David Huffman	New Directions
accountant	Jeff Brooks	Dramatists Play Svc.
hospital psychiatrist	Leonard Hicks	Samuel French
NY Times journalist	Bob Dishy	Samuel French
very-Off Broadway actor	Don Parker	Samuel French
owner of Honeymoon Holidays, Cuban	Richard Bauer	Dramatists Play Svc.
Manhattan yuppie	Mark Blum	Dramatists Play Svc.
pastor of First Existential Church	Richard Schaal	Random House
tennis pro	Brian Tarantina	Hill & Wang
airline steward	Joe Pichette	Dramatists Play Svc.
surrogate father	Kevin Gardiner	Dramatists Play Svc.
Bronx-Italian hothead	John Turturro	Dramatists Play Svc.
male stripper	Rick J. Porter	Dramatists Play Svc.
Chinese-American preppie	Loren Fong	Avon Books
street pimp, London	Ian Holm	Evergreen
advertising executive	*Paul Rudd	Dramatists Play Svc.
postnuclear DJ	John Horn	Broadway Play Publishing

* = NYC cast, not original production

Play	Role	Age
Pastorale	John	mid-20s
Savage in Limbo	Tony	32
Scooter Thomas Makes It to the Top of the World	Dennis	20s
Serenading Louie	Carl	30s
Short Eyes	Ice	late 20s
Tracers	Little John	young

MEN—YOUNG—*Dramatic*

Play	Role	Age
Balm in Gilead	Fick	any age
The Blood Knot	Morris	young
The Blood Knot	Zachariah	young
The First Breeze of Summer	Sam Green	mid-late 20s
Fishing	Robbie	30
The House of Ramon Iglesia	Javier Iglesia	22
Ma Rainey's Black Bottom	Levee	early 30s
A Prayer for My Daughter	Jimmy	early 20s
The Sea Horse	Harry	late 30s
Short Eyes	Clark	early 20s
Soap Opera	Johnny	mid-20s
Still Life	Mark	28
Streamers	Billy	mid-20s
The Sun Always Shines for the Cool	Cat Eyes	young
The Sun Always Shines for the Cool	Willie Bodega	any age
Tracers	Baby San	young

Character Description	Original Actor	Publisher
New England hippie	Jeffrey Fahey	Samuel French
Bronx-Italian stud	Larry Joshua	Dramatists Play Svc.
mourning friend	John Pielmeier	Dramatists Play Svc.
real estate developer	Edward J. Moore	Dramatists Play Svc.
convict, black	Ben Jefferson	Mermaid
soldier in Vietnam	Merlin Marston	Hill & Wang
heroin addict	Neil Flanagan	Hill & Wang
light-skinned South African Coloured	Athol Fugard	Oxford U. Press
dark-skinned South African Coloured	Zakes Mokae	Oxford U. Press
railroad worker, southern black	Carl Crudup	Samuel French
rich hippie drifter	Guy Boyd	Samuel French
Puerto Rican college grad	Giancarlo Esposito	Samuel French
trumpet player, black	Charles S. Dutton	New American Library
junkie	Alan Rosenberg	Samuel French
merchant seaman	Edward J. Moore	Samuel French
child molester	William Carden	Mermaid
auto mechanic	N/A	Dramatists Play Svc.
Vietnam vet, photo artist	John Spencer	Dramatists Play Svc.
Army recruit	John Heard	Samuel French
pimp, Hispanic	Jaime Tirelli	Arte Publico Press
street hustler	Bruce Waite	Arte Publico Press
soldier in Vietnam	Vincent Caristi	Hill & Wang

N/A = not available

Play	Role	Age
The Transfiguration of Benno Blimpie	Benno	20
The Transfiguration of Benno Blimpie	Father	early 30s
The Typists	Paul	20s
A Weekend Near Madison	Jim	early 30s
The Woolgatherer	Cliff	20s-30s
Zooman and the Sign	Zooman	young

MEN—MIDDLE-AGED—*Comic*

The Lisbon Traviata	Mendy	mid-age
The Marriage of Bette and Boo	Father Don-nally	mid-age
Thieves	Martin Cramer	40

MEN—MIDDLE-AGED—*Seriocomic*

Glengarry Glen Ross	Roma	early 40s
Lakeboat	Joe	40s-50s
The Madness of Lady Bright	Leslie Bright	40
Old Times	Deeley	early 40s
Orphans	Harold	mid-age
Reunion	Bernie	53
The Wake of Jamey Foster	Brocker Slade	53

MEN—MIDDLE-AGED—*Dramatic*

Blues for Mister Charlie	Meridian Henry	mid-age
Curse of the Starving Class	Weston	mid-age
Fences	Troy Maxson	53

Character Description	Original Actor	Publisher
Italian-American, 500 lbs.	James Coco	Dramatists Play Svc.
working-class Italian-American	Roger Serbagi	Dramatists Play Svc.
typist & night-school law student	Eli Wallach	Dramatists Play Svc.
art gallery worker	Randle Mell	Samuel French
truckdriver	Ray Baker	Samuel French
mugger, urban black	Giancarlo Esposito	Samuel French
opera lover	Seth Allen	Dramatists Play Svc.
priest	Richard B. Shull	Dramatists Play Svc.
NYC grade school principal	Richard Mulligan	Samuel French
real estate salesman	Jack Shepherd	Grove Press
able-bodied seaman	Larry Shue	Samuel French
fading queen	Neil Flanagan	Hill & Wang
English	Colin Blakely	Evergreen
gentleman crook, Chicago	Lane Smith	Samuel French
ex-alcoholic	Don Marston	Grove Press
pig farmer, Mississippi	Brad Sullivan	Dramatists Play Svc.
minister, southern black	Percy Rodriguez	Samuel French
avocado farmer, western California	James Gammon	Dramatists Play Svc.
garbage collector, black	James Earl Jones	New American Library

Play	Role	Age
Ma Rainey's Black Bottom	Toledo	mid-50s
A Prayer for My Daughter	Sean	40s
The Real Thing	Henry	40ish
A Soldier's Play	Tech/Sgt. Waters	mid-age
Teeth 'n' Smiles	Saraffian	early 50s
MEN—OLDER		
Mad Dog Blues	Waco Texas	old
A Midnight Moon at Greasy Spoon	Joe	late 60s

Character Description	Original Actor	Publisher
piano player, black	Robert Judd	New American Library
crook, a "weird"	Laurence Luckinbill	Samuel French
playwright, English	Jeremy Irons	Faber & Faber
drill sergeant, black	Adolph Caesar	Samuel French
rock-and-roll manager, English	Dave King	Faber
country-western cowboy	John Bottoms	Winter House
restaurant owner, former vaudevillian	Harvey Pierce	Arte Publico Press

AFTERWORD

A Conversation
with Christopher Durang

Christopher Durang was born in Berkeley Heights, New
Jersey. He received a B.A. from Harvard and an M.F.A.
from the Yale School of Drama. He has won Obie Awards
for *Sister Mary Ignatius Explains It All for You* and *The
Marriage of Bette and Boo*, sharing a second Obie for Out-
standing Ensemble Acting for his performance as Matt in
Bette and Boo. Durang's other plays include *The Actor's
Nightmare*, *A History of the American Film*, *Beyond Therapy*, *Baby with the Bathwater*, *Titanic*, *The Idiots Kara-
mazov* (written with Albert Innaurato), and *Das Lusitania
Songspiel* (written and performed with Sigourney Weaver).

In the published introduction to Titanic, *you wrote that
since that play was miscast in an early production, you had
been involved in casting all subsequent productions of your
plays. Is that still true?*

I have been involved if it's in New York, where I live,
or if it's a premiere of a play, regardless of where it is. If
it's a subsequent production in a regional theatre, I actually
have not been involved. I've been lucky enough to be produced so often that I wouldn't have time left for anything
else. It's strange, it's probably good for me to let go of plays
after a while and let people interpret them as they have
to, or as they see fit. But it makes me long for a good movie
version of something of mine. For instance, *A Streetcar
Named Desire*, even with the changes they had to make
due to the Production Code, is a good film version. So you
don't see, for instance, Blanche DuBois being played as a
cracker. People know there's sort of an archetype, and that's
not true in my plays. Sister Mary Ignatius, for example,

can be played as a total virago, and it's not how I like it done.

What do you look for when you are there in casting?

My work requires a comic flair, but with a foot in reality. When people audition for my plays, I would say that a third of them clearly get the style instinctively. And that means two thirds don't. They come in and the scenes literally do not work. In a lot of my plays, particularly the earlier ones, the comedy is very broad, as written. It's exaggerated. In those really exaggerated plays, if the actor exaggerates more, it becomes like telling a joke too loud, or underlining the punchline. Suddenly it isn't funny. Some actors think, "Oh God, I'm in a comedy, I have to be funny."

There is that cliché, which is true, mostly, that the better comedy comes from a real place. Diane Keaton, in *Annie Hall*, is acting from a real place, and she's very funny at the same time.

When I say, for instance, that Sister Mary can be played as a virago or just as a bitch. . . . Imagine if Cloris Leachman played Sister Mary like she played that nurse in Mel Brooks's *Young Frankenstein*. The audience might laugh hilariously, because Cloris is very funny, but the play would not be the play I wrote. It would be this cartoon about this awful, awful, *awful* woman ruining all these children. But when the play turned serious at the end, the audience would resist it. (Cloris Leachman *did* play Sister Mary, by the way, quite brilliantly. She's a wonderful actress.)

It's really a fine line, because if you go to the other extreme of playing it overly seriously, the play becomes deadly. That's happened less frequently to my work, but it usually ruins the play. I recently had the experience of seeing Matt, the part I played in *The Marriage of Bette and Boo*, done by someone who played it very, very self-pityingly. All the words can support that, but it changes the tone, making the play about this person who is destroyed by his background. That's not how it came off in New York. I think the ending of *Bette and Boo* is about forgiveness, without anyone saying it. We really discovered that through Jerry Zaks, the director. And that's one reason why it was so painful to watch this other production, because the ending, the meaning of the play, was totally different.

What was it like to play that role?

It was exciting, and also very dangerous. Matt is clearly very close to my biography—or rather, Bette and Boo are close to my parents' biography. Matt's character is really implied rather than presented in the play, and I didn't write it with the idea that I would play it. In fact, I saw other people play him in an earlier one-act version, including a black actor once.

Unlike most of my plays, which I've tended to write in a chunk all at once, or over a few months, I really wrote *Bette and Boo* over ten years, putting it aside for five years. When I finally completed the full-length version, it was Joe Papp's idea that I should play Matt. I was worried about it, because I thought my presence might turn him self-pitying, or would make it too eerie. It was a scary thing to do, but I was very excited that Joe Papp, who runs such a powerful theatre, wanted me to be in my own play.

When you act in your own plays, do they feel very different from inside?

The Actor's Nightmare felt just as I thought it would, and I enjoyed it enormously. The role of George is rather more mysterious to play than one would think. In auditions people would come in, and if they didn't have the right instinct for it, it just wouldn't be funny.

First of all, George is very innocent. He doesn't know where he is or how he got there—he's a bit of a blank slate. I've seen some actors bring their own awareness of how upsetting it would be to be on stage and not remember their lines. They play it with sheer, building terror. I don't find that interesting. If an actor just plays fear, there's no playfulness going on. One of the keys is that in the beginning of the play he says he's an accountant. Now, a lot of people have gotten hung up saying, "Well, an accountant would never dream this, so he must really be an actor who *thinks* he's an accountant." Once they think that way, they're probably thinking too hard about the play anyway. If I had to choose, I'd make him an accountant so he's a real innocent who doesn't know where the hell he is. It's also more existential, we're all accountants in this theatre of life, you know, wandering about. . . . But I think it's important to let the audience enjoy the playfulness of watching George try to figure out what his cue might be. Each line has a logic to George.

In your notes to the published edition of some of your plays you wrote that there's a very moment-to-moment quality to your work, that the actor must commit fully to whatever is going on in each moment.

Kate McGregor-Stewart, who's been in a lot of my plays, once advised some other actors who were new to my work that when she does my plays, she just commits to each line fully and doesn't actually worry where it comes from. She presumes I've done that work.

Talk a bit more about the specific characters whose monologues appear in this book. Let's start with Bette and Father Donnally, from The Marriage of Bette and Boo.

I think Bette's monologue and Father Donnally's monologue are probably two of the better ones for actors to try. Bette's has a lot of ties to realistic writing, actually. It's the first clear cue to the audience that they don't have to find everything funny—as a matter of fact, there's a lot in the play they're not meant to find funny. One can theoretically go through that whole speech and never get a laugh, and that's fine with me. There are little laughs in there, but the purpose is not to get laughs. It's a character monologue about Bette's sadness and vulnerability and her sort of childish girlishness. I think it's less in the "Durang style" than a lot of my writing, and thus easier, in a way, for actors.

Was it in the one-act version of the play?

No, it wasn't. I wrote it later, in the middle of a period when I wasn't working on the play, but suddenly thought of it. I remember writing it in a notebook and liking it, but also feeling it was very different that there's nothing like it in the short version. Frankly, it's sort of dead-on poignant, which is fine, but there's not a lot of that in my work.

What about Father Donnally?

Oddly enough, I have never seen that monologue done badly. Even when I've seen productions of *Bette and Boo* that I haven't liked, usually the Father Donnally is very good. And I have also seen many different interpretations of it. For instance, I just saw a very funny one at Arena Stage—by Terrence Currier, a member of their company—where he was extremely Irish, as Terrence himself is. He basically did a drunken priest, but didn't push it over the top. It was rooted in reality, not a Mel Brooks drunken turn. The more he drank, the more his logic got screwed up, and his temper got caught up.

Now Richard B. Schull, who did it in New York, was also drinking wine, but that was less important in his performance. Richard is a very funny character actor and has a great character look as well. He simply played it as a priest who had been through this for many years. At first he felt, "Let's just get through this quickly, I've done this before," but as he got more into the argument itself, he started to get irritated at all these people wanting him to solve their problems. The last part of his speech is about exasperation. I've never seen anyone play the end without exasperation, and it probably wouldn't be right to. Though every so often, someone can surprise you with a weird interpretation. Just avoid the Mel Brooks stuff.

How about Jane's Peter Pan speech in 'dentity Crisis?

That seems to work best when she just reports it with a certain quizzical quality: "Isn't this strange that this happened?" If she pushes how crazy the events were, the scene stops being funny—again that problem of taking writing that's exaggerated, and exaggerating it further. It's a good monologue, but I don't think it gives opportunities to show a lot of acting colors. It lets you show simplicity and timing, but if you want something to show off an array of emotions, you probably shouldn't choose it.

And Vivian's monologue in Death Comes to Us All, Mary Agnes?

Oh, I'd love to talk about that one, because I know so little about it! I've seen only one production in my entire life, at the Yale School of Drama, and I've never seen it auditioned for, so in a way I don't know its pitfalls. Going back to my thoughts when I wrote it, Vivian is a narcissist to the most extreme degree: she wants all eyes upon her. You could either play her as grand, or you could play her as just *assuming* everyone's looking at her. She also probably likes the sound of her own voice. She talks a lot, and some of her speech is actually contradictory, but she doesn't care, as long as it sounds good. Whatever she says is true at that moment.

How about Baby with the Bathwater—*Daisy's first psychiatric session?*

What I said about *'dentity Crisis* is also true here: there is an awful lot of benefit in being factual about it, a quizzical factualness. Both Jane and Daisy feel, "Gee, something seems wrong in the world."

Daisy has had just a ghastly upbringing, but he doesn't have any idea of how ghastly it was because he's shut down his emotions. He's presenting it as if he were saying, "I remember my birthday, I was three and they bought me a cake." But instead he's saying, "My parents dressed me as a girl because they didn't know which sex I was."

Both *'dentity Crisis* and this Daisy speech might be very good exercises for simplicity for somebody who tends to overcomplicate things and wants to work on being simple. This is something I think actors are sometimes afraid of.

What about Diane in Sister Mary?

That speech is really tough. The material about the rape and the mother's death is so obviously sad and volatile and upsetting for Diane that it's very tricky not to push it too far: "Oh, pity me, pity me," or taking it into red hot rage, or reliving the experience. Also, the speech is extremely verbal. She carries on an intellectual argument throughout the whole speech. My notes in the published edition were actually based on one particular actress from her audition, who really distressed me with what she did—every single word at the top of her lungs, near screaming and tears. In the midst of that hysteria, no one could believably present the logic of the speech. Whoever plays Diane has to have a gift for making the intellectual argument both followable and interesting.

Jerry Zaks found something in the Off Broadway *Sister Mary* that I hadn't intended but that turned out to be great. What Jerry and Polly Draper, who played Diane, chose to do was to find a place in the middle of the speech to let the vulnerable emotion break through. When Diane says, "I wasn't even asking that she live, just that He end her suffering"—she's in the middle of talking logic, but she starts to get tears in her voice. It also gave Elizabeth Franz, the actress playing Sister Mary, a great moment to be sympathetic. She went over and held Polly Draper's hands, and you saw that Sister was not this person without feelings, that she could respond to Diane's vulnerability for a moment. But because the speech had to keep going, Diane put the lid back on, pulled away from Sister and said, "So why was He letting her suffer? Spite?" And she's back to her logic again.

Anyway, it's a very hard speech, I must say. I'd almost recommend it more for an acting class than for an audition.

Talk a little bit about Sister Mary herself, how you think that character works best.

The first time *Sister Mary* was performed, Jerry Zaks was the director and Elizabeth Franz was Sister. I was very excited by what Elizabeth brought to the part. So many people said, "Oh my God, she's *just* like such and such Sister I had!" Her face happened to look very much that

way, but she also caught a lot of realistic things. She had
a delicacy very much like certain nuns, and she was very
sweet to Thomas. Also, there was something about her
whole manner that seemed so sexually repressed. I don't
know how you act that, and I don't mean that Elizabeth
Franz herself is that, but when she put on the nun's habit,
she took that on. She brought a lot of very realistic colors
to it.

In her lecture at the beginning of the play, Sister Mary
is basically listing what to her are facts, so there's nothing
surprising about any of it. I love that part of the humor.
Elizabeth would explain how many billion years you would
be in Purgatory in the most offhanded manner, as just
another fact.

*Do you want to talk about the controversy surrounding
that play?*

It is a heated issue for me. The protests bother me on
two fronts. The political one is, I genuinely feel, a threat
to free speech. The groups protesting the play say, "You
can't make fun of people's beliefs, if they hold them sincerely." That's pretty crazy, because what *anybody* believes, they believe sincerely. And what the play actually
pokes fun at is ideas. Mortal and venial sin is an idea. If I
can't criticize an idea, suddenly the meaning of free speech
is pretty skewed.

So I'm very concerned about it politically, because I think
this country is getting pretty conservative. Also, free speech
doesn't just protect liberals: There are lots of feminist groups
or gay groups who would also protest certain plays. Having
been through this, I'm really with the A.C.L.U. in saying
that the best remedy for speech you don't agree with is
more speech, not limiting speech. And that really does
include allowing plays that we're all horrified by to be performed. We can protest them; but saying that they can't
be heard is the real danger.

The other way the controversy upsets me—and this is

really less important, but important enough for me—is that it affects me personally. I feel misunderstood.

Has anyone ever told you that you're a very serious person to write such funny plays? That you seem to have a good twin and a bad twin?

I know, isn't it strange? Actually, my early plays—*Death Comes to Us All, Nature and Purpose of the Universe,* and *'dentity Crisis*—offended some people, because the humor was so far out and kind of violent. *Nature and Purpose* in particular was very violent. So was *Better Dead Than Sorry,* which hasn't been published. And *Titanic.* I was relieved that people meeting me would say, "Gosh, you're not at all what we expected," because I thought if I was anything like these plays, I would be very unpleasant to be around.

My early plays—*Titanic* and *Nature and Purpose of the Universe* are good examples—presented alarming behavior, and there was no way for the audience to know what the author thought of it. So a lot of them thought he must be insane, he thinks this behavior is fine. Later on—actually it starts with Diane's speech in *Sister Mary*—you do get a sense of what the author thinks. And that's also true in *The Marriage of Bette and Boo* and, oddly enough, in *Baby with the Bathwater.* So I feel the side of me that is more serious or more sane is starting to show through in my writing.

A Conversation
with Lanford Wilson

Lanford Wilson was born in Lebanon, Missouri, and is a founding member of New York's Circle Repertory Company. His full-length plays include *Balm in Gilead, The Rimers of Eldritch, Lemon Sky, The Hot L Baltimore, The*

Mound Builders, Serenading Louie, Angels Fall, and the
Talley cycle: *Fifth of July, Talley and Son,* and the Pulitzer
Prize-winning *Talley's Folly.* Wilson's many other awards
include the Drama Critics Circle Award, the American In-
stitute of Arts and Letters Award, and a special Obie for
Sustained Achievement. This interview took place during
a break in rehearsals for his new play, *Burn This,* at the
Mark Taper Forum in Los Angeles.

Do you know when you're going to write a monologue?
Not very often. In *The Rimers of Eldritch,* I knew that
I was going to write Skelly's monologue, because I wrote
the whole play without it and knew that it had to be there,
but didn't know quite where. I didn't want it to be at the
top of the second act, because I had just done *Balm in
Gilead,* which has a monologue at the top of the second
act. But there was no way out of it.
When I wrote Darlene's long monologue in *Balm in
Gilead,* I wrote it as a short story, to help me understand
the character. It wasn't a piece of the play, it was research.
But when I finished it, I knew it had to be in the play. I
thought it was just going to be Darlene speaking, but Ann
started answering. And then it got longer and longer—I
couldn't believe I was making it quite that long—but it was
very exciting. The monologue usually runs between sixteen
and twenty minutes, a very major portion of the second
act. It's almost a one-act play.
*You write two kinds of monologues. Some are addressed
to the audience, and some come out of a scene. Talk a little
bit about audience address, because that's something that
you do wonderfully, and in a very particular way.*
When I first started writing, I was playing a lot more
with audience/actor relationships and character/audience
relationships. It was great fun. I think it's revealed best in
the way that *The Great Nebula in Orion* works. The characters are much more honest with the audience than they
are with one another.

At the same time, they overhear one another's asides, which I've never seen anywhere else.

I couldn't help that. I was playing with two people on-stage and with a stage convention, and then I thought, "Why on earth are we going to pretend that she didn't hear that? She's sitting right there!" So I had great fun throwing the convention of "You're not supposed to hear this" to the wind.

Does this call for a different kind of approach for the actor?

When I rewrote *Serenading Louie,* I took certain speeches that were addressed to the audience and put them in the context of the play. For example, when the characters were reminiscing about school, Mary turned to the audience and said about her husband, "I don't really think that I loved him then. But I love him then now." And there was a pause, and they all went back to talking. In the original *Louie,* none of the other characters heard her say that. But in the new version not only do they hear it, they have to deal with it, and it changes the whole mood of the party. Everyone has to be saddened by it, or ignore it, or at least have an individual reaction. That changed the scene a lot.

You often write roles for particular actors.

Since we started Circle Rep, since '69—really, since *The Hot L Baltimore.*

Do you think that hearing a particular actor's voice affects the way you write monologues?

Say I'm writing something for Conchata Farrell. When the big, blowsy whore came down the stairs in *The Hot L Baltimore,* I wondered, "Who in the hell is this?" And then I thought, "Oh, this would be perfect for Chatty Farrell," and aimed it straight as a challenge for her.

So you see the character first.

Almost always the character first, and then, "Who can do this?" From time to time you take shameless advantage of something you know the actor can do very well, but usually it's more fun to aim it as a challenge.

Have you sometimes found that when you're thinking of a particular actor for a role, and someone else comes in to read it, that you rediscover the character in some way?

Sometimes, yes. I very often use the actor as a stimulus to me. If you're writing *Talley's Folly* for Judd Hirsch, you want to take advantage of everything he could possibly do. You want to show those incredible depths that he has, but also the lightness, the jokes, the dancing, the funny voices and the imitations—everything you can possibly come up with. He even sings at one point. It made the character so much richer to challenge Judd to take advantage of that instrument—and to challenge myself to take advantage of that instrument.

But the real challenge with Judd, since he'd been in comedies, was to see how deep I could go. How soulful? And the answer was, pretty goddamned soulful! That was a direct challenge, and consequently I wrote one of my richest characters.

And other actors have come up to me, saying they had more fun playing that part than any other part they've ever played. A lot of people have done it now, so I guess it's a challenge to anyone.

What about Carl's monologue in Serenading Louie, *when he's talking about his religious period and the promise to his mother?*

That is directly from my experience. Carl says he was fourteen. I was a little younger, probably about eight. Mother had a thyroid operation, and I very well remember doing all those things. It was really quite an extraordinary period. I had to go live with my grandmother for a month, and when I came back, of course, Mother was perfectly fine. It wasn't a difficult operation at all, but it had terrified me.

And you did make a pact with God?

Oh yes, absolutely! And I gradually decided it really hadn't been His intervention, so I could start doing all those things that I swore I'd give up. I did them very gradually, so God wouldn't notice.

Many things in my plays come from my own experiences. The Satori experience in *Brontosaurus* is direct as a plank; it happened exactly that way. The challenge, of course, is to change it into a character speaking, and in this case I wanted to write it as simply as I could for him, because he's a no-frills sort of person.

Do you think you borrow more from your own experience when a character is telling a story in monologue form?

Sometimes I borrow from others' experiences. For Darlene's monologue in *Balm in Gilead*, I didn't get the marriage license, but I went with someone who did. And everything Darlene says is true, except that Cotton was not Cotton. Cotton was somebody else. Only the names have been changed to protect the innocent. And the physical descriptions. But all of that happened.

That play feels so much like a documentary. You keep thinking, "God, he was lucky to overhear this!" Then of course you realize that it's not luck, it's knowing what to do with what you hear.

I overheard an awful lot.

The monologue I chose for the book is Fick's, at the end of Act One.

I had no money to give to Fick. I was very, very poor. I was working on *Balm in Gilead*. I would go into this coffee shop at night and drink a cup of coffee. The counterman got to know me, and he knew what I was doing. He'd refill my cup and pretend I wasn't there, and I'd sit there for six hours writing down everything I heard, then orchestrating and organizing it if I wasn't hearing much. I was really quite far into the play, but Fick wasn't yet in it at all.

I was living on Seventy-fourth Street, and the closest subway stop is Seventy-second. One night at four in the morning—*pouring* rain, rain like you've never seen—I got off the subway, and this *kid*, this little tiny kid latched onto me and started running sideways like Ratso Rizzo. I had no umbrella or anything. I was walking as fast as I could, and he was walking backwards and sideways beside me. I had not a nickel on me, and I really didn't want to be his buddy forever. He was high on God knows what—heroin, he said.

When I finally got to the door of my building, I said, "I'm sorry, they won't let you come up. I have to say good-bye here. I have absolutely nothing for you." I went upstairs and said, "Well, one thing I *can* do is write down every damn word he said."

So that speech was said to me almost verbatim between Seventy-second Street and Seventy-fourth. He really did say, "It's getting cold. What is it, October?" I just couldn't believe that someone didn't know the month. And it *wasn't* October, it was November. So he automatically went in the play.

Did any of the people on whom you based characters come to see Balm in Gilead?

One. Dopey. Dopey was named . . . it doesn't matter. He read the play. He didn't come to see it because by the time it got onstage a year later, I had moved and didn't know how to reach him. But he was kind of a buddy of mine. I liked him a lot. When he read the play, he said it was more or less okay, it was kind of fun, but I was a little easy on the drug scene. I had gotten some of my information on drugs from him. He sort of "corrected my paper" for me.

What about Louise in The Great Nebula in Orion?

That's one of those incredible things you just fall into. A producer friend of mine who cooks was talking to me one day before rehearsal at her house, and she did that entire speech. It was about an acting award, not the Coty Award, but she did the whole speech, and I was dumb Carrie saying, "That is astonishing, that's . . ." And I remembered it. I have a very, very good memory—or did have, when I was young. A year or two later, I was working on *Serenading Louie*. I was going to put that speech into it, and I thought no. So I put *Serenading Louie* aside and wrote *The Great Nebula in Orion*.

So you really wrote the play around that speech.

Louise's whole character came from that speech. The woman who told me the story was not gay, but I liked the idea of Louise being gay and having a sort of odd relationship with her mother. It doesn't often happen, but Fick and Louise just dropped right in my lap.

What about Jean's speech in The Mound Builders, *about the spelling bee?*

Oh! I'm the worst speller in the world, so that certainly didn't come from my experience! However, my grandmother used that kind of syllable spelling, which was just the most melodic thing in the world. I loved it. When I was writing, suddenly Jean said, "I won the spelling bee." And I said, "My God, you did?" And it just came out.

What about Zappy's speech in Angels Fall, *about tennis and finding his calling?*

That happened to me. That's the way I discovered I was a playwright.

How old were you?

I was nineteen. I had written several stories, sent them off, and gotten them back. I always say I have rejection slips from the best magazines in the country—quite a collection, too, from back then. I had been involved in acting in high school, and once in college I was a stage manager. But it never crossed my mind that plays were *written*. Certainly not by anyone we know.

But I'd thought of this idea, and probably because it was so much like *The Glass Menagerie*, I thought, Oh, that's not a story, that's more like a play. So I sat down and started writing it, and by the middle of the second page I said out loud, "I'm a playwright." It was the most astonishing, wonderful experience that's ever happened. I knew instantly that this was what I should do for the rest of my life. And I knew that it was so enormous an undertaking that I'd never be able to get it right, so it's always a challenge, a very large challenge.

But I would have forgotten that experience except that

on television—see, something *can* come from watching television—they were interviewing some basketball player (I think it might have been Kareem Abdul Jabbar) and they said, "Have you always played basketball? When did you know you were going to be a great basketball player?" just as a stupid question. He said, "My father gave me a basketball for my sixth birthday. He threw it to me, I took two dribbles, and said, "I'm a basketball player. And that's what I want to do with my life."

That connected back to my own experience, and when I got to *Angels Fall*, which talks so much about work and those choices we make, I knew from the beginning that Zappy was going to have this speech. So as long as you know he's going to have the theme-of-the-play speech, you have all the freedom in the world to make him nutty and crazy and ridiculous and silly. You laugh at him all the way through, because you know he's going to fool you.

Have you been involved with auditions for a lot of your plays? Have actors brought in monologues, or have they usually read from the script?

They've read from the script. Sometimes we do plunge right into some of those speeches, but usually with a little preparation.

What grabs your eye when you're looking at an actor? What do you look for them to find in your work?

I look for them to find the character in themselves—if they *believe* him and understand him. It's astonishing how many actors will come in with something they really haven't understood at all, that means nothing to them. They really haven't found it yet. But when they do understand it, and find it in themselves, I love it. I also love it when they surprise me, make it different from what I expected or heard in my head, but still true. That's hard, though. You can't go for being kooky or weird or having an oddball rhythm. It has to come organically from you, and when it does it can be very exciting.

Now, you still might be completely wrong for the part.

The best reading we had for *Lemon Sky* was by a girl named Mari Gorman, who was absolutely and completely wrong for the part. She's a gamine, a little street gamine, and Carol is much more sophisticated than that. We tried to get more sophistication, but we were just ruining what Mari had brought to it. She had brought *herself* to it—brilliantly—but we couldn't use her. So I wrote Jackie in *The Hot L Baltimore* for her. It changed that part completely.

In rehearsals, actors are always coming up with line deliveries that are different from what I heard, and I yak with laughter, just yak-yak-yak. For a long while actors thought I was laughing at my own play! No, I was laughing at a twist they brought to it that was completely different from what I'd imagined. It's just wonderful to have that happen.

A Conversation with Tina Howe

Tina Howe was born in New York City. She is the author of *The Nest, Birth and Afterbirth, Museum, The Art of Dining, Painting Churches,* and *Coastal Disturbances.* Ms. Howe is the happy recipient of an Outer Critics Circle Award, a Rockefeller Grant, an N.E.A. Fellowship, and an Obie Award for Distinguished Playwriting.

How would you define a monologue?

A monologue, to me, is the writer's and the character's chance to explore those darker, spongier places of the human spirit that you can't show in simple action, in simple behavior. My monologues tend to be rather dark confessions. Even though a lot of them have a comic overtone, they tend to come out of something neurotic. A monologue has to do with revealing things that the character has been unable to reveal before. So it's a very precious moment.

One of the characteristics of my writing is that I always feel that every one of my plays has to have a killer monologue in it. I love to try and see if every character can have a moment of revelation when something really ghastly, something really private and rather ugly, is revealed. I usually write monologues for all my characters, mainly to explore their depths: what it is that animates them, what their secrets are. I think that a monologue is a way of investigating a character's darker side.

So you use monologues as background material when you're first working on the characters?

Yes. It's something that's always on my mind, that every character should be capable of giving a killer monologue, and that if push came to shove and the characters are put into a situation of utter desperation, they should be able to stop everything cold with something harrowing and gorgeous. And if they can't do that, then there's something wrong with the way I conceived them. I invariably end up dispensing with a lot of these monologues because they won't have any dramatic function.

And how does a killer monologue make it onstage?

For me, when a character gets to the point of giving a monologue, it means that everything else has broken down, that all normal channels of communication have collapsed. Things have gotten so out of hand that the only way the character can regain his equilibrium is to say, "STOP! Wait a minute! I have to say this!"

And even then . . . There's something very peculiar and quite wonderful about a lot of your monologues: the person they're addressed to is often not listening at all.

(Laughs.) Right!

In Painting Churches, *when Mags is describing her first gallery show, and it's very urgent for her to tell her parents about this, they're busy posing as paintings. So that what reads as a monologue from Mags's point of view, a continuous story she's telling, actually looks on the page like a scene. And Tink's monologue in* Museum. *There seems to be this theme of not listening. Do you have any theories about that?*

Oh, God. I'm not very psychoanalytical, but I suppose it's because I grew up in a household with all these very brilliant talkers, and everyone was always *talking* and being terribly smart and terribly entertaining, and I suppose it was hard to be heard.

Also, I think it's because I see monologues coming out of desperation, that the character is so frustrated and so thwarted. . . . I suppose it's a kind of a little suicide, a little suicidal dance the person is performing. And to me, it makes it even more dramatic if the other people *aren't* listening, because it forces the person giving the monologue to be even more daring and extravagant in the things that he's saying in an attempt to get their attention.

So it ups the dramatic urgency.

And the longer the listener *doesn't* pay attention, the more exquisite chance that you the writer have to try to win it. If the person giving the monologue is fighting a losing battle, then it forces you the writer to go deeper and deeper into that character's own torment, into his visual bank, his memory bank, and become more and more extreme.

The danger, of course, is that you can get totally carried away. I was working on a failed play for about a year, and there was this huge killer monologue in it that kept getting longer and longer, and more and more baroque and outrageous. There comes a point when you can feel that you're going off into outer space. And when that happens, when the character is starting to shred in front of your eyes, it's usually a pretty good indication that you've lost the momentum of the scene. When killer monologues kill themselves, it's a sign that you've got to back off!

You have to key the tone and the nature of the monologue to the piece that you're writing. If you have a piece of work that is very decorated, in *Painting Churches*, for example, all of the characters tend to be rather eccentric and talk a

lot, so Mags's monologues had to be even more heightened
than my normal characters' monologues would be. Whereas
in *The Art of Dining*, which doesn't have all that many
monologues, I have one character, Elizabeth Barrow Colt,
who is terrified of food. For her, the monologue is a chance
to avoid having to eat. There is a certain amount of talking
in *The Art of Dining*, but there's much more eating. Most
of the talk is just about ordering, and the familiar behavior
of eating and dieting and all those little one-phrase ex-
changes that people have. Because none of the characters
really got into expressing themselves that much, I knew I
had a real potential for fireworks with Elizabeth.

*But for the actress playing Elizabeth, it's very practically
motivated. Talking becomes a substitute for eating, and a
way of avoiding her fear of food.*

I guess the trick of writing that play was turning my own
fear of food into a love of food, and into rejoicing over the
whole phenomenon of dining and how it's been exalted into
an art form. It's curious, I believe that plays come from
previous plays, that every play is in some way an attempt
to redress the inadequacies or the questions that were un-
answered by the play that went before. In *Museum*, I had
shown people coming to look at the work of artists, and it
left me wanting to write a play showing the artist actually
caught in the moment of creativity. I got it in my head that
I wanted to write something that would show an artist
enthralled by her materials. You think of a writer, but that's
so *boring*, because all you do is sit at a typewriter. Or you
think of a painter, but it's a nonverbal, rather quiet art
form. I was trying to think of different kinds of artists and
how you could get an audience involved in their creation,
and then I thought of a cook, because you see all that food
getting slung around.

And I have very strong feelings about food, mainly sort
of negative, because of the way I grew up. Mealtime was
the time when you were supposed to be social and entertaining, and we'd all sit at the big dining room table and

try to be as clever as we could. So that I always felt this responsibility to entertain my parents, and their guests, and my brother, and the *food*—I just couldn't cope with the food! The onus of being entertaining was so strong that the food was just impossible to deal with. And it's funny, my husband suddenly raised a very interesting question, and that was, "Was the food any good?" Maybe the food wasn't that *good*! It had never occurred to me! Maybe our Irish cook Dodie wasn't a great cook, and it was just sort of mediocre cooking. It had never crossed my mind that the *food* might have been at fault. I immediately assumed it was my fault!

And the other thing is that my father, as is true in *The Art of Dining*, ate very fast. He *gobbled* it down. It was on the plate and then—WHOOSH—it disappeared. And my mother did play with her food, and she put on all this lipstick. It was on all the time. She put it on before meals and after meals and during meals, so that the lipstick would come off on her fork and stain her food pink. And she played with it, because I don't think she enjoyed eating very much either.

We had *very* entertaining mealtimes, mind you! My father was the only one who would eat, because my mother would play with her food, and I would just look at mine. We had very comical evenings. I mean, they were a scream. We would laugh a lot, and do accents, and tell stories and carry on. But somehow the spectacle of my father bolting his food and my mother playing with hers . . . it really turned my stomach.

I hadn't really thought about it—I'm not a very reflective person, I tend to be very involved in the moment and not think about the past or what things mean. And so in writing this play I had sort of blithely stumbled onto the idea, "Oh, wouldn't it be great to set a play in a restaurant!" I also find food terribly funny. To me, nothing is funnier than a fancy restaurant and waiters walking to tables with their arms laden with dishes beautifully prepared. I just find food

hilarious. I think it's so full of potential sight-gags. So I
tend to relate to food in that way—the dramatic possibilities
of grapes, for instance, or a fish with a thousand bones in
it that you have to carefully de-bone, or broccoli. . . .
There are certain kinds of foods that just make me helpless
with laughter.

*So you started with the restaurant. How did you pick
the characters for that setting? How did you choose Elizabeth?*

Well, it seemed beholden on me, if I were writing a play
about diners, to show the other side of the spectrum: someone who was afraid of food. Because I think that part of
what you attempt to do when you animate a setting is to
show all the extremes in that setting, all the extremes who
are drawn to it. You have the couple that loves to eat, and
the dieters who are *dying* to eat but are guilty about doing
so, and to me it made perfect sense to have a girl who is
terrified of eating—who, as many people have pointed out,
is really the other side of Ellen, the cook. Elizabeth and
Ellen in many ways are the same person. They're both
creative, they're both obsessed with their art. Elizabeth is
a writer and Ellen is a cook, but both of them have rather
obsessive personalities. They're both very female, and they're
creative, and they come together in this one remarkable
moment, in this one evening: one whose art form happens
to be preparing this wonderful food, and one who can't deal
with it but can *talk* wonderfully about food and what it
evokes in her. It's funny, in the various productions that
the play has had, sooner or later, somebody has pointed
out that they are in fact the same character.

And then you created Mags in Painting Churches, *who
also has a history with food and fear of food, and is herself
an artist.*

Yes, right. So I made a point in my new play, *Coastal
Disturbances*, not to deal with food at all! I have *done* the
food thing to the end! And I wanted to see if I could write
a play where nobody talks about food at all. It's an adoles-

cent hangup of mine; I see it as being part of my youth. And I wanted to climb out of the nursery, out of my absorption with my childhood and my parents, and see if I could step into womanhood.

I think what a monologue should do is lead the listener down the garden path. The whole nature of a monologue is that it starts very innocently, and that the person giving the monologue doesn't quite know where it's going to end. It begins as, "Oh, do you know what happened to me once?" And then as the teller of the monologue gets deeper and deeper into the story, more and more unexpected, disturbing things are revealed. I've always seen monologues as leading an audience into some forbidden landscape.

I think a good monologue should have tension in it, that it should be a narrative; that it's not just an explosion of random feeling, but has a beginning, middle, and end. And part of building a beginning, middle, and end has to do with suspense and surprise, and pulling the rug out from under. That's something I consciously do whenever I'm working on a killer monologue. A killer monologue tricks you. It tricks the audience. And it tricks the person saying it.

Does it trick the writer? Do you often find, when you're writing a monologue, that it goes off in a direction that's completely unexpected?

Yes, oh yes, absolutely! And I think it's very key for the actor, with my monologues anyway, that he shouldn't be aware of where the monologue is going. That is always the first rule. As an actor, *you* don't know where this is going to lead you, you don't know how much you're going to reveal. You mustn't play the result. You're going down the garden path along with everyone else. You don't know where it's taking you. To me, it's that element of discovery. Monologues are about discovery.

Do actors often trip over your monologues? Do they find it hard to make the jump from the scene to that different rhythm of speech?

Often they do. Because I also think that there should appear to be something natural and colloquial and *spontaneous* about a monologue. Some monologues come out very neatly, like a silken toss, and one of the things I'm always trying to do is rough them up. I think it's important—particularly if you have a character who's enthralled in high emotion—that the delivery be roughed up, and that the imagery be roughed up, and that the logic and the sequence be roughed up, so that you maintain that edge of high feeling and of freshness, so that the whole thing is erupting as it's being spoken.

There's a wonderful quote I read, Martha Graham talking about modern dance, saying that the Navajo women, when they wove their blankets, always left in a flaw to let the soul out. And that's particularly true in monologues, I think, because that's when you're right on the pulse of a character. And if the writing is too controlled, and the images are too lush, you're not letting the soul out.

Is there any other advice that you generally give to actors, besides not knowing where a monologue is leading, not playing results?

Well, if it's one of these neurotic monologues revealing some blinding moment of pain, I try as much as I can to encourage actors to recall something similar that happened to them, to try and personalize it as much as they can. The irony is that I think the best-written monologues are the most quirky and the most specific, the most unique and the most individual, but the way that actors can convey that is by relating it to something utterly unique and specific and individual that they have gone through. The better the material, the easier it is for the actor to do that. You know that you haven't really written a true killer monologue if the actor is lost and flagellating and floundering around.

I think monologues are an integral part of a theatre piece, because they give the writer and the character a chance to go into another dimension: into the dream dimension, into the fantasy, into horror, into terror, into something tre-

mendously private. And because so much of the theatre is
about behavior and the way people interact, the monologue
seems to be that one chance for the character to fall into
his insides and explore the terrain.

Sometimes I think that what I would really like to do is
to set a play within a character's body, within different parts
of the body. Maybe you'd begin inside the ear, and then
you'd move into the throat—not that it would be a realistic
throat or a realistic ear, but it would be clear that the play
is taking place inside one person. And then the monologue
would become something totally different! I suppose it would
be a blasting *out* of the body and doing something on the
outside, something that *isn't* introverted.

But I am very intrigued with the interiors of people's
imaginations, with the interiors of their neuroses, of their
fears. And I know that at some point in every play I write,
there's got to be that moment where that horrible exami-
nation takes place. And if the person to whom the monologue is being delivered *isn't* listening, so much the better.
Because then the person reciting the monologue has to go
deeper and deeper to try to grab his attention. I think it's
a wonderful exercise, as a writer and as a dramatist, looking
for that truth. Oh, it's the thing to talk to me about, monologues! You're talking about the right subject! Because
they're very, very precious.

I think the reason we write plays is that we want attention, that our plays are monologues in a way. I've always
had the feeling—this is a simpleminded thing to say—that
the reason one writes is that one doesn't *live* very well. If
we could live a little more successfully, we wouldn't have
to write. The reason we write is to be able to do things
better, to present ourselves better, to rewrite our lives.
And I think the reason we write for the theatre in particular
is that we get this fantastic chance to make everything come
out the way we want it to, either for the good or for the
bad. Dramatists have this extraordinary luxury of being able
to relive our fantasies over and over and over again. When

you have a play running, it's this incredible moment of drawing an audience into your world and having it played out night after night, either the way you wanted it to happen, or exaggerating the way it did or didn't happen. You start with the personal, and then you enlarge it and make it enormous, and you disguise it. And that's the fun of it. The fun of it is disguising the personal, taking an Elizabeth character who's very close to you and disguising her, putting her in an outlandish situation, in an extreme situation—I never had a meal like that in my life! But that's the perverse enjoyment of it, that you get to make it preposterous. You get to take something very familiar and painful and private, and make it public through its preposterousness. And the lure of that, the lure of reinventing your life and pulling it in one direction or another, is so exhilarating! The whole ritualistic aspect, that it's done night after night after night, the exact same way . . . it really gives me chills to think about why one writes plays. There's nothing like it.

PERMISSIONS

Grateful acknowledgment is made for permission to reprint excerpts from the following plays:

The Actor's Nightmare by Christopher Durang. By arrangement with Helen Merrill, Ltd., 361 West 17th Street, New York, NY 10011.

Angels Fall by Lanford Wilson. Copyright © 1983 by Lanford Wilson. Reprinted by permission of Farrar, Straus and Giroux, Inc.

The Art of Dining by Tina Howe. © 1978 by Tina Howe. All rights reserved. Selections used by special permission from Flora Roberts, Inc.

Aunt Dan and Lemon by Wallace Shawn. Copyright © 1985 by Wallace Shawn. Reprinted by permission of Grove Press, Inc.

Baby with the Bathwater by Christopher Durang. By arrangement with Helen Merrill, Ltd., 361 West 17th Street, New York, NY 10011.

Balm in Gilead by Lanford Wilson. Copyright © 1965 by Lanford Wilson. Reprinted by permission of Farrar, Straus and Giroux, Inc.

Between Daylight and Boonville by Matt Williams. Reprinted by special arrangement with Rick Leed, Agency for the Performing Arts, 888 Seventh Avenue, New York, NY 10106. For any use or rights other than stock and amateur stage rights, contact agent at the above address. For stock and amateur rights, contact Samuel French, Inc.

Birdbath by Leonard Melfi. Copyright © 1967 by Leonard Melfi. All rights reserved.

The Blood Knot from *Three Port Elizabeth Plays* by Athol Fugard. Copyright © 1963, 1964 by Athol Fugard. Reprinted by permission of Viking Penguin Inc.

Blue Window by Craig Lucas. Copyright 1984, 1985 by Craig Lucas. All rights reserved. CAUTION: Professionals and amateurs are hereby warned that *Blue Window* is subject to a royalty. For information regarding amateur and stock production rights, address Samuel French, Inc., 45 West 25th Street, New York, NY 10010. For inquiries concerning all other rights, address Peter Franklin, c/o William Morris Agency, Inc., 1350 Avenue of the Americas, New York, NY 10019.

Blues for Mister Charlie by James Baldwin. Copyright © 1964 by James Baldwin. Reprinted by permission of Doubleday Publishing Group.

Bosoms and Neglect by John Guare. Copyright © 1980 by St. Jude Productions, Inc.

Brontosaurus by Lanford Wilson. Copyright © 1978 by Lanford Wilson. Reprinted by permission of Farrar, Straus and Giroux, Inc.

Calm Down Mother by Megan Terry. Copyright 1965, 1970 by Megan Terry.

Christmas on Mars by Harry Kondoleon. © Copyright 1983 by Harry Kondoleon. © Copyright 1982 by Harry Kon-

The Dance and the Railroad by David Henry Hwang. By arrangement with Helen Merrill, Ltd., 361 West 17th Street, New York, NY 10011.

Danny and the Deep Blue Sea by John Patrick Shanley. Copyright 1984 by John Patrick Shanley.

A Day in the Death of Joe Egg by Peter Nichols. Copyright © 1967 by Peter Nichols. Reprinted by permission of Grove Press, Inc., and Faber and Faber Ltd.

The Days and Nights of Beebee Fenstermaker by William Snyder. © Copyright 1963 by William Snyder. The excerpts included in this volume are reprinted by permission of the author and Dramatists Play Service, Inc. The use of excerpts in question must be confined to study and reference. Attention is called to the fact that these excerpts, being duly copyrighted, may not be publicly read or performed or otherwise used without permission of the author. All inquiries should be addressed to Dramatists Play Service, Inc., 440 Park Avenue South, New York, NY 10016.

Death Comes to Us All, Mary Agnes by Christopher Durang. By arrangement with Helen Merrill, Ltd., 361 West 17th Street, New York, NY 10011.

The Death of a Miner by Paula Cizmar. Copyright © 1980, 1982 by Paula Cizmar. Used by permission.

'dentity Crisis by Christopher Durang. By arrangement with Helen Merrill, Ltd., 361 West 17th Street, New York, NY 10011.

The Effect of Gamma Rays on Man-in-the-Moon Marigolds by Paul Zindel. Copyright 1970 by Paul Zindel. All rights

by David W. Rabe. Reprinted by permission of Grove Press, Inc.

Jesse and the Bandit Queen by David Freeman. Copyright © 1976 by David Freeman. Reprinted by permission of International Creative Management, Inc.

Kennedy's Children by Robert Patrick. By arrangement with Helen Merrill, Ltd., 361 West 17th Street, New York, NY 10011.

The Lady and the Clarinet by Michael Cristofer. © Copyright 1985 by Onicca Corp.

Lakeboat by David Mamet. Copyright © 1981 by David Mamet. Reprinted by permission of Grove Press, Inc.

Landscape of the Body by John Guare. Copyright © 1978 by St. Jude Productions, Inc.

Later by Corinne Jacker. © Copyright 1979 by Corinne Jacker. The excerpt included in this volume is reprinted by permission of the author and Dramatists Play Service, Inc. The use of the excerpt in question must be confined to study and reference. Attention is called to the fact that this excerpt, duly copyrighted, may not be publicly read or performed or otherwise used without permission of the author. All inquiries should be addressed to Dramatists Play Service, Inc., 440 Park Avenue South, New York, NY 10016.

Life and Limb by Keith Reddin. Reprinted by special arrangement with Rick Leed, Agency for the Performing Arts, 888 Seventh Avenue, New York, NY 10106. For any use or rights other than stock and amateur stage rights, contact agent at the above address. For stock and amateur rights, contact Dramatists Play Service, Inc.

354   **PERMISSIONS**

Gardner. Reprinted by permission of International Creative Management, Inc.

Tracers conceived by John DiFusco and written by the original cast: Vincent Caristi, Richard Chaves, John DiFusco, Eric E. Emerson, Rick Gallavan, Merlin Marston, and Harry Stephens, with Sheldon Lettich. Copyright 1983, 1985, 1986 by John DiFusco, Vincent Caristi, Richard Chaves, Eric E. Emerson, Rick Gallavan, Merlin Marston, Harry Stephens, and Sheldon Lettich. "I lost my sense of judgment yesterday" written by Vincent Caristi. "Been out in the fuckin' bush" written by Eric E. Emerson.

The Transfiguration of Benno Blimpie by Albert Innaurato. By arrangement with Helen Merrill, Ltd., 361 West 17th Street, New York, NY 10011.

The Typists by Murray Schisgal. Copyright © 1963 by Murray Schisgal. Reprinted by permission of International Creative Management, Inc.

Uncommon Women and Others by Wendy Wasserstein. Copyright © 1978 by Wendy Wasserstein.

The Wake of Jamey Foster by Beth Henley. Copyright 1983 by Beth Henley. All rights reserved. CAUTION: Professionals and amateurs are hereby warned that *The Wake of Jamey Foster* is subject to a royalty. For information regarding stock and amateur production rights, address the Dramatists Play Service, Inc., 440 Park Avenue South, New York, NY 10016. For inquiries concerning all other rights, address Gilbert Parker, c/o William Morris Agency, Inc., 1350 Avenue of the Americas, New York, NY 10019.

A Weekend Near Madison by Kathleen Tolan. © Copyright 1983 by Kathleen Tolan.

FOR THE BEST IN PAPERBACKS, LOOK FOR THE

In every corner of the world, on every subject under the sun, Penguin represents quality and variety—the very best in publishing today.

For complete information about books available from Penguin—including Penguin Classics, Penguin Compass, and Puffins—and how to order them, write to us at the appropriate address below. Please note that for copyright reasons the selection of books varies from country to country.

In the United States: Please write to *Penguin Group (USA), P.O. Box 12289 Dept. B, Newark, New Jersey 07101-5289* or call *1-800-788-6262*.

In the United Kingdom: Please write to *Dept. EP, Penguin Books Ltd, Bath Road, Harmondsworth, West Drayton, Middlesex UB7 0DA*.

In Canada: Please write to *Penguin Books Canada Ltd, 90 Eglinton Avenue East, Suite 700, Toronto, Ontario M4P 2Y3*.

In Australia: Please write to *Penguin Books Australia Ltd, P.O. Box 257, Ringwood, Victoria 3134*.

In New Zealand: Please write to *Penguin Books (NZ) Ltd, Private Bag 102902, North Shore Mail Centre, Auckland 10*.

In India: Please write to *Penguin Books India Pvt Ltd, 11 Panchsheel Shopping Centre, Panchsheel Park, New Delhi 110 017*.

In the Netherlands: Please write to *Penguin Books Netherlands bv, Postbus 3507, NL-1001 AH Amsterdam*.

In Germany: Please write to *Penguin Books Deutschland GmbH, Metzlerstrasse 26, 60594 Frankfurt am Main*.

In Spain: Please write to *Penguin Books S. A., Bravo Murillo 19, 1° B, 28015 Madrid*.

In Italy: Please write to *Penguin Italia s.r.l., Via Benedetto Croce 2, 20094 Corsico, Milano*.

In France: Please write to *Penguin France, Le Carré Wilson, 62 rue Benjamin Baillaud, 31500 Toulouse*.

In Japan: Please write to *Penguin Books Japan Ltd, Kaneko Building, 2-3-25 Koraku, Bunkyo-Ku, Tokyo 112*.

In South Africa: Please write to *Penguin Books South Africa (Pty) Ltd, Private Bag X14, Parkview, 2122 Johannesburg*.